HOW BLAIR KILLED THE CO-OPS

MANCHESTER
1824

Manchester University Press

How Blair killed the co-ops

Reclaiming social enterprise from its neoliberal turn

Leslie Huckfield

MANCHESTER UNIVERSITY PRESS

Published by Manchester University Press
Oxford Road, Manchester M13 9PL

www.manchesteruniversitypress.co.uk

British Library Cataloguing-in-Publication Data
A catalogue record for this book is available from the British Library

ISBN 978 1 5261 4973 2 hardback

First published 2021

Typeset
by Sunrise Setting Ltd

Contents

Figures

Acknowledgements

I am profoundly grateful to so many colleagues and friends who generously gave advice and support throughout the research for this book. Especially, thanks are due to Professor Alex de Ruyter, Dr Geoffrey Whittam and Dr Anne Smith as supervisors for their understanding and support and to all who gave their time to participate in meetings and interviews, including a Focus Group in September 2016. I'm also grateful to Dr Alan Southern, who was my external examiner, for continuing support, to Dr Matt Thompson for his final detailed book review and to Professor Peter Lloyd – all from Liverpool University.

At Glasgow Caledonian University (GCU) I received considerable help from Grace Poulter in the Graduate School, Margaret Brown in Academic Development, and Joanne Piraino, Raymond O'Brien, Lynn Irvine and Julie Smith in GCU Library. Karen McDairmant in the GCU Yunus Centre office was indefatigable in coping with incoming funds and outgoing expenses for interview journeys and visits. My thanks are also due to Stefan Dickers at the Bishopsgate Institute in London, IDOX staff in Glasgow for Planning Exchange material, Paul Evans for his boxed archive collection and Geoff and Rachel Fordham who worked with Victor Hausner throughout the 1980s and 1990s. For other material I am grateful to John Goodman, previously a Co-operative Development Officer and policy advisor to Co-operatives UK, to Rodney Stares, a fellow director of SENSCOT, for his signposting to former colleagues working on community regeneration, and to Jenny and Ismail Saray at the ArtZone Co-operative in Tower Hamlets, for providing a London base during my first interviews.

For funding, this research was completed with an initial GCU Part-Time PhD Stipendship for part of the time. I am grateful to Glasgow School for Business and Society and the Yunus Centre for Social Business and Health for extending this for a further period. I am also grateful for support and encouragement to Aidan Pia, formerly SENSCOT Executive Director and SENSCOT colleagues, to Andrew Robinson from CCLA Investment Management, to Paul Bell, UNISON National Local Government Officer and to the Unite Edinburgh Not for Profit Branch. All these, through funding for attending other meetings and working with them, enabled many trips from Scotland to London and elsewhere, without which interviews and data collection would not have been possible.

I would also like to thank Alan Kay at GCU and Philipp Golka in Hamburg for many encouraging conversations.

Finally, and most of all, I will always be grateful to Margaret, my wife, and my family, for tolerating my intermittent but continuing absences since 2013.

Abbreviations

ALMP	active labour market policies
CDP	community development project
CIC	community interest company
CIRIEC	International Centre of Research and Information on the Public, Social and Cooperative Economy
DETR	Department of Environment, Transport and the Regions
DTI	Department of Trade and Industry
EMES	L'Emergence de l'Entreprise Sociale en Europe Research Network
ESF	European Social Fund
EU	European Union
ICA	International Co-operative Alliance
ICOF	Industrial and Common Ownership Finance
ICOM	Industrial and Common Ownership Movement
ILM	intermediate labour market (for "work insertion" or "work integration")
IPS	industrial and provident societies
MSC	Manpower Services Commission
OTS	Office of the Third Sector
PIC	public interest company
PIU	Performance and Innovation Unit
RMI	Revenu Minimum d'Insertion
SEC	Social Enterprise Coalition
SEL	Social Enterprise London
SENSCOT	Social Entrepreneurs' Network Scotland
SEU	Social Exclusion Unit
TSO	third sector organisation
WISE	Work Integration Social Enterprise

This overall policy direction was soon reinforced at a Downing Street breakfast for co-op leaders on Tuesday 26 February 2002, hosted by Prime Minister Blair (Former Senior Civil Servant III 2016):

> [H]e (Blair) then sort of told them very clearly in the nicest possible way that they ... that social enterprise is going to be this way. ... [Anon] took us off into another room and then she basically put her very pointed stiletto heels in and made it quite clear what was and what was not going to be counted within social enterprise.

> I knew that Patricia Hewitt was very much a supporter of the coop but didn't want the whole social enterprise agenda dominated by them. She said ... there's a huge cooperative agenda here that we within the Labour Party have got to sort out ... but don't let it overwhelm the work you're doing on social enterprise.

1

Introduction

Organisations labelled "social enterprises" are now redefined, reinvented and written up widely as though they were for low-cost delivery of public services. Social enterprise today is also frequently presented as an alternative to, as an amendment or even resistance to neoliberalism and capitalism. But in this book the author shows that, far from forming an alternative to neoliberalism, social enterprise and much of the third sector now feature as platforms for its incursion into ever wider spheres of public life. As a central part of this process, especially for the Labour Party, a previous emphasis on co-operatives and locally controlled democratic organisations is now largely jettisoned. Had their previous community control been retained, their transformation for this new purpose would not have been possible. A further motive for this shift of emphasis from co-operatives and community controlled structures to more loosely defined social enterprise structures is that all this encourages the growth of social finance and social investment – an infusion of external private funds to deliver so-called impact investment, which is nowadays even encouraged in university incubators. In its more recent incarnation of social impact bonds private investors receive payments when public service outcomes are achieved. Social enterprise is now promoted globally by the British Council and the Global Strategy Group for Impact Investment as an instrument of financial liberalisation and the dilution of the role of the public sector in delivery of public services.

As a former Member of the House of Commons and the European Parliament, followed by a career in further and higher education and in training and funding third sector organisations (TSOs), the author is uniquely positioned to write with personal first-hand experience of these developments throughout the entire period of this book. Having been first elected to Parliament in 1967, one year before Labour's first Urban Development Programme in 1968 with its community development projects (CDPs), he was later joint leader of the occupation of the Triumph Motorcycle Factory in Meriden in 1973 to form a workers' co-operative. He was then an Industry Minister in the Callaghan government, which introduced the 1976 Industrial

Common Ownership Act and 1978 Co-operative Development Agency Act. He was a member of the London Co-operative Society Political Committee from 1978 until 1993. As a member of the Labour Party National Executive Committee, where he represented co-operative societies, he chaired the National Executive Committee Working Group on Worker Co-operatives, whose 1980 report formed the basis of co-operatives policy in Labour's 1983 General Election Manifesto. As a Member of the European Parliament from 1984 till 1989, he developed the use of European funding for community and third sector structures. From 1989 to 2004, working for Merseyside Colleges and the Association of Colleges in the West Midlands, he promoted and developed projects for TSOs.

After moving to Scotland in 2004, he set up the Plean Community Trust in one of Stirling's Eastern Villages in 2008 and in 2009 became a Director of the Social Entrepreneurs' Network Scotland (SENSCOT). After working on a series of third sector projects, in 2015 he conducted 11 EU Funding Master-classes across Scotland for SENSCOT, Social Firms Scotland, the Development Trusts Association Scotland and Scottish Community Alliance. From 2016 he has lectured in social enterprise at GCU, where he gained his PhD in 2018. In 2018 he became a member of the Shadow Chancellor's Implementation Group which produced recommendations for Labour's 2017 and 2019 manifesto commitment to double the size of the co-operative economy. He continues as a director of the Sheffield Co-operative Development Group.

The author's role in policy development and implementation offers a first-hand witness account from the 1960s and 1970s to the present day, which is reinforced by data collection and interviews with key participants over the same period. However, he recognises that others involved in social enterprise, co-operative and third sector narratives may not share his per-spective and may offer different interpretations. For objectivity and in search of a more independent perspective, as described in Chapter 2, this book has been written with a Critical Realist philosophy (R. Bhaskar 1989):

> "Philosophical under-labouring" is most characteristically what critical realist philosophy does. The metaphor of "under-labouring" comes from John Locke who said:
>
>> "The commonwealth of learning is not at this time without master-builders, whose mighty designs, in advancing the sciences will leave last-ing monuments to the admiration of posterity: but everyone must not hope to be a Boyle or a Sydenham; and in an age that produced such masters as the great Huygenius and the incomparable Mr Newton, with some others of that strain, it is ambition enough to be employed as an under-labourer in clearing the ground a little, and removing some of the rubbish that lies in the way to knowledge." (Locke 1959)

Chapters in this book

The author is critical of a dominant interpretation of social enterprise in the UK as a market-oriented public service delivery vehicle, promoted under New Labour and augmented since 2010 by Conservative governments. His alternative narrative for social enterprise and the third sector consists of seven chapters, which are structured as follows:

- Chapter 1: Introduction, explaining this book's chapters and the author's approach, setting out the book's context and recurring themes.
- Chapter 2: Background, which describes how research for this book was carried out, using Critical Realism as its basis and how this approach differs from other current contributions.
- Chapter 3: Theoretical foundations and conceptual interpretations for the third sector, summarising literature contributions from North America and European concepts of a social economy, including the approach of French Regulationists. These contrast with the narrower market approach of L'Emergence de l'Entreprise Sociale en Europe Research Network (EMES) and UK social enterprise.
- Chapter 4: 1960s–1980s regeneration, showing local indigenous structures in the UK as a response to deindustrialisation and job losses, especially following the 1976 Industrial Common Ownership Act and Beechwood College, Leeds. These are the true antecedents for UK social enterprise.
- Chapter 5: New Labour, co-operatives and social enterprise, showing key developments including Social Enterprise London (SEL) 1998, the Department of Trade and Industry (DTI) Social Enterprise Unit 2001, the Social Enterprise Coalition (SEC), Department of Trade and Industry "Strategy for Success" document, HM Treasury Cross Cutting Review and "Private Action, Public Benefit" in 2002. The years 1998 to 2002 saw major changes.
- Chapter 6: Explanations, offering reasons for possible misrepresentations and misconceptions in other UK academic contributions. These include their borrowing from North American and selective European academic contributions, UK exclusion from the initial period of the Social Chapter in the European Union (EU) and an apparent neglect of enhanced EU funding and influences in mainland European and other contemporary developments.
- Chapter 7: Conclusions, outlining reasons for this book's different conclusion in contrast to other UK contributions, with suggestions for further research and alternative policy development.

The policy issues

North American discourses

The concept of independent social entrepreneurship, imported from North America, rather than community organisations, is becoming more dominant in the UK. Though social enterprise in North America started from a different position and operates in a different environment, for the UK the influence of American business schools at Stanford, Harvard and Duke Universities has been significant (Nicholls 2010, 618). United States nonprofits operate alongside private corporations and are significantly influenced by the policies of foundations and tax exemption, with a significant expansion following Reagan's and Bush's "roll back neoliberalism" from the 1980s onwards (Peck and Tickell 2002). Because North American business schools dominated early literature on social entrepreneurship (Dees and Anderson 2006; Nicholls 2006; Austin 2006), their influence constitutes "a legitimating strategy in which organizations actively engage in processes that align field-level and internal logics to shape emergent institutional fields as closed systems of self-legitimation" (Nicholls 2010, 617).

Mainland EU social economy discourses

Apart from US contributions, UK discourses have been heavily influenced by the EMES, with its restricted focus on social enterprise as a marketised variant in a social economy. Earlier mainland European interpretations of social enterprise as collective, associational or mutual activities were closer to the International Centre of Research and Information on the Public, Social and Co-operative Economy (CIRIEC) view of a social economy. Typically, EMES now focuses on Work Integration Social Enterprises (WISEs), in which social enterprises frequently compete for contracts to deliver public services.

The EMES approach dominates many European discourses, despite mainland European interpretations of previous earlier institutionalisation of co-operative, mutual and associational structures (Vivet and Thiry 2000, 33) with public service delivery projected under Christian Democracy (Van Kersbergen 2003; Esping-Andersen 1999; Huber, Ragin and Stephens 1993).

Neglect of earlier indigenous structures

Apart from the influence of North American and EMES discourses, for the author the major problem in most current UK interpretations of social enterprise is that large numbers of community-based regeneration structures in the 1970s and 1980s have been neglected, though they originated as community defences during a period of massive deindustrialisation and job losses, and were the genuine antecedents of social enterprise in the UK. Following Labour's 1976 Industrial Common Ownership Act (Watkins 1976) and the 1978 Co-operative Development Agency Act, during the 1970s and 1980s the size of the co-operative economy more than doubled.[1] Labour's 2017 and 2019 General Election manifestos (Labour Party 2017; 2019) included a commitment to double the size of the co-operative economy.

Voluntary, community organisations and social enterprise

Most UK contributions do not synchronise voluntary, community and social enterprise developments, despite many policies to encourage voluntary and community sector participation in a marketised public service delivery which prefaced similar later policies for social enterprise. Other contributions support the author's contention. "In such a perspective, the third sector can no longer be viewed as fully separated from the private for-profit and the public sectors; instead, it appears as an intermediate sector" (Defourny, Nyssens and EMES 2012, 11). The third sector definition is extended specifically in order to include social enterprises, which, until that point, were institutionally dealt with as businesses, and part of the market, rather than the third sector (Carmel and Harlock 2008, 160).

Social enterprise policy shift

The components of the major policy shift running throughout this book are, firstly, New Labour's marginalisation of co-operatives and the wider Co-operative Movement in favour of social enterprise and, secondly, UK and other academic contributors' complete neglect of the genuine antecedents of social enterprise, many of which were themselves co-operatives, registered by the Industrial Common Ownership Movement (ICOM). The underlying motive behind this policy shift was to enable social enterprise activities to refocus on public service delivery. All this involved a political rupture with the Co-operative Movement which was at least as politically significant as Labour's repudiation of Clause Four of its constitution in 1995. As shown in Chapter 4, most 1980s and 1990s co-operatives were registered as companies limited by guarantee, rather than as industrial and provident society (IPS) or Financial Conduct Authority co-operatives. These were similar registrations to most of today's social enterprises.[2] Data and interviews in Chapter 5 show that rather than a transfer of emphasis from co-operatives in the 1990s to social enterprise in the 2000s, this was a more intense policy divergence between the Labour and Co-operative Movements. Labour's turn to social enterprise was as much a political move as a structural change.

Political encouragement for New Labour social enterprise structures was heralded by publications such as *Marxism Today* and pamphlets from the think tank Demos by Mulgan and Landry (1995) and Leadbeater (1997). Many still refer to Leadbeater's contribution as a founding document for social enterprise in the UK. But a further motivation for these contributions was welfare reform and greater private sector involvement (Leadbeater 1997, 78), which became a New Labour mutation from US President Clinton's 1996 Personal Responsibility and Work Opportunity Act, which he described as "the end of welfare as we know it". This replacement of welfare by "workfare" was part of a process often described as the "Clintonisation of the Labour Party" (Rustin 1996).

All this represented a significant departure from the policies of ICOM as the main registration body for co-operatives, which had operated as part of alternative local social economies and alongside local enterprise support agencies (Patel, Carter and Parkinson 1999a; 1999b; Wood, Reason and Egan 1999; Martinelli et al. 2003; Cornforth et al. 1988; Knight 1993). New Labour policies represented a policy shift from radical community economic development to increased dependence on the skills of individuals (Chapman, Forbes and Brown 2007; Parkinson and Howorth 2008; Parkinson 2005). This involved a change in governance from collective, co-operative and mutual organisations to those with less democratic accountability. UK contributions which omit this "paradigm shift" in voluntary, community and social enterprise policy – as interpreted by Kuhn (1962) and Hall (1993) – not only neglect social enterprise and co-operative antecedents from twenty years previously but also discard contemporaneous concepts of an alternative local social economy as described by Lipietz (1996), Mayer (2003) and Amin et al. (2002).

Though social enterprise emerged as a novel policy initiative during these major political changes, there has been almost no analysis of the wider political context. For the author, the totality of this paradigm shift ranks alongside Hall's (1993) description of the abandonment of Keynesian demand management and its replacement with monetarism in the 1980s (Baumgartner and Jones 1991; Daigneault 2014; White 2012).

Policy entrepreneurs

Today's interpretations of UK social enterprise and third sector policy development are strongly driven by policy entrepreneurs. The qualities of a successful policy entrepreneur are useful in the process of softening up the system. They lie in wait for a window to open. "In the process of leaping at their opportunity, they play a central role in coupling the streams at the window" (Kingdon 2011, 181). "As to proposals, entrepreneurs are central to the softening-up process … They float their ideas as trial balloons, get reactions, revise their proposals in the light of reactions, and float them again" (Kingdon 2011, 205). Quoting from Majone (1988, 160), Mintrom stresses that "before the dialectic of conflicting positions can unfold", there must be agreement about the nature of problems then facing the community (Mintrom 1997, 739). Policy entrepreneurs can therefore be thought of as being to the policy-making process what economic entrepreneurs are to the marketplace (Mintrom 1997, 740). "[P]olicy networks, or professional-bureaucratic functional alliances … restrict who contributes to policy-making and policy implementation … They are also a form of private government; much of their work is invisible to the parliamentary and public eye" (Rhodes 1994, 147).

Academic and third sector policy entrepreneurs

There is a strong history of influential academic and third sector policy entrepreneurs in North America and the UK. Indifference or hostility of the state and the weakness of US sector organisation were counterbalanced by the development of a strong and well-resourced non-profit academic community and lobby (Rochester 2013, 45). North American policy was particularly driven by the Johns Hopkins Global Non Profits study (Salamon and Anheier 1997b). Because the institutionalisation of non-profit public service delivery followed different paths in North America, though UK academics have borrowed from these discourses, it is questionable whether these are appropriate as UK policy precedents.

In the US, there was a major output of PhDs and widening postgraduate education for the managers and leaders of non-profit organisations (Rochester 2013, 45). Business investment in higher education made possible the establishment of academic disciplines as powerful elements in policy entrepreneurship for political and industrial self-government. Historians were both propagandists and apologists for the new order (Dobkin Hall 2001, 5). Defending the role of academics, Salamon replied to David Horton Smith: "Those of us who sought to bring the dark matter of the staffed non-profit world into view therefore had the same sense of discovery that you seem to exhibit" (Salamon 1998, 89). Though rarely mentioned in UK contributions, papers from the Open University Research Unit provided academic underpinning for the expansion of co-operatives in the 1980s and 1990s (Cornforth et al. 1988; Spear 1999). During the early days of New Labour, Westall and Grenier performed the same function (Grenier 2002;

Westall 2001a). Though these performed similar policy entrepreneur roles in their respective periods, 1980s contributions are not mentioned in those of the 2000s.

In the UK there are strong policy entrepreneur precedents for voluntary organisations. The "voluntary sector", as a concept created a new policy field as well as developing a policy sub-elite made up of those who lead the intermediary bodies and those who act for government at central and local level, together with some "useful" fellow-travelling intellectuals (Rochester 2013, 52). "Modernisation of the sector helped to create or entrench the power of this sub-elite, identified by 6 and Leat (1997) as the inventors of the concept of a sector ... Government has identified sector 'leaders' and co-opted them to its 'modernisation' project" (Rochester 2013, 77). 6 and Leat say of contributions from academia that "to weave numbers around the concept of 'sector' created for political purposes, one needs intellectuals" (6 and Leat 1997, 39). This view is echoed by Alcock and Kendall (Alcock and Kendall 2010, 8):

> In an analysis of the structures set up to review research and seeking to set the agenda for policy from Wolfenden (1978) to Deakin (1995), 6 and Leat (1997) argued that these "committees" had essentially operated to politically construct "the voluntary sector" as an entity.

Those benefiting most from the idea of "voluntary sector unity" have been, on the one hand, the "top 2%" of voluntary agencies and those like NCVO (National Council for Voluntary Organisations) and ACEVO (Association of Chief Executives of Voluntary Organisations), which promote their interests and, on the other, those in government bent on privatising public services (Rochester 2013, 214). Of academic contributions on the voluntary and community sector, Harris describes their "inclination to focus their attention on the grand questions of policy development and policy outcomes rather than on the messy practicalities of the mediating organisation though which social policy implementation is achieved" (Harris 2001, 222). There are also contributions,[3] which, though descriptive, lack analysis of developments. With a few exceptions,[4] most contributions have failed to provide a critique of these developments (Rochester 2013, 126). This has paved the way for "welfare pluralism" in the UK. "'Welfare pluralism' could replace 'welfare statism' as a central plan of social policy" (Rochester 2013, 46).

Rochester calls in evidence DiMaggio and Powell's institutional isomorphism (DiMaggio and Powell 1983; Rochester 2013, 128). NCVO and voluntary and community sector organisations willingly engaged in the rolling out of government policies. "There remains the issue of how far the voluntary sector is being harnessed to New Labour's project 'for itself', and how far it is still a matter of it serving government's ends" (Lewis 1999, 265). The third sector policy agenda is driven by the sector itself (Lewis 1999), with "identifiable interlocutors in the form of the National Council for Voluntary Organisations (NCVO) and other national bodies" (Carmel and Harlock 2008, 159).

Conclusion

Social enterprise and third sector policy development in the UK has been heavily influenced by discourses from North America and by the EMES in mainland Europe. But the UK social enterprise policy agenda has also been dominated by the failure of many contributions to revisit the lessons of earlier community and third sector development in the 1970s and 1980s, in which the author was heavily involved. The contemporary roles of academics and TSOs as policy entrepreneurs are frequently overlooked. This has been important not only for the "invention of the voluntary sector" (Rochester 2013; 6 and Leat 1997) and the role of North American business schools (Grenier 2009; Salamon and Anheier 1997b), but also for the expanding roles of UK third sector representative organisations like SEL and the SEC, especially between 1998 and 2002.

From the author's political and personal experience, this book will show that all this has resulted in a UK social enterprise policy within a marketised and neoliberal framework. Co-operatives and locally accountable TSOs have been major casualties throughout these developments. As chapters 6 and 7 show, many of these structures now struggle for survival.

Notes

1   In 2018 and 2019, the author was a member of Labour Shadow Chancellor John McDonnell MP's Implementation Group to carry forward Labour's manifesto commitment to "double the size of the cooperative economy". He has written elsewhere of his surprise that many involved in Implementation Group discussions had no understanding that "doubling the cooperative economy" had already happened in the 1970s and 1980s.
2   Further details of different registrations are shown in Appendix 2.
3   Paola Grenier wrote her PhD thesis while New Labour social enterprise policy was unfolding and places social entrepreneurship within a contemporary current economic and political framework rather than as challenging it (Grenier 2002). Alibeth Somers worked for SEL during this initial period. Though her PhD thesis provides a contemporary interpretation, it lacks analysis of antecedents and policy. See A. Somers, "The Emergence of Social Enterprise Policy in New Labour's

Second Term", Goldsmiths College, University of London, 2013, http://research.gold.ac.uk/id/eprint/8051/.

4   A smaller number of academic contributions on social investment also describe the roles of policy entrepreneurs, including in higher education. See J. Morley, "Elite Networks and the Rise of Social Impact Reporting in the UK Social Sector", *SSRN Scholarly Paper No. ID 2736167* (Rochester, NY: Social Science Research Network 2016).

2

Background

This chapter seeks to explain the theoretical basis for the author's approach, how this contrasts with others and how research for this book was undertaken. Many other contributors write about policy development for co-operatives and social enterprises and its implementation as though these are loosely related discourses. These approaches are based on the assumption that "discourse makes the world" or that material conditions and social relations have no ontological status or explanatory relevance unless and until they are discursively constituted (Outhwaite 1998).

Most UK contributions on social enterprise development have followed a "roll with it neoliberalist" turn, which "prefers straight to 'ecological dominance' as a 'natural' and often unquestioned condition of life under capitalism today" (Keil 2009, 232). But the author believes that social enterprise and third sector developments are more significant. Wendy Brown describes the emergence of "governance" in state, business, non-profit and NGO endeavours, with "significantly altered orientations and identities of each as everything comes to comport increasingly with a business model and business metrics" (2015, 124). She notes that "NGOs, nonprofits, schools, neighbourhood organizations, and even social movements that understand themselves as opposing neoliberal economic policies may nonetheless be organized by neoliberal rationality" (201).

The author's approach shows that changes described throughout this book have deeper underlying causes and shares Reed's analysis from a Critical Realist viewpoint (Reed 2005, 1627):

> explanations of the long-term material consequences of these underlying structural contradictions and their impact on the development of managerial control strategies and practices in contemporary capitalist organizations, that were once so central to the historical sociology of work-based power and control, are marginalized ... Indeed, the overwhelming importance given to discourse and identity has reached a position where political economy and social structure have all but disappeared from the explanatory agenda.

Critical Realism has emerged in response to dissatisfaction with the many academic representations of loosely connected events, many of which are grounded in social constructionist approaches similar to that of Giddens (1984), which underwrote much New Labour policy. As a legitimate criticism of many current contributions on social enterprise, Reed believes that we need to develop an adequate analytical and empirical grasp of underlying dynamics and mechanisms of institutionalised power relations, since power structures have a temporal, spatial and social continuity and reach that cannot begin to be grasped by conceptions of power which are only episodic (Reed 2005, 1628, 1630):

> Critical realists insist that it is possible to assess competing scientific theories and explanations in relation to the comparative explanatory power of the descriptions and accounts that they provide of the underlying structures and mechanisms that generate observable patterns of events and outcomes. (R. Bhaskar 1978; Outhwaite 1998)

"We are shaped and affected by social structures, which act upon us. Social structures limit our range of possible choices of action and thought ... We do not 'create' social structure. We reproduce and transform it. But social structure causally affects us" (Potter and Lopez 2001, 15).

As an example of a loosely related or "episodic" approach of which the author is critical, Nicholls refers to "contests for the control of the legitimating discourses that will determine the final shape of the social entrepreneurial paradigm" – a "characteristic of a field that is at a less well-developed stage of legitimacy than the key paradigm-building actors within it" (2010, 611). He refers to Suchman's (1995) contention that organisations actively construct and promote new rationales and logics of social reality and DiMaggio and Powell's suggestion that "isomorphic processes represented examples of structuration between organizations and larger institutional forces" (1983). Rather than leading to any historical analysis or comparisons with mainland European or international policy regimes, as in chapters 3 and 5, this view enables Nicholls to refer to "paradigm building actors" from 1998 onwards (2010, 617). Similarly, Grenier (2002, 3) writes of social enterprise organisations as "relatively young, established mainly in the late 1990s and early 2000s", and not existing before New Labour (Nicholls 2010, 618).

Neither of these contributions heeds Bhaskar's caution that "underlying structures and mechanisms are not directly accessible to sense experience ... which critical realists call 'retroduction'" (1989, 1). As shown in Chapter 4, before the arrival of New Labour there was evidence of underlying causal mechanisms which ultimately sought to move local community structures into market delivery of public services in competition with the private sector. Most UK academics have neglected these historical contexts and causal mechanisms.

In his Introduction to Bhaskar's *Reclaiming Reality*, Hartwig describes Bhaskar criticism of the "new realism" or "empiricism" already emerging in Labour circles in the 1980s, "empt[ying] the social world of any enduring structural dimension and playing a vital role in the 'demarxification' of social theory and philosophy in the UK, France and elsewhere" (Bhaskar 1989, ix). This "unthinking materialism" is a label for the positivism against which Bhaskar had warned, along with "the new idealism" or "poststructuralism". He continues (1):

> An indication of the extent to which the right – echoed in the Labour movement – has managed to seize this ground is that it has not only succeeded in achieving political dominance; it has, under the guise of the "new realism", even appropriated the very concept of reality and realism for itself!

This forms an apposite summary of the many UK contributions which describe in detail the emergence of social enterprise as a New Labour phenomenon (Grenier 2009; 2002; Nicholls 2010; Teasdale 2012; Westall 2009; 2001a) while neglecting significant social economy structures emerging contemporaneously in mainland Europe and Quebec, as described in Chapter 3, with important historical antecedents in Chapter 4. Grenier is typical in describing the emergence of social enterprise as a contemporary concept and "something significant" (2009, 38):

> The authors and publishers were well connected and highly regarded, and the reports succeeded in familiarizing a number of politicians, political commentators, and policy makers with the term social entrepreneurship. The reports sparked debate and a growing excitement that social entrepreneurship was something significant.

Reed provides a summary of these contributions, which have "little or no engagement with the structurally embedded and historically contextualized power struggles between collective actors that generate new forms of corporate agency and the political potential that the latter embody and carry for subsequent phases of institutional change and transformation" (Reed 2005, 1636).

In contrast with Nicholls and others, the author's approach in chapters 4 and 5 shows that social enterprise was neither a New Labour phenomenon nor a straightforward or almost seamless shift from democratically controlled co-operatives to less accountable and individually controlled structures. The author thus rejects any approach or interpretation of social enterprise policy as an innovative institutional event. Following Jessop's analysis, Critical Realists assume that events are contingently necessary because a particular combination of tendencies and counter-tendencies in specific historical conditions typically makes one particular outcome (or set of outcomes) rather than another necessary (Jessop 2005, 4). Rose writes on more deep-seated causes of moves to an "'intelligent' welfare state ... that is 'personalized and flexible, designed to promote individual choice and personal responsibility'" (1999, 257). New Labour social enterprise policies formed an essential component of these moves "from welfare to workfare" described in Chapter 3. Chapters 4 and 5 show several references to initial causal mechanisms from the 1970s onwards which led ultimately to the emergence of social enterprise as a lower cost delivery vehicle for public services, to be funded increasingly with external private investment. Chapter 7, 'Conclusions', shows that while this process of transformation continues, it is today almost complete.

Critical Realism and social enterprise

While much has been written about Critical Realism's general principles (Archer et al. 1998; Archer 1982; Bhaskar 1978; 1989; 2015; Jessop 2005), the author has been influenced by the smaller number of more recent and relevant contributions which apply Critical Realism to qualitative research (Danermark et al. 2002; Fletcher 2020; 2016; Meyer and Lunnay 2013).

The author's response to the "New Labour phenomenon" interpretations above is summed up by Carter and New, Bhaskar, Jessop, O'Mahoney and Vincent and others (Archer 1982; Archer et al. 1998; Bhaskar 1978; 1989; 2015; Carter and New 2004; Jessop 2005; O'Mahoney and Vincent 2014). We confront a world "which is not directly produced or constructed by us, but is rather the complex outcome of earlier interactions between people and their structural contexts" (Carter and New 2004, 12). "Critical realists do not deny the reality of events and discourses; on the contrary, they insist upon them. But they hold that we will only be able to understand – and so change – the social world if we identify the structures at work that generate those events or discourses" (Bhaskar 1989, 2). "Critical realists also assume that events are contingently necessary because a particular combination of tendencies and counter-tendencies in specific historical conditions typically makes one particular outcome (or set of outcomes) rather than another necessary" (Jessop 2005, 4). "The layperson's predilection to accept widely accepted socially constructed versions of reality is often part of the problem in the first place, so unless our ontology is able to separate people's beliefs from the reality they represent we will end up with another form of thin explanation" (O'Mahoney and Vincent 2014, 6). In contrast to the many UK contributions which either describe social enterprise as an innovative

New Labour phenomenon or a straightforward policy shift from co-operatives to social enterprises, this book seeks to pierce these thin explanations by explaining their underlying, deep-seated and ambitious motives and causal mechanisms from the 1970s onwards.

There are underlying phenomena which explain the appearance of New Labour's social enterprise. Throughout the entire period covered in this book, the author hopes that his background enables the deciphering of causal mechanisms which other contributions may not have recognised or may have omitted. While everyday concepts must be included in conducting research and forming concepts, concepts of reality, including "science", "everyday knowledge" and "common sense" often constitute the social phenomena making up the field of research itself (Danermark et al. 2002, 33). "As researchers we will only be able to understand what is going on in the social world if we understand the social structures that have given rise to the phenomena that we are trying to understand" (Saunders, Lewis and Thornhill 2012, 115).

"(U)nlike relativism/idealism, Critical Realism contends that there is a real world, independent of our knowledge about it and that it is possible to gain knowledge so determined" (Danermark et al. 2002, 202). Critical Realism challenges researchers to move beyond mere description of social situations to "a more critical assessment of the relationship between structural factors and human agency" (Blundel 2007, 4, 12). Reality is not a series of events, where one thing follows another with observable regularity. The relation between reality and our knowledge about it comprises three distinct ontological domains: the empirical (our experiences), the actual (events), and the real, where the mechanisms are what produce the events in the world (Danermark et al. 2002, 203). Approaches simply based on social construction – such as those of Nicholls, Grenier, Westall and Teasdale above (Grenier 2009; 2002; Nicholls 2010; Teasdale 2012; Westall 2009; 2001a) – impede "the development of a more nuanced understanding of the role of human activity in the reproduction or transformation of entities" (Fleetwood 2004, 22). To the author, these recent approaches struggle to find a contemporary meaning or relevance for social enterprise. In contrast to various Third Way approaches (Giddens 1998), this book explores their neglect of pre-existing domains and their resistance to other infrastructures from mainland Europe.

Programme of interviews and data gathering

For the author, Critical Realism not only ensures greater methodological rigour, independence and objectivity but offers some relief from any perceived bias from personal experiences. It is necessary here to explain briefly some underlying components of this approach which feature throughout this book.

Reed (2005) conducts exploration in painstaking detail of each historical case, "revealing the complex interaction between relevant corporate agents, structural conditions, and situational contingencies" (Edwards, O'Mahoney and Vincent 2014, 6–7). Easterby-Smith et al. provide further context for this book (2012, 29):

> Two other features are important in Critical Realism. First is the idea that causality exists as potential, rather than the automatic correlation of events that is normally associated with strong positivism. Second is the idea, drawn partly from critical theory, that many of these underlying mechanisms do not work in the interests of ordinary people and employees, and that greater awareness of their underlying causes will provide potential for emancipation from their effects.

Especially in chapters 4 and 5, the author examines causal mechanisms which enable his conclusions. "And the essential movement of scientific theory will be seen to consist in the movement from the manifest phenomena of social life, as conceptualized in the experience of the social agents concerned, to the essential relations that necessitate them" (Bhaskar 2015, 28). As a basis for these chapters, formal interviews of various "social agents" took place in London from September 2015 onwards. These provided further suggestions for interviews for the remainder of 2015 and the beginning of 2016 on a "snowball" basis. During interviews throughout 2016 and 2017, the author ensured a wide range of views on key topics, from social agents supporting and opposing policy changes. From a range of 50 original contacts, 25 interviews were selected from a representative sample from each group in time, including 6 Former SEL board members, five former senior civil servants, eight different representatives from the wider Co-operative Movement, former government advisors and key participants. These were key players, especially those former senior civil servants and representatives from organisations previously involved in policy development and implementation.

Further research and data collection included detailed analysis of hard copy, internet literature and documentary archive data, including from Bishopsgate Library and Institute, London, the IDOX Group, Glasgow (for documents from the original Planning Exchange, Glasgow), the Co-operative Union, SEL and SEC. Archived material was also generously provided by former senior civil servants and representatives of co-operative and social enterprise organisations.

The author also convened a Focus Group at GCU's London Campus during September 2016 as a "neutral venue", with key players and representatives, to discuss developments based on their personal involvement during the period 1998 to 2002.[1] From the outset, it was made clear to Focus Group participants that as facilitator the author would only seek to steer discussion in relevant directions (Morgan and Krueger 1993, 5), taking a peripheral rather than central role (Farnsworth and Boon 2010, 608). The author was careful not to let participants rehearse their positions without further evaluation (Bristol and Fern 2003, 435) and took note of attitude shifts (439). Focus Group dynamics were recognised and attended to in a theoretically informed way (Farnsworth and Boon 2010, 620).

Components of Critical Realism

Interviews and data collection described above were coded using NVivo software. Since all were considered as important, dominant codes were then used to identify regular patterns or demi-regularities (Fletcher 2016, 186). "Demi-regularities are imperfect patterns or trends that indicate the probable operation of a causal mechanism, although its operation may sometimes be mitigated by other conditions or mechanisms in the openness and complexity of the social world" (Danermark et al. 2002; Fletcher 2020, 181). Preliminary identification of such causes is similar to pre-coding, which "may give rise to provisional codes which are subsequently firmed up and 'validated' by ongoing data collection and analysis and may eventually be adopted as core codes and categories" (Meyer and Lunnay 2013, 6; Fletcher 2016, 186; Fletcher 2020, 191). Coding from interviews and data, whether on co-operatives or new structures, showed emerging patterns or demi-regularities for the increasing marginalisation of public ownership, public sector delivery, collective structures and more democratic control.

Abduction combines observations, often with theory identified in literature, to produce the most plausible theoretical explanation of the mechanisms that caused the events. Abduction re-describes the observable everyday objects of social science provided by interviewees or from data collection in an abstracted and more general sense in order to describe the sequence of causation that gives rise to observed regularities in the pattern of events. If the explanation of the mechanisms is successful, theory and data will be consistently and effectively "fitted together" in such a way as to show the nature of the mechanism more clearly (O'Mahoney and Vincent 2014, 16). Abduction thus moves from the descriptive level of interviews and data collection to a more abstract analysis of the data. The author follows this approach throughout chapters 3, 4 and 5, where relevant examples are elaborated. Abduction thus enables forming associations that enable the researcher to discern relations and connections that are not otherwise evident or obvious.

Through data and interviews and following discussion during the Focus Group, the author discerned a political shift to looser governance structures in a more competitive marketplace, with resistance to the concepts of redistribution and reciprocity inherent in more social and community structures of a social economy. Much of this was fundamentally different to social economy approaches outside the UK.

The most important stage of Critical Realism, retroduction, focuses on causal mechanisms and conditions – which may not be those immediately observable or decipherable. "[How] do we identify the deeper structures from which these powers and liabilities originate? The goal of retroduction is to constantly move between empirical and deeper levels of reality to fully understand the phenomenon under study" (Fletcher 2016, 189). The author is also guided by Meyer and Lunnay's (2013, 2) interpretation of Critical Realism for practical research:

> Abduction is a way of (re)interpreting data and used in conjunction with retroduction, often leads to the formation of a new conceptual framework or theory (Danermark et al. 1997). Retroduction is a way of conceptualising by identifying the circumstance without which something (eg. trust) cannot exist.

Retroduction seeks to ascertain what the broader context must be like in order for the mechanisms observed to be as they are and not otherwise. This involves identifying patterns over different times and contexts to ask creatively 'what if?' to identify hidden causal mechanisms. This, in turn, suggests a number of other causal processes which affect the mechanism observed, with an opportunity to understand more about the relationship between the mechanisms observed and the contexts in which these operate (O'Mahoney and Vincent 2014, 17). "Critical realism is committed to a retroductive mode of inference in which putative causal relations are imputed by reasoning backwards from the phenomena under investigation and asking 'what, if it existed, would account for this phenomenon?'" (Reed 2005, 1631).

While abduction uses theory to provide an explanation that fits the data, retroduction involves a more vertical movement through in-depth ontology to identify the most pertinent causal structures and mechanisms. Retroduction is defined as the movement from "the manifest phenomena of social life, as conceptualised in the experience of the social agents concerned, to the essential relations that necessitate them" – that is, the movement from empirical to structural/causal (Bhaskar 2015, 26) (Fletcher 2020, 186). It is retroduction which prompts the author to examine deeper pollical economic roots – the features of capitalism and neoliberalism described below (Fletcher 2016, 186, 188, 189, 190). As shown in chapters 4 and 5, this is not simply "advanced capitalism", but refined gradual and continuing processes to reposition the third sector as a low-cost and flexible public service delivery mechanism.

Fletcher recognises the risk of failing to retroduce the deep causes of various infrastructure and policy guidelines. As shown in Chapter 4, a simple attribution to NCVO's 1980s managerialism and to 1990s Demos policies for a mixed economy in welfare state delivery fails to explain why these happened in the first place. They do not acknowledge the deeper political economic guidelines which could eventually lead us to a much more basic mechanism: capitalism as a structure (Fletcher 2020, 188). The need for capitalism to replenish itself yields underlying structures and mechanisms for social enterprise and the third sector (Boltanski and Chiapello 2005, 30):

> [F]unctioning as a recording chamber, resonance-box, and crucible where new compromises are formed, we find the spirit of capitalism. It is renegotiated, challenged, or even destroyed prior to emerging anew, through transformation of the mechanisms geared towards profit and justice alike, and continuous metamorphosis in the need for justification under fire from critique.

Using abduction and retroduction, an unbroken causal chain is interpreted from 1980s National Council for Voluntary Organisations' (NCVO's) managerialism through 1990s' state pressure to fashion the third sector to deliver public services, through to implementation of procurement and contracts under New Labour. The most recent manifestation of this transformation is a constant rebadging of social enterprise alongside impact investment.

Conclusion

Against a Critical Realist background, the author believes his approach is relevant for a debate where most other UK contributions show little linkage between current social enterprise literature and previous practice in the 1970s and 1980s or mention other contributions reflecting mainland European and other contemporary developments. Reed provides a fitting conclusion for this chapter:

> By linking local changes in organizational forms and control regimes to deeper structural changes within the political economy of contemporary capitalism, realist-based research and analysis provides the opportunity to understand and explain the complex interplay between managerial agency and structural constraint over time and place. (Reed 2005, 1639)

Note

1 The following background information was sent in advance by the author to the focus group:

These are some issues for discussion at the Focus Group:

- During this period and the early years of Social Enterprise London, was there a shift from cooperatives to social enterprise? If so, why was this taking place?
- Did the direction of Social Enterprise London reflect or precede changes "on the ground"?
- How much discussion was there in the wider cooperative and social enterprise movements of any changes taking place?
- How were any changes taking place in structures and policies seen in the wider third sector at the time and what reaction and responses did these produce?

3

Theoretical foundations and conceptual interpretations for the third sector

Background to this chapter

To set this book in a wider context, in this chapter the author surveys alternative discourses. UK contributions on social enterprise and the third sector have been highly selective in their references to and reliance on other countries' policy regimes. As an example, though North American discourses are often quoted, through their operation in a market economy, the author contends below that these are often not helpful to UK comparisons. There are also wide-ranging discourses in mainland Europe, from which UK contributions have only imported the smaller, more marketised EMES variant. Regulationist approaches and those in Quebec are also covered below, since though they were contemporaneous with social economy and social enterprise developments in the UK, these are rarely mentioned.

In view of the policy entrepreneur role of many academics, which is elaborated in Chapter 1, models and frameworks included or excluded from UK contributions often have a significance beyond their basic publication and promotion. This is particularly relevant following approaches made to UK academics during the 1970s from the CIRIEC, which are described below. The consequences of a selective reliance on a limited number of policy regimes by UK academics as policy entrepreneurs are further described in Chapter 6.

In contrast, O'Mahoney and Vincent summarise the author's approach throughout this chapter (O'Mahoney and Vincent 2014, 13):

A standard review of the literature for a Critical Realist (CR) researcher will attempt three things. It will first aim to distinguish more realistic from less realistic theorizing, often drawing on a historical analysis of the phenomena under study. Second, having identified the more realistic theories, it will seek to identify the mechanisms that a researcher might expect to be at play in the research area and the contexts in which these might be best studied. Third, the literature review might seek to identify gaps concerning the interplay of mechanisms and contexts which warrant further study.

Many UK academic contributions either rely on North American individual social entrepreneurship and non-profit models or an interpretation of market-oriented WISEs from mainland Europe, as typified in contributions from EMES. Because these discourses exclude other significant mainland European and Canadian literatures, for nearly 20 years UK contributions on social enterprise and third sector development have been dominated by the market. In particular, these rarely mention earlier social and solidarity economy approaches to deindustrialisation, job losses and the development of third sector policy elsewhere, including French Regulationist and social solidarity approaches from organisations like CIRIEC from the 1970s onwards. The author contends that these neglected approaches and interpretations are relevant since they were directly contemporaneous with the growth of UK community indigenous structures during the 1970s and 1980s described in Chapter 4. These differences are described elsewhere as the two "'tensions' of 'social enterprise' – between those enterprises which offer their output for sale and those whose activities are 'non market'" (Defourny and Nyssens 2006, 8).

North America

A difficulty for those UK contributions which seek to borrow from North American contributions is that there is no equivalent of the third sector or a social economy in North America. Defourny and Nyssens provide a European interpretation of the social economy (Defourny and Nyssens 2010c, 39):

> [A]ccording to most European traditions (Evers and Laville 2004), the third sector brings together cooperatives, associations, mutual societies and increasingly foundations, in other words, all not-for-profit organisations, ie. organisations not seeking profit maximization for those who control them. The third sector they form together is labelled the "social economy" in some European countries.

Because of their completely different context, the author seeks to show below why North American antecedents for nonprofits and social entrepreneurs are hardly reliable for the UK. Many of these were influenced by the marketisation of North American nonprofits under Ronald Reagan and George H. W. Bush "thousand points of light" polices which coincided with Thatcher and Major Conservative governments' expansion of quasi-market public service delivery. North American literatures from the 1970s and 1980s onwards show a growth of nonprofits which was market-driven, with their fiscal exemptions allowing different structures and developments from mainland Europe and the UK. Alongside reductions in US Federal government spending, non-profit growth was funded through philanthropy, foundations and earned income in the market. North American social entrepreneurship is essentially based on the market and social innovation by individual social entrepreneurs, promoted by Dees and others and networks through the Ashoka, Schwab and Skoll foundations. As exemplified by Austin et al., North American approaches make no mention of social causes or needs and instead focus on "actors" and "key attributes of social entrepreneurs" as if there are no other participants in social welfare (Austin 2006; Grenier 2009, 17). Though UK contributions on social entrepreneurship have freely borrowed from North America, few have commented on a fundamentally different context and structures.

Non-distribution, transaction costs and fiduciary duty

One of the main difficulties for UK contributions in making comparisons with North American interpretations is that non-profit concepts of non-distribution, transactions costs and a fiduciary duty to stakeholders are central.[1] In contrast, many UK and European structures, including co-operatives, make distribution to members. Much non-profit literature derives from the theory of the firm and business management, with a difference between classical and institutional approaches. Neoclassical theory seeks to explain resource allocation as a process guided by prices. Institutional approaches describe resource allocation as guided by management. Coase described how the supremacy of the price mechanism as the key influence on firms' behaviour, with management's "reacting to price changes" and "rearranging factors of production" (Coase 1937, 405).

In contrast, Demsetz rejects a core model for the competitive firm from classical economic theory, suggesting that management's judgement is paramount. But he supports Coase in recognising that firms may be more efficient than open market transactions for some economic activities (Demsetz 1997, 428). Badelt also describes entrepreneurship theories which can be viewed as "institutionalist" for the non-profit sector – which makes it difficult to compare them with more formal neoclassical theories. So a detailed description of entrepreneurship theories has to deal with the motives of the entrepreneurs (Badelt 1997, 165, 166).

Hansmann's non-distribution constraint is the most important characteristic used to define a non-profit typology – which is the main reason for the author's contention that the theoretical underpinning of nonprofits has less relevance in the UK. He summarises the advantages of non-distribution for nonprofits (Hansmann 1980a, 879):

[N]onprofit firms are at a disadvantage relative to for-profit firms in various respects, including access to capital, efficiency of operation, and speed of entry and growth in expanding markets. Consequently, whether non-profit firms are more suitable than for-profit firms in any given industry depends upon the balance of competing factors. Only if, in any given case, the protection afforded patrons by the non distribution constraint is so valuable as to outweigh the disadvantages just mentioned will non-profit firms have a competitive edge.

Because Hansmann sought to distinguish nonprofits, he wrote that this constraint limits the possibility of profit maximising organisations being able to label themselves social enterprises to obtain unwarranted fiscal and reputational advantages. Based on non-distribution, nonprofits can thus be trusted not to exploit any advantage over the consumer resulting from contract failure (Hansmann 1980b, 896). The non-profit abandons any benefits from full ownership in favour of stricter fiduciary constraints on managers, which are governed by a "fiduciary duty" to customers rather than a profit motive (Hansmann 1996, 228; 1980b, 879). Where the value of protection to stakeholders and patrons outweighs a traditional market approach, nonprofits may have a competitive edge (Hansmann 1996, 228).

"The informational role of public benefit non profits reflects the importance of economising on bounded rationality-induced transaction costs as opposed to opportunism-induced costs emphasised by the conventional transaction cost approach" (Valentinov 2007, 9). Hansmann also concludes that the main strength of nonprofits which produce goods or services is often their being well established incumbents in the market, since they do not gain significant comparative advantages from mitigating the cost of contracting (Bacchiega and Borzaga 2001, 281).

Management approaches

A further difficulty for UK contributions in borrowing from North America is that social entrepreneurs have always operated alongside private competitors in the marketplace. Dominated by Dees (1998a; 1998b), earlier North American management literatures viewed social entrepreneurship as a branch of mainstream entrepreneurship, management and organisation studies, based on individual entrepreneurs, and taking a positivist, determinist and objectivist view. Though these are relevant in explaining the development stages of social entrepreneurship research, contributions confined to this North American market context have less relevance to the UK. However, Dees accepts that there is a wider "bottom line" for social entrepreneurs, based on their intended social impact, whether "housing for the homeless, a cleaner environment, improved access to health care, more effective education, reduced poverty, protection of abused children, deeper appreciation of the arts, or some other social improvement" (Dees 2003, 2) But his difficulty is that social value in this wider bottom line cannot be easily measured by the market mechanism. The discipline of these "markets" is frequently not closely aligned with the social entrepreneur's mission (Dees 1998a; Petrella and Richez-Battesti 2014, 146).

Because North American social entrepreneurship discourses originated in business schools and MBA programmes, social entrepreneurship was constructed in management terms within non-profit organisations (Badelt 1997; Young 2006; Dees and Anderson 2006). These focus on organisational processes, performance measurement, access to finance, legal form, and growth strategies (Mair et al. 2006; Nicholls 2006; cited in Grenier 2009, 17). Management and business studies dominate literature on social entrepreneurship (Dees and Anderson 2006; Nicholls 2006; Austin 2006). Approaches and constructs stemming from research on entrepreneurship in the business sector shaped the first attempts to conceptualise social entrepreneurship (Mair and Marti 2006, 39). "The control systems developed by journals and university departments alike exert a confining if well-meaning hold on the jugular of scholarship, which threatens to strangle the development of new possibilities" (Morgan 1990, 29). Social entrepreneurship definitions are thus "a subset, or specific application of entrepreneurship as conceived as a business school discipline" (Haynes 2012, 59). Based on these business school interpretations, the role of North American and UK academics as policy entrepreneurs is elaborated in Chapter 1.

Mair and Marti emphasise social value. Social entrepreneurship deserves attention as a field of research, with a potential to inform and enhance the field of entrepreneurship and an opportunity to challenge central concepts and assumptions (Mair and Marti 2006, 39, 42). Daft and Lewin also urge the breaking out of this "normal science" straightjacket through what they call "symbol creation research" in contrast to "symbol communication research". "Symbol creation research, on the other hand, involves the creation of new grammar, new variables, and new definitions, thus spawning new paradigms" (Daft and Lewin 1990, 5).

Many earlier contributions which describe a transition from the classical economics approach to a more institutional setting for social enterprise have also been influenced by DiMaggio and Powell on institutional isomorphism (DiMaggio and Powell 1983). Suchman describes the role of academics as policy entrepreneurs, with universities as "important centres for the development of organisational norms among professional managers and their staff", elaborating on legitimisation through their institutional theories (DiMaggio and Powell 1983; Suchman 1995, 571).

Social enterprise – two schools of thought

Dees' patterns of individual social entrepreneurship behaviour are supplemented with proposals made by Drucker (1985) and Peredo and McLean (2006, 58). But he was criticised by practitioners for his lack of focus on earned income. If "traditional non profits" had a better understanding of social enterprise they would "summon the courage to begin emphasising earned income, sustainability and self sufficiency instead of charitable contributions, government subsidies and eternal dependency rather than returning to the same individual donors, foundations and government agencies" (Boschee and McClurg 2003, 2, 3). Dart views Dees' definition of social entrepreneurs as "change agents" as too broad and prefers the narrower focus of Boschee on business and revenue generation. The decline of welfare state ideology has meant the "emergence of a renewed and pervasive faith in market and business based approaches and solutions". Dart's conclusion is that social enterprise is conferred with moral legitimacy because "as business becomes a more preeminent organisational model and as increasingly wide swaths of human society become conceptualized as markets, then the business-like hybrid face of social enterprise is legitimate and in fact responsive to the times" (Dart 2004, 412, 418, 422).

To widen the acceptability of his original 1998 definitional contribution, Dees later developed two social enterprise schools of thought (Dees and Anderson 2006, 41). The first and dominant school (the "earned income school") refers to the use of commercial activities by non-profit organisations in support of their mission. They developed commercial activities to solve funding problems after cutbacks in public grants and encountered increasing difficulties in mobilising private donations from individuals or foundations (Petrella and Richez-Battesti 2014, 148). Discussion in North America has been strongly influenced by the role of foundations and consultancy firms "that developed a whole industry focusing on business methods and earned income strategies to be adopted by non profits looking for alternative or more stable sources of funding" (Defourny and Nyssens 2010c, 39).

Dees and Anderson's second social innovation school focuses on establishing new and better ways to address social problems or meet social needs. This school showed that, irrespective of sector, social value was central. The "social entrepreneur's value proposition targets an underserved, neglected, or highly disadvantaged population that lacks the financial means or political clout to achieve the transformative benefit on its own" (Martin and Usberg 2007).

Bornstein's originators of change include St Francis of Assisi. "Across the world, social entrepreneurs are demonstrating new approaches to many social ills and new models to create wealth, promote social wellbeing and restore the environment" (Bornstein 2004, 9). Bornstein portrayed social entrepreneurs as "transformative forces: people with new ideas to address major projects who are relentless in the in the pursuit of their visions" (Dees and Anderson 2006, 46). This social innovation school adopts a Schumpeterian conception of the social entrepreneur as a change maker – an entrepreneur with a social mission, as advocated by foundations such as Schwab and Ashoka which "encourage the professionalization of social entrepreneurs" (Defourny and Nyssens 2010c, 40; Petrella and Richez-Battesti 2014, 148). However, Dees and Anderson's examples of CafeDirect, Delancy Street Foundation, Grameen Bank, Virginia Eastern Short Corporation and Habitat for Humanity are hardly typical social enterprises (Dees and Anderson 2006, 52, 53). Because, according to this interpretation, the social entrepreneur aims for value in the form of large-scale, transformational benefit that accrues either to a significant segment of society or to society at large (Martin and Osberg 2007), the author questions its actual potential for innovation, since repeated censi of social enterprises show that only a minority achieve a scale needed to realise this kind of transformative benefit. At the time of Dees' contributions, there was also considerable North American evidence[2] that most social enterprises did not have the size, scale, resources or ambition to achieve this scale of transformation (Emerson and Twersky 1996; Massarksky and Beinhacker 2002; Zimmerman and Dart 1998).

Europe

Though there is a much wider definition of the social economy in mainland Europe, as explained later, most UK contributions borrow only from a narrower and marketised EMES variant. Laville further explains the social economy (Laville 2010b, 229):

> the social economy includes all economic activities conducted by enterprises, primarily co-operatives, associations and mutual benefit societies, whose ethics express the following principles: placing service to its members or to the community ahead of profit; autonomous management; a democratic decision-making process; the primacy of people and work over capital in the distribution of revenues.

Though in mainland Europe there have been numerous contributions on a social and solidarity economy (Jean-Louis Laville, Dennis Young, and Philippe Eynaud 2015; Fecher and Lévesque 2008; Laville 1996; 2011; 2013), reference is rarely made to these in UK contributions. There were also debates initiated by CIRIEC in its Annals of Public and Co-operative Economics (Gelard 1997), including contributions by Fecher and Lévesque (Fecher and Lévesque 2008; 2015).

European theory

From the nineteenth century onwards, there have been important legal distinctions for social economy structures in mainland Europe. Co-operatives, mutual societies and associations are defined as social economy organisations so that "a ban on the distribution on profits is not the decisive criterion, but rather the material interest of investors is subject to limits". This means a "boundary between capitalist and social economy organisations" (Laville 2010b, 228).

In both Belgium and France there was a historical concept of mutual aid associations in the nineteenth century, regulated by the state and integrated into the non-market economy to complement social transfers (Laville et al. 1999, 18). The Bismarckian corporatist concept of social insurance for wage earners in Germany, France and Belgium in a regulated service regime gave rise to a non-market isomorphism of Third System structures that brought them closer to government and prompted them to form large national federations. These structures were linked to political parties, churches, the Red Cross and non-aligned organisations in Germany, to lay and Catholic bodies in France, and to socialist and Christian bodies in Belgium (Laville et al. 1999, 20). Defourny and Nyssens describe these Christian Democrat welfare systems (Defourny and Nyssens 2010c, 34):

> In the countries with a Bismarckian tradition – which, according to the Esping-Andersen (1999) typology, can also be referred to as the countries belonging to the "corporatist" group – (namely Belgium, France, Germany, and Ireland), non-profit private organisations, mainly financed and regulated by public bodies play an important role in the provision of social services (Salamon et al. 2004).

Though these are nonprofits, in contrast to the United States, most distribute payments and benefits to their members. The "co-operative model becomes the point of reference for the whole of the social economy, so that only entrepreneurial associations that have a company form are included" (Laville 2010b, 230). According to most European traditions (Evers and Laville 2004), the third sector includes co-operatives, associations, mutual societies and, increasingly, foundations – in other words, organisations not seeking profit maximisation. They are usually called the social economy and involve "the quest for democracy through economic activity" (Defourny and Nyssens 2010c, 39). This social and solidarity economy is underpinned by Polanyi's core principles of the market, redistribution and reciprocity, so that citizens can escape from traditional forms of philanthropy (Laville 2010b, 231).

Alongside this broad array of social economy solidarity organisations across mainland Europe, there is a narrower, marketised EMES version of WISEs (Defourny and Nyssens 2010b, 290), which are described in more detail below. In many countries, WISEs are officially recognised, with a specific public scheme supporting their mission at the national level (as in the case in Portugal, France, Ireland and Finland) or at regional level (for example in Belgium, Spain and Italy) (Nyssens 2008, 8). Despite this, it is from this narrower EMES interpretation which many UK contributions have borrowed.

Mainland European differences from North American approach

These different approaches in North America and mainland Europe described above are not interchangeable. "It is clear that supporting the development of social enterprise cannot be done just through exporting US or European approaches." A European approach to the third sector priori-tises governance arrangements. "In Europe, the notion of social enterprise focuses more heavily on the way an organisation is governed and what its purpose is rather than on whether it strictly adheres to the non-distribution constraint of a formal non profit organisation" (Defourny and Nyssens 2010c, 48, 49).

Social enterprise in Europe belongs to the "social economy", where social benefit is the main driving force, with a social co-operative or association formed to provide employment or specific care services in a participatory framework. In the United States, it generally means any type of non-profit involved in earned income generation (Kerlin 2006, 249, 250). The European social economy approach with its emphasis on democratic participation contrasts with the Johns Hopkins non-profit approach (Salamon and Anheier 1997b), which through prohibition of profit distributions, in prac-tice excludes all co-operatives and mutual aid organisations. By prohibiting distribution of profits, nonprofits exclude co-operatives, since these gener-ally redistribute a share of their surplus to members and mutuals which refund surpluses to members as lower premiums (Defourny and Develtere 1999, 18).

Much of this divergence between North America and Europe rests on different perceptions of the role of a third sector or "third system" in society. Many mainland European contributors argue against Hansmann's (1987) and Weisbrod's (1988) concept of nonprofits' emerging from market failure to reduce informational asymmetries and state failure to respond to minority demands (Lewis 1999). Nonprofits represent a hierarchical structure in which the market and state are pillars of society, with the third sector only an auxiliary force (Laville et al. 1999, 11). In contrast, European theory sees the "third system" as part of the public sphere of modern democratic societies within civil society as a whole (Evers 1995). The public sphere is not a homogeneous whole but a "plurality of public spheres" (Chanial 1992, cited in Laville et al. 1999, 12). European contributions view US nonprofits as a "second or third rank option" when the market or state were inadequate, with society the result of individual choices and individuals considered as consumers. This North American concept of society is invalidated by a "history more than two centuries long" (Laville 2010c, 225–7). In further criticism, Habermas questions whether rational choice theory can explain "how society can possibly exist if all persons exclusively make decisions based on their own individual preferences and benefits". Social enterprise models premised on egocentric decision making fail to explain how individuals are embedded in social structures and thereby disregard "how changes in interests and value orientations relate to social context" (Hulgård 2010, 294).

European solidarity-based TSOs operating with public funding suggests these organisations' linkages to trust, "which is considerably richer than the legal-economic perspective of Hansmann (1987), with its heavy emphasis on legal constraints on profit distribution". The non-distribution constraint is insufficient for building trust (Ortman and Schlesinger 1997) and solidarity organisations show ways to develop as collective entities based on an interactive process among different types of stakeholders (Laville et al. 1999, 28). So there is no North American equivalent of European concepts of solidarity, mutual aid and associations, which emerged in the nineteenth century after the French Revolution as a social-democratic link, with solidarity as a debt to society, as proposed by the solidarity theorists (Leroux 1851, 170, cited in Laville et al. 1999, 15).

Approaches outside the UK: the social and solidarity economy

"Solidarity based" organisations differ from the traditional functioning of the structures of the third sector and the market-based economy at large (Laville and Nyssens 2000, 68). An initial legal definition from the Belgian Walloon Council for the Social Economy includes the "aim of providing members or the community a service, rather than generating profit; independent management; democratic decision-making, and priority given to persons and work over capital in the distribution of income" (Laville and Nyssens 2000, 68: footnote). Compared with the three poles of the market, the state, and private households, the civil and solidarity-based economy triangle gives the same importance to the dimension of public space inherent in third sector collective action" (Laville and Nyssens 2000, 82).

There are three basic principles for the solidarity economy – the market, redistribution and reciprocity (Laville 2010b, 1465), principles which derive from Polanyi (Hodgson 2017, 3). Polanyi (1944, 272) suggested that "'Reciprocity and redistribution are principles of economic behaviour which apply not only to small primitive communities, but also to large and wealthy empires'" (cited in Hodgson 2017, 4). The economic activity of social enterprises is embedded – a concept central to Polanyi (1944) and Granovetter (1985). "Initiative and solidarity are reconciled since individuals are uniting voluntarily to undertake joint action that will create economic activity and jobs, while simultaneously forging a new social solidarity and reinforcing social cohesion" (cited in Laville 2003, 400). Veltz (1998) argues that the market economy can only function by mobilising all kinds of non-market social resources – material and intangible collective infrastructures (physical facilities, education, health, etc.), "an accumulation which is often 'forgotten' by the private players in our countries" (cited in Laville 2003, 402). This context of a "plural economy" (OECD 1996) is based on different economic principles from the market and redistribution, including the principle of reciprocity – the relationship between groups and individuals through "services that derive their meaning from the desire to develop a social link between the parties involved (Mauss, 1950; Polanyi, 1957, 19)" (Laville and Nyssens 2000, 78).

Proximity services

As a central component of a social and solidarity economy, "proximity services" are "sub-categories such as community, personal and social services show notable particularly strong growth" (Laville 2003, 394). In 1990 these services totalled 30% of employment in France, 38% in Sweden and 32% in the UK. These services respond to individual or collective needs based on a definition of proximity that can be "objective, in that it is anchored within a specific social space, or subjective, in that it refers to the relational dimension of the service" (Laville 2003, 396). "The quasi-collective nature of many proximity services and the relevance of equity implies market failure and calls for public regulation" (Badelt 1997). The externalities at stake tend to be "nondepletable" and cannot be "internalised" by the market mechanism (Mas-Colell, Whinston and Green 1995). The European Commission refers to many of these as "local initiatives for development and employment" (Laville 2003, 395), which from the 1980s benefitted from EU funding. Though proximity services clearly occupy a significant status in mainland European third sector discourses, they rarely achieve mention in UK contributions.

Associations

There are significant differences between the history of co-operatives in France and the UK. After the French revolution of 1848, the institutionalisation of French third sector structures began under Emperor Napoleon III from 1860 to 1870. "In the nineteenth century, the extension of market generated reactions on the part of society, among which the setting up of associations, followed by the construction of a protecting welfare state. Associations were 'the first line of defence'" (Laville 2010b, 1465). For the UK "late 19th century Britain had effective central government institutions, but a small central bureaucracy (in stark contrast to the late 20th century) and a strong desire to limit the activities of central government" (Lewis 1999, 258). In France, these were followed by other components of the social economy – non-profit organisations, co-operatives and mutuals, with a legal framework. This compartmentalisation and forms of economic integration contributed to the multiplication and fragmentation of subdivisions among the different components of this social economy (Laville 2010b, 1466). In a UK interpretation, Knight writes these that associations "played a role that would be the envy of the Poverty Lobby in Britain. The key difference of course was that groups concerned with poverty were out of step with the philosophy of the Government" (Knight 1993, 261).

Buchez (1866) promised "the association of work and not that of capital" by "the constitution of a common social capital which would be inalienable and indivisible" (cited in Demoustier and Rousselière 2004, 6). The French approach to the creation of associations was driven by "the republican ideal deriving from the French Revolution that denied any organised mediation between the individual and the state, and the anti-individualist tendencies that stressed the importance of intermediary structures (Barthelemy 2000, cited in Moulaert and Ailenei 2005, 2039). During the 1970s associations became "a major economic force in industrial nations", sometimes accounting for 10% or more of the active labour force. In France, Germany and the United States, they "contributed more to growth in employment in the 1980s than any other economic sector (Ben-Ner and Anheier 1997, 336)" (Fecher and Lévesque 2008, 694) This is a totally different situation compared with the UK, where equivalents such as Friendly and Benefit Societies operated with only a minimal role following the post-war advent of National Insurance and the NHS.

Laville describes the UK perspective of charitable associations' previous role in welfare administration. These institutions acted as intermediaries between the state and the citizens, while being at the same time "an integral part of the State fabric (Lewis 1997, 169)" (Laville et al. 1999, 14). There were earlier UK possibilities. "The first socialism I would describe as associationism … associationism (like socialism, an early-nineteenth-century word) can be contrasted with statism" (Yeo 2001, 56). These were working people's associations long before political parties became dominant and "the soil in which a Party for Labour grew, to a greater extent than anywhere else in the world" (Yeo 2001, 8). But the "classical theory" of democracy through consumer-oriented, market-based, machine political parties was preferred over the Webbs' "Industrial Democracy (1897)" (Yeo 2002, 14). The common origins of co-operatives and mutual societies have been forgotten in the UK, so that they are today commonly referred to as "the third sector" rather than the social economy (Laville, Lévesque and Mendell 2005, 4). Yeo's narrative rarely enters any UK contribution on the emergence of co-operatives or social enterprise.

Co-operatives

Using Pestoff's analysis (1998), Laville writes of the "cooperatisation of social services". This "cooperatisation" developed to increase the role of users, such as parents, in the organisation of childcare services, and has been accepted because of the financial pressures on the public sector. The legal status of co-operatives was used to propose services that the public sector was unable to provide (Laville 2003, 397). The social economy in France has been dominated by co-operatives. Following Fauquet and Colombain (1965), and Vienney (1980) the co-operative model became the reference for the whole of the social economy, including associations which are enterprises. The social economy thus comprises non-capitalist enterprises active in the market (Laville 2011, 7).

In Italy, social co-operatives became popular through their ability to deliver services such as the creation of jobs for those excluded from the labour market (primarily women) and the creation of new services. Social co-operatives first emerged in the 1970s and grew rapidly. Borzaga's estimate (1997) shows about 3,000, representing approximately 100,000 associates and providing services for several hundred thousand people (cited in Laville 2011, 7). Other countries followed Italy in 1991, with Portuguese models in 1998 of social co-operatives that bring together "salaried" members, paid skilled workers employed in the services and "voluntary" members contributing to the production of the services. At a national level the French government initiated a State Secretariat of Civil and Solidarity-Based Economics for the first time between 2000 and 2002 (Laville 2003, 390). This represented a joint development of supply and demand for services for the purpose "not only of soliciting individual users as consumers within a private functional framework but also of integrating them as citizens in the political arena and as community and family members in an informal environment (Evers, 1997, p. 55)" (Laville 2010b, 1467).

Though a legal form for some co-operatives dates from UK Industrial and Provident Society Acts in 1852 and 1893, associations and mutuals were never institutionalised in their own right into the UK legal system or its political or social economy. Following the Labour Representation Committee in 1900, Labour Party linkages with labour movement associations and co-operatives have been progressively diluted. In contrast, in France and elsewhere, components of this social economy are directly linked with the political framework. In the "plural economy" of Hart et al. (2010, cited in Laville 2011, 9), the market is only one of the components, "which cannot occult the existence of redistribution and reciprocity". Civil society initiatives are thus "in the public space of modern democratic societies" (Laville 2011, 8, 9).

Chapter 4 describes the significance of co-operatives in the UK from the 1970s and 1980s onwards. Despite this, the author notes that few UK or mainland European contributions mention the proliferation of papers from the Open University Research Unit (Cornforth 1988; 1989; 1984; 1983; Cornforth et al. 1988; Cornforth and Thomas 1991; Spear 2006; 2000; 1999), which provided considerable academic underpinning for the doubling of the size of the co-operative economy after the 1976 and 1978 Acts under local Co-operative Development Agencies and the ICOM. These Open University papers on co-operatives amplify an ongoing academic policy entrepreneurship role in the face of Conservative government policies, which sought to reduce the economic development powers of local government. Though called co-operatives, because most of these were actually registered as companies limited by guarantee by ICOM, most were no different to New Labour's later social enterprises. The growth of these structures thus represents a major part of the author's central contention on the neglect of social enterprise antecedents.

Approaches from CIRIEC

Especially during the 1980s, there were major differences between French and UK approaches. "In France, the contemporary re-emergence of the social economy as 'social and solidarity economy' is narrowly linked to the reaction against neo-liberal principles and individualist ideology. The term social economy is of relatively recent currency in the UK and its meaning is still evolving and susceptible to many often-contradictory interpretations

(Pearce and European Network for Economic Self-Help and Local Development 1999, p. 2; Amin, Cameron and Hudson 2003)" (Moulaert and Ailenei 2005, 2041, 2043). Though Anglo-Saxon countries have always seen a division between public and private domains, in continental Europe this has never been clear-cut, as nonprofits have from earlier times been involved in delivering public services. There is also a long corporatist tradition, affording trade unions, employers' representatives and others a more central role in economic and social policy (Brandsen, van de Donk and Putters 2005, 757).

It was desirable to restrict the market "to prevent it from expanding to include all spheres of human life and to preserve relationships based on solidarity", with "institutional innovations grounded in social practice" and "shaping the economy by democratic forms" (Laville 2010a, 81, 82). During the deepening 1980s fiscal crisis of the French welfare state, with slowing economic growth and the rise of unemployment, public agencies sought co-operation from organisations in the social economy. In 1982 the Mitterrand government's decentralisation policy increased public awareness of these organisations (Archambault 1997, 105, 106).

> This social economy, called the 'third sector' in the French Ninth Plan (1986–89), included 'associations', 'co-operatives', and 'mutualist' entities. One estimate was that 1.5mn people worked in the social economy. The creation of a 'Delegation a l'Economie Sociale' (Social Economy Unit), attached to the Prime Minister, reflected the extent to which the Government recognised the social economy, and was concerned to promote its development. (Knight 1993, 251)

Though there has been little focus in UK contributions on a wider mainland European range of contributions on the social and solidarity economy, approaches were made from the CIRIEC to UK academics to participate in discussions on the social economy (Gelard 1997, 67):

> During the 1970s, after numerous fruitless contacts with the United Kingdom at the regular invitation of British rapporteurs to the international congresses, a small group of specialists interested in research in public enterprises came forward as the British Section of CIRIEC … The Group publishes a bulletin entitled "Public Enterprise" which is no less interesting for consisting of only a few pages.

> Beyond attending various congresses and contributing some articles to the "Annals", the Group never had firm relations with the International Centre.

Founded in 1947, CIRIEC was relaunched from 1978 to 1988. From 1978 onwards, its Annals of Public and Co-operative Economics "received a distinctly academic impulse, with issues on special themes, mainly carried out under the management of qualified colleagues and attracting high level contributors" (Gelard 1997). European contributors commented on this absence of UK input and CIRIEC continued to seek UK contributions.

The author maintains that had UK academics responded more favourably, the UK might have witnessed the development of a mainland European social economy as in France or Quebec. A recent comment in support of the author's contention is that "CIRIEC could have been just one of the organizations needed to contribute to increasing the capacity and strength of CMEs (Co-operative and Mutuals Enterprises) in the UK economy" (Parnell 2020, 4).

The French tradition, which was the basis for CIRIEC, including regulation, state, convention, and societal effect theories, offers many observations about the operation of labour markets. The Anglo-Saxon approach is based on the "English principle" of the separation of sciences, which consists of "political economy as having to constitute itself as the science of wealth in order to place itself outside the entirety of human knowledge" (Ott 1851, 5). The harmful effects of competition, as a factor of crises and disorder in production and consumption, leads the authors to refute the theory of Say (which is "nothing but pure chance") and it follows that auto-regulation of the market must be replaced by social prevision (Demoustier and Rousselière 2004, 5).

CIRIEC made other approaches, including to Germany. Partly in response, the Technical University of Berlin set up its own research institute. "During the last two decades, the Technical University of Berlin (together with its partners from the European Network for Economic Self-Help and Local Development) was one of the few research organizations dealing explicitly with issues of social economy and social enterprise" (Birkhölzer et al. 2015, 17). The Network was founded in 1992 and carried out a number of transnational projects, using an operational definition which was different to the EMES (Birkhölzer et al. 2015, 5). Though John Pearce at Community Enterprise in Strathclyde, whose work in Scotland is detailed in Chapter 4, responded through participation in setting up this European Network, and though this represented a different approach to both CIRIEC and EMES, the author notes no refences in UK contributions.

Despite participation from John Pearce, continuing abstention from UK academia meant that any policy entrepreneur role was diluted. Though not in direct response to CIRIEC, one of the few UK academics later to recognise the potential of Birkhölzer's wider approach was Peter Lloyd from the University of Liverpool, who also worked for the European Commission. He wrote that the "Third System should be valued for is its ability to tackle Birkhölzer's 'shadow economy' in a way that can deliver jobs, quality services and a degree of local solidarity to the fabric of society as a whole" (Lloyd 2005, 200).

The characteristics of growth in this "Third System" in continental Europe are "(a) the object of providing a service to members (common or mutual interest) or the community (general interest) (b) the primacy of people over capital (c) democratic functioning and (d) a management system which is independent of the public authorities" (Vivet and Thiry 2000, 10). There are national differences. This Third System enjoys the highest degree of development in France and Spain, with Belgium (particularly in the Walloon Region) to a lesser extent (Vivet and Thiry 2000, 30). Greece, Denmark, Luxembourg, United Kingdom, Germany, Austria and The Netherlands "appear much more restrained in their acceptance of the potential represented by the diverse features of Social Economy" (Vivet and Thiry 2000, 33). The organisations of social economy play a role in crisis regulation as the "post-Keynesian solution" in targeting the interest of solitary members towards social utility (Vienney 1995, cited in Demoustier and Rousselière 2004, 16).

Other social and solidarity approaches, especially in France, have also been largely ignored in UK academic contributions. The lack of English translation means that this rich vein goes untapped by non-French speakers, though the French tradition has much to offer (Fleetwood 2006, 3). Since most contributions do not appear in UK discourses or contributions on social enterprise, a summary is provided below.

Approaches outside the UK: regulationist approach in France

Apart from UK contributions' scant references to the mainland European contributions on a social economy, there are even fewer references to a Regulationist approach. The participation of French Regulationists in the 1981 François Mitterrand "Union de la Gauche" government coincided with Labour's heavy electoral defeat in 1983, despite Labour's General Election manifesto in that year advocating similar policies. A range of significant Regulationist approaches are omitted, from Aglietta (1979) and Lipietz (Lipietz 1992) to Boltanski and Chiapello's "New Spirit of Capitalism" (Boltanski and Chiapello 2005). Lipietz and others specifically refer to developments in the third sector (Catterall et al. 1996; Lipietz 1996; 1989; 1992; 1988; Lipietz et al. 1990; Lipietz and Jenson 1987). It is difficult to understand how these contributions have been overlooked, especially since they were contemporaneous in the 1970s and 1980s with doubling the size of the co-operative economy in the UK, as shown in Chapter 4.

The French Regulationist approach represents an important theoretical and conceptual response in a post-Fordist period, as summarised by Jessop (1994, cited in O'Toole 1996, 79):

> A Post Fordist system would underpin/encourage the conversion of productive and reproductive processes to flexible templates, increase the availability of new technological infrastructures, encourage an innovative pattern of

accumulation, polarise the position and incomes of skilled workers and service classes and encourage interaction with global competitive markets.

Peck and Tickell argue for "a supralocal regulatory framework which would involve co-ordination at national and supranational level to harness and exceed the institutions thrown up by neoliberalism" (2002). Mayer argues for "an expansion in the sphere of local political action (to involve unions, local authorities, investors, planners, research centres, training agencies, voluntary agencies, etc.) and the rise of "new bargaining systems based on negotiation" (2003). Lipietz argues for the transformation of the welfare state (based on income redistribution) into the "welfare community" (in defence of the welfare of communities) (cited in Amin 1994, 28, 29).

Two key elements are the "regime of accumulation" and "modes of social regulation" as the background of the Regulationist approach (Aglietta 1979). Jessop describes "an alternative economic strategy for France that could be pursued by a relatively autonomous state in order to promote a new class compromise and new structural forms and norms of production and consumption appropriate to the new economic circumstances" (Jessop 1997, 504). The social economy concept seeks to establish collective well-being and recreate social bonds between the people within their communities in order to provide alternatives for services usually rendered by the state (Moulaert and Ailenei 2005, 2041).

Mitterrand's 1981 "Union de la Gauche" Government followed a period of orthodox neoliberalism under Valéry Giscard d'Estaing (1974–1981). "Modes of social regulation" during this period are identified in numerous contributions by Lipietz and others following a Regulationist approach (Barbrook 1990; Catterall et al. 1996; Leborgne and Lipietz 1988; Lipietz 1997; 1996; 1992; 1989). But despite their advice, market pressures for convergence of economic and social structures resulted in France's moving closer to Germany, where neoliberalism had constituted the official economic ideology since 1949 (Denord 2017, 91). Though many contributions from Regulationists sought to define a social sector more specifically, these are rarely mentioned in contemporary descriptions of a UK third sector. Lipietz criticises the "Fordist Left" which "has died because it did not know how to impart the spirit of initiative, or human warmth, to solidarity. It neglected the importance of direct initiative on the part of workers and citizens" (Lipietz 1996, 142). His approach to deindustrialisation and Post-Fordism includes a specific contribution from a "third sector" (Catterall et al. 1996, 88):

> So, maybe, if you subsidise a kind of semi-private, semi-voluntary, semi-natural community-based sector, maybe you could produce goods and services at a price that the community could accept. And this is the idea of a third sector.

Lipietz calls it a democracy in the making, not a protected outcome since it involves radically new, non-Fordist, forms of political engagement in pursuit of a radically new set of expectations of social and economic progress. (Amin 1994, 29)

Lipietz sought a third sector with intermediate agencies of socially useful work, a new sector of activity, restricted to something like 10% of the active population, or the prevailing rate of unemployment. Those in the third sector would have a job which was socially recognised and more rewarding for their self-esteem than moonlighting or precarious casual work. The welfare state would be transformed into a welfare community (Lipietz 1996, 141, 142, 144).

Mayer describes a "proliferation of measures, institutions and coalitions, and their orientation towards 'the entrepreneurial mobilization of indigenous potential' as a genuine replacement for the overbearing, hierarchical Fordist state" (Amin 1994, 28). Third sector and social economy programmes aim to compensate for the simultaneous fragmentation of the traditional structures of market and state (Mayer 2003, 124). Almost alone in UK contributions, Amin later provided a wider and inclusive definition of the social economy which was closer to Lipietz. While forms of ownership and control vary considerably within the social economy (e.g. co-operatives, charities, community ventures and informal exchange networks), the sector is distinctive from the state and the private sector, belonging to the "third" sector or system (Amin 2009, 31). "[N]on state actors to meet the burden of delivering social welfare" with "community-led social economy initiatives offered flexible and cost-effective services directly in response to local need (Amin, Cameron and Hudson 1999, 2034). But Amin and others recognise these UK interpretations of the social economy as different to the CIRIEC and Regulationist approaches in mainland Europe, with domination of a UK third sector by local authorities and national programmes (Amin, Cameron and Hudson 1999, 2037). "There are very few community-based social enterprises in the UK that have been able to develop and flourish without public money" (Amin, Cameron and Hudson 1999, 2041).

The absence of UK contributions which mention Lipietz's approach is even more surprising since he attended at least one London Conference in May 1996, where, as quoted above, alongside English contributors, he explained in detail his concept of the third sector (Catterall et al. 1996, 86).

Lipietz's report for Martine Aubry

Lipietz produced a major report on the social economy for Martine Aubry, France's Minister for Employment and Solidarity in September 2000. As the daughter of former European Commission President Jacques Delors, Aubry held senior Cabinet positions so the Liepietz report was significant. Delors had been a major driver for the Social Chapter in the 1992 Treaty of Maastricht, from which Conservative Prime Minister John Major secured a UK opt-out. The author is surprised that though this report on the social economy coincided with the development of New Labour social enterprise policy, it receives no mention in UK academic contributions. Aubry's "Mission Letter" gave Lipietz these terms of reference (Aubry 1998):

> to think about the creation, alongside integration companies, of a status of company with a social purpose. These companies, while exercising their actions in the market sector, would be likely to pursue activities that meet needs that are not currently satisfied by the market and to integrate specific objectives of social utility.

In his preliminary Progress Report of January 1999, Lipietz calculated that expenditures, including making up for a contributions shortfall, would be self-financing. He stressed the need for the third sector to be regulatory and fiscally compatible with public and private sectors, which feared unfair competition (Lipietz 1999). His final report recommended a statutory basis for a new category of enterprises – those with a "social goal". A "third sector" exempt from social contributions and commercial taxes and subsidised at the level of a Revenu minimum d'insertion (RMI) per person employed, "would not cost the general government anything".[3] Though this report was not implemented when Aubry was no longer a Minister after 2000, there is no mention of its significance in UK contributions.

Approaches outside the UK: Quebec social economy

Bouchard distinguishes between Anglo-Saxon, European and Quebecois approaches. In the European approach, democracy allows market activities to be included to make them compatible with the collective interest (Bouchard 2013, 26). The Anglo-Saxon approach to non-profit organisations emphasises non-distribution, whereas European and Quebecois approaches to the social economy emphasise governance and democratic functioning, including co-operatives, mutual societies and non-profit organisations. This difference is not profit seeking versus non-profit orientation but between capitalist and "'a-capitalist' organisations" (Demoustier 2001; Draperi 2009), or "socio-economic" organisations (Evers and Laville 2004). These emphasise enhanced collective wealth, rather than a return on individual investment (Bouchard 2013, 4). The Quebec social economy blends the characteristics of legal and institutional forms of organisations – co-operatives, mutual societies and non-profit organisations (Desroche 1983) – and the values, principles and rules that these share: service to members and community, democratisation of the economy (Defourny and Monzón 1992; Vienney 1980) and hybridisation of the economic principles identified by Polanyi (1944) (Bouchard 2013, 4).

The Forum for Full Employment during the 1980s, the 1995 Quebec Women's March on Poverty and 1996 Social Economy Summit with representatives from the state, market and civil society (including unions, women's groups, and community organisations) all came together in the Working Group on the Social Economy which in 1999 became the Chantier de l'Economie Sociale. The Chantier was an overarching framework for the social economy in Quebec, which the women's movement defined (Laville, Lévesque and Mendell 2005, 11):

> the women's movement proposed a broad definition of the social economy in order to include community action, ie. initiatives for poverty reduction and combating exclusion and unemployment, as well as initiatives to increase social awareness and build solidarity – a definition that is thus not limited to the production of goods and services nor to the market portion of the social economy.

"This became the apotheosis of the state's recognition of the social economy as a focus for job creation" (Dancuse, Bouchard and Morin 2013, 112). While the economic recession of the 1980s speeded the shift in the centre of gravity of Quebec's community movement from mobilising political demands to providing autonomous services, it was in the 1990s that the term "social economy" entered the policy lexicon (Graefe 2005, 13). The Quebec government directly contributes to funding the Chantier, rather than subcontracting or outsourcing as in the UK. "There is no resemblance to neoliberal strategies elsewhere to disengage the state and transfer responsibility to its citizens, but represents the re-engagement of the state as a partner in socio-economic development strategies in the ... Chantier de l'économie sociale" (Mendell, Lévesque and Rouzier 2000, 38, 40). "The Chantier allows organisations to retain autonomy, so that in pursuing these objectives they will not be obliged to become subcontractors or even accomplices of the neo-liberal state (Bardos-Feltoronyi 2004)" (Klein and Tremblay 2013, 236).

The Quebec Provincial Government recognises the Chantier as a full partner in economic and social development (Lévesque 2013, 36). Unlike the UK, significant funding also comes from trade unions. "It not only mobilizes capital, but also expertise and social capital"; social economy enterprises need public sector support and intervention (Bourque, Mendell and Rouzier 2013, 183, 184). Social economy initiatives have a positive impact on forging social bonds and improving people's living environment and cultural development. Lipietz (2001, p. 74) calls this the "'halo' effect in a community" (cited in Klein and Tremblay 2013, 234).

Since these developments in Quebec coincided from 1998 onwards with New Labour's Social Exclusion Unit (SEU), its Policy Action Teams and the setting up of the Social Enterprise Unit at the DTI, the author is surprised that so little mention of these Canadian developments features in any UK contribution.

EMES and work integration subsidies

Apart from North American influences, in other UK contributions there has been excessive reliance in UK contributions on an interpretation of social enterprise by the EMES.

Various EMES WISE models as active labour market policy delivery structures are not a new model of social enterprise or a new economic category or organisation. Though most WISE structures predated EMES literature on social enterprise and social entrepreneurship, their role was augmented through increased EU funding. "Work integration social enterprises (WISEs) have existed in Europe for nearly 50 years, though many were born in the last 20 years in the framework of policies set up to fight unemployment" (Davister, Defourny and Grégoire 2004, 21). Kerlin (2006, 252) also describes the narrower EMES approach:

> Most of these pioneering social enterprises in Europe were founded in the 1980s by civil society actors: social workers, associative militants, and representatives of more traditional third sector organizations, sometimes with the excluded workers themselves (Nyssens and Kerlin 2005). These addressed those areas the welfare state had retreated from or had not been able to meet demand – employment programs for the long-termed unemployed, personal social services.

The WISEs approach involves "hiring people in intermediate capacities or as household workers, in what are considered as fill-in jobs" (Laville 1996, 49). There is also a wariness of public sector involvement in this narrow market approach "when stakeholders from civil society and the social economy are forgotten or instrumentalised in the relationship with the state, public policy is impoverished, because it reproduces the downside of competitive or bureaucratic regulation" (Vaillancourt and LeClerc 2013, 139).

An initial definition from EMES appeared in 1999 (Defourny and Develtere 1999, 16):

We define the social economy as follows: "The social economy includes all economic activities conducted by enterprises, primarily co-operatives, associations and mutual benefit societies, whose ethics convey the following principles:

a) placing service to its members or to the community ahead of profit
b) autonomous management
c) a democratic decision-making process
d) the primacy of people and work over capital in the distribution of revenues."

But EMES research later narrowed its focus to WISEs, an approach which many came to regard as restrictive. "A restricted view on the social economy coupled with a silo-approach in the development of supportive policy measures is still hindering the development of the field, as well as the measurement, assessment and recognition of this social economy" (De Cuyper, Jacobs and Gijselinckx 2015, 268). The criteria used by the EMES and others are still – as the EMES itself underlines – defining an "ideal-type"; the real-life situation is much more complicated (Birkhölzer 2015, 24). The EMES approach refers only to part of the social economy (De Cuyper, Jacobs and Gijselinckx 2015, 273):

> EMES researchers use the term "social enterprises" (Borzaga and Defourny 2001, Defourny and Nyssens 2010, 2013) to refer to "those organisations that are at the crossroads of market, public policy and civil society" (Nyssens 2006). According to Monzón Campos and Chaves (2012) it refers to the market sub-sector of the social economy.

"There is a more dominant view of EU integration that reduces all activity to a single market that leaves no room for a civil society based perspective" (Laville 2003, 391). These organisations have obvious links with the market, as recent reforms foster market principles and competition, which creates another source of tensions (Hulgård 2010)" (Defourny, Nyssens and EMES 2012, 12, 13).

The origins of the EMES interpretation of social enterprise, WISEs and the role of the RMI placement subsidy on which these are based are discussed more fully in Chapter 6.

US WISEs

The Clinton 1996 Personal Responsibility and Work Opportunity or Welfare Reform Act enforced two-year time limits for the able bodied to be on welfare and life-time limits for recipients, making work and welfare even more a punitive individual responsibility (Albo and Fast 2003, 22). The public subsidy approach for WISEs in Europe is thus less available in North

America (Laville, Lemaitre and Nyssens 2006). Without the greater funding available in Europe, especially from the European Social Fund (ESF), the challenge for US WISEs is generating resources "to buffer pressures of competitive isomorphism to establish supportive employment conditions in business niches where the prevailing employer practices may be less than desirable"[4] (Cooney 2011, 103).

The author reflects that despite these growing difficulties with mainland European EMES and US WISE models, these approaches still influence UK discourses and contributions.

UK literature contributions

This section shows a brief cross-section of UK contributions on social enterprise, which underline the author's concern about the reliance of many UK contributions on inappropriate North American and EMES models and their omission of more appropriate UK antecedents.

In response to earlier US management and business approaches, Grenier mentions various approaches to which reference is made later (2009, 18):

> There is a growing number of other disciplinary perspectives present in the literature which offer some alternative insights into social entrepreneurship and social enterprise, and are generally more critical: Cho (2006) embarks on an analysis rooted in political science; Dey (2006) uses rhetorical and discursive analysis; Parkinson (2005) employs critical discourse analysis; Dart (2004) approaches from sociology; Edwards (2002) applies postmodern social welfare theory; and Amin, Cameron and Hudson (2002) come from the discipline of geography.

Westall, who played a prominent role in New Labour's early social enterprise development, provides an interpretation which is similar to Austin. Discussions need to emphasise the social aim first and not the specific organisational model. In other words, form follows function. The clearest way to distinguish social enterprise is probably by social aim (Westall 2001a, 30). Haugh seems equally influenced by the EMES approach when writing about "assisting the unemployed and disabled to enter the workforce by developing work-related and life-skills" and "community care services ... either filling gaps and/or reducing inequalities in service provision" (Haugh 2005, 4).

"Following the creation of a social enterprise unit within the DTI, the social enterprise construct expanded to fully incorporate social businesses. A policy environment of 'what works' was receptive to the argument that organisational form was irrelevant (Newman 2007)" (Teasdale 2012, 110). Teasdale and Nicholls seek to show that "the neoliberal macro paradigm" governing social enterprise during the periods of New Labour and Conservative coalition has "remained intact" (Teasdale and Nicholls 2015, 2). But this conclusion is only achieved through their confining interpretations of social enterprise within a period from 1997 to 2012, founded by Nicholls' "paradigm building actors" in the UK (2010, 617) as recently as 1998 onwards. Teasdale contends that "An early alliance of co-operative and community enterprise practitioners utilising the language of New Labour helped embed social enterprise on the policy landscape in 1999" (2012, 108).

Huybrechts and Nicholls write that social entrepreneurship has developed differently in the UK and US "Anglo-sphere" compared with continental Europe. A US focus on commercialisation of the non-profit sector and private initiatives to deliver public welfare goods is compared with a European focus on collective entrepreneurship and analyses at organisational level (Defourny and Nyssens 2008; Kerlin 2006; Huybrechts and Nicholls 2012, 33). Despite this, in complete contrast to Fecher and Leveque (2015, 184, 185) they view the social economy as narrower than social entrepreneurship because it only includes organisations with specific legal forms – not-for-profits, charities, co-operatives, mutuals and foundations. For Huybrechts and Nicholls, social entrepreneurship is "not a discrete sector but a set of hybrid organisations and processes in different institutional spaces and across existing sectors" (2012, 37). They view collective action almost as an "additional extra". Though they recognise that the "hero" social entrepreneur has been criticised as reflecting Western cultural values, collective action is "where social change cannot be the result of social entrepreneurship alone" (37). This approach is at variance with the collective values of UK social enterprise antecedents.

Doherty et al. explain "social entrepreneurship" as a "product of the evolutionary development of non profit or voluntary, co-operatives and mutual organisations and include co-operatives and mutual organisations". This blurs boundaries between different organisational forms and positions social enterprise at the intersection of private, public and non-profit sectors (Defourny and Nyssens 2006; Doherty, Haugh and Lyon 2014, 421). Social enterprise discourse in North America is dominated by market-based approaches to income generation and social change (Austin, Stevenson and Wei-Skillern 2006), whereas in Europe, social enterprise is located in the co-operative tradition of collective social action (Borzaga and Defourny 2001; Defourny and Nyssens 2010; Nyssens 2006). Because the UK borrows from both traditions, Docherty et al. refer to the DTI 2002 definition (Doherty, Haugh and Lyon 2014, 420). But Doherty et al.'s survey of 129 social enterprise research papers is dominated by Austin et al., where "social entrepreneurship is not defined by legal form, as it can be pursued through various vehicles. Indeed, examples of social entrepreneurship can be found within or can span the non profit, business, or governmental sectors" (Austin, Stevenson and Wei-Skillern 2006, 2).

On UK Conservative government initiatives on Big Society Capital, and EU endeavours on social business and social innovation, Doherty et al. write that "these policies have encouraged the establishment of new SEs and the adoption of commercial activity by non-profit organisations". Though they write that "Mason (2012) argues that successive UK governments have attempted to influence the SE discourse in order to facilitate reform in the public sector", they give no reference to the background of organisations from which these changes are sought (Doherty, Haugh and Lyon 2014, 430). They continue that social enterprise missions "require managers to craft a balance between social/welfare logic and market/commercial logic (Santos 2012)", and that "hybridity makes it difficult for financiers to categorise SEs, so they are poorly understood by mainstream sources of finance (Battilana and Dorado 2010; Brandsen and Karré 2011)" (Doherty, Haugh and Lyon 2014, 427). They advance the concept of hybridity to explain how social enterprises sustain relationships with different stakeholders with competing objectives and develop market-based strategies (Doherty, Haugh and Lyon 2014, 430). But the author observes that most social enterprises operate in hybrid fashion as a matter of routine.

As a good example of the predominant UK view of the policy origins of social enterprise, in an earlier work Nicholls describes social entrepreneurship as "a field that has yet to achieve a paradigmatic consensus and which lacks a normal science or clear epistemology". Key paradigm building actors have more legitimacy than the field itself (Nicholls 2010, 611). He mentions the Office of the Third Sector (OTS) in the DTI, the American Skoll and Ashoka Foundation (founded in 1999 and 1982) Community Action Network (founded in 1998) and SEC (founded in 2002). "Collectively, these paradigm building actors have been highly influential in establishing the discourses, narratives, and ideal types that characterise the early stage development of social entrepreneurship" (Nicholls 2010, 618). His "reflexive isomorphism" is a legitimating strategy in which "organisations actively engage in processes that align field-level and internal logics to shape emergent institutional fields as closed systems of self-legitimation" (2010, 617). But none of Nicholls' "paradigm building actors" precede New Labour.

When Haugh and Kitson explain the growth of the third sector by its "distinctive organisational capabilities", there is no mention of antecedents or precedents (2007, 981). Equally significant is their warning about social enterprise and cut-price welfare delivery (991), as if they were responding to Leadbeater (1997, 81):

The main challenge facing New Labour is to ensure that the sector maintains its distinctive capabilities and does not simply absorb and replicate the business objectives and strategies of the private sector. They must not let it become a cut-price source of welfare provision to those unable, for whatever reason, to acquire the goods and services they require and indeed are entitled to.

In support of the author, Parkinson is concerned that research agendae are moving away from a more practical implementation of social enterprise. In the rise of social enterprise from its roots in community (economic) development with a radical political agenda, community has been sidelined. The "'everydayness' of entrepreneurship (Steyaert and Katz 2004; Steyaert 2004) has replaced the 'empowering of the many'" (Pearce 2003, 69; Parkinson 2005, 2). The shifts towards "dominant entrepreneurship discourse ... driven by policy makers, funders, the sector and academics do not necessarily infiltrate ideology at the level where the action is located" (Parkinson 2005, 12, 14).

Parkinson and Howarth recognise that much current work comes from business and management disciplines (Mair and Marti 2006) instead of as a complex social movement in its own right (Parkinson and Howorth 2008, 287). "Social and community entrepreneurship in the UK emerged out of structures aimed at anchoring the benefits of the local economy within communities." Echoing the author's contention throughout this book, they refer to "research from a management or entrepreneurship discipline that fails to take account of the political sociology of the movement" (2008, 291, 305).

Literature reviews

Throughout this book, the author has argued that many UK literature contributions on social enterprise have misinterpreted the development of social enterprise policy in the UK through failing to recognise earlier antecedents of social enterprise. The literature reviews described below support this contention.

Literature review October to December 2013

During a thematic literature review during October to December 2013, it was found that after removing duplicates and those which were irrelevant, which concerned another topic or contained nothing on ICOM and worker co-operative origins, only 115 sources remained from 1169 possible sources reviewed. Judgement was exercised on sources and, in mitigation against any bias, this review accessed fourteen different databases.

There were only four out of 115 sources which describe 1970s and 1980s social enterprise origins in significant detail with references to the previous period. This is the "Gold Standard" (Young et al. 2002). Ridley-Duff (2009) is the only source in this whole review which makes links to social enterprise and worker co-operative developments in the 1970s and 1980s. Ridley-Duff and Southcombe (2012) describe some precedents but make no linkages between examples from different periods. Shaw (Shaw, Carter 2007) includes reference to earlier structures, but reaches only general conclusions and omits reference to 1970s and 1980s worker co-operatives. Spear (2006) describes earlier co-operatives but does not carry these forward as antecedents of current social enterprises.

Only 15 out of 115 made some reference to the previous period or mention social enterprise origins in the 1970s and 1980s but without linkages to current discourses.

Second literature review September 2017

To ascertain whether any significant changes had taken place since his original thematic literature review in 2013, using three major databases and Google Scholar with a minimum 100 citations, the author conducted a follow up review in September 2017. This basically confirmed earlier 2013 results. In this September 2017 review, it was found that after removing duplicates and those which were irrelevant, concerned another topic or contained nothing relevant on a previous period or described collective origins, only 50 sources remained from 5698 possible sources reviewed. This review included a larger number of possible sources than in 2013, following changes in Google Scholar operator procedures.

Only two out of 50 sources made detailed references to the previous period in the research question and describe 1970s and 1980s social enterprise origins in significant detail, with linkages to current discourses. These were Ridley-Duff and Southcombe (2012) and Shaw (Shaw and Carter 2007), which are described above.

Only 3 out of 50 made some reference to the previous period or mentioned social enterprise origins in the 1970s and 1980s, and these were without linkages to current discourses.

There are other literature reviews considered by the author, which also support his contention of a minimal focus on social enterprise antecedents.[5]

Conclusion

Through UK academic reliance on North American non-profit and individual social entrepreneurship discourses, through their emphasis on the narrower EMES version of social enterprise, and through non-participation in mainland European discussion, most UK contributions describe a UK third sector which now operates within a competitive market economy for public service delivery. UK contributions have been influenced by North American neoclassical approaches on nonprofits and from business management schools, especially following Dees (Dees 1998a; 1998b; Dees and Anderson 2006). Most view nonprofits as resulting from either market or public failure, with production and distribution of their services based on individual rational choice theory (Hulgård 2010).

In complete contrast, in mainland Europe from the nineteenth century there has been a gradual institutionalisation of mutuals, co-operatives and associations within civil society structures (Laville et al. 1999). UK contributions have largely ignored these and continued with an excessive reliance on EMES and WISE models, while neglecting the RMI programme, which propelled their development, as explained in Chapter 6.

After Labour's General Election defeat in 1983 in the UK, Le Grand and others began to develop the concept of "quasi markets" (Le Grand and Estrin 1989). These and other UK approaches departed from contributions from French Regulationists (Aglietta 1979; Lipietz 1989; 1992) and those arguing for a social and solidarity economy in France (Lewis 2004; Laville et al. 1999) and in Quebec (Lévesque 1999; Mendell, Lévesque and Rouzier 2000). Arising from this, in many UK contributions, notions of "collective action" have been marginalised, with UK contributions on social enterprise increasingly describing hybrid organisations and processes in different institutional spaces and across existing sectors (Huybrechts and Nicholls 2012, 37).

Notes

1 For a more comprehensive discussion on US nonprofits, including the concepts of trust and fiduciary duty, transaction costs and contract failure, see Bacchiega and Borzaga (2001); A. Ben-Ner and T. V. Hoomissen, "Nonprofit Organizations in the Mixed Economy", *Annals of Public and Cooperative Economics* 62 (4) (1991): 519–50; H. Hansmann, *The Ownership of Enterprise* (Cambridge, MA: Harvard University Press, 1996); E. James, "Economic Theories of the Nonprofit Sector: A Comparative Perspective", in Helmut K. Anheier and Wolfgang Seibel (eds), *The Third Sector: Comparative Studies of NonProfit Organisations* (Berlin: De Gruyter, 1990), 21–30; B. R. Kingma, "Public Good Theories of the Nonprofit Sector: Weisbrod Revisited", *VOLUNTAS: International Journal of Voluntary and Non-profit Organizations*, 8 (2) (1997): 135–48; B. A. Weisbrod, *To Profit or Not to Profit: The Commercial Transformation of the Nonprofit Sector* (Cambridge: Cambridge University Press, 2000); O. E. Williamson, "Public and Private Bureaucracies: A Transaction Cost Economics Perspective", *Journal of Law, Economics, and Organization*, 15 (1) (1999): 306–42.

2   For further direct information on the fragility of many US social enterprises, see Dart (2004); Dees and Anderson (2006); E. L. Edgcomb, J. A. Klein, and T. Thetford, 'Pursuing Sustainability in the Micro Enterprise Field: Findings from a Literature Review', Aspen Institute (2007), https://www.aspeninstitute.org/wp-content/uploads/2007/03/PursuingSustaintability.pdf; Emerson and Twersky (1996); S. Johnson, 'Literature Review on Social Entrepreneurship', Canadian Centre for Social Entrepreneurship (2000); Massarksky and Beinhacker (2002); Zimmerman and Dart (1998).

3   For details about Lipietz's significant report and his Regulationist approach, see Aubry (1998); Biewener (2006); M. R. Jones, 'Spatial Selectivity of the State? The Regulationist Enigma and Local Struggles over Economic Governance', *Environment and Planning A*, 29 (5) (1997): 831–64; Lipietz (1999); A. Lipietz, 'The Opportunity of a New Type of Society with a Social Vocation' (Ministry of Employment and Solidarity, 2000).

4   For further information on US WISEs, see Cooney (2011); K. Cooney, 'Work Integration Social Enterprises in the United States: Operating at the Nexus of Public Policy, Markets, and Community', *Nonprofit Policy Forum*, 7 (4) (2016): 435–60; E. E. Garrow, 'Competing Social Service and Market-Driven Logics in Nonprofit Work Integration Social Enterprises: A Comparative Study', *Nonprofit and Voluntary Sector Quarterly* (2013): 1–32; E. E. Garrow and Y. Hasenfeld, 'Social Enterprises as an Embodiment of a Neoliberal Welfare Logic', *American Behavioral Scientist*, 58 (7) (2014): 1–19.

5   For details of further literature reviews which support the author's contention on lack of connected mention of appropriate antecedents, see W. Cukier, S. Trenholm, D. Carl and G. Gekas, 'Social Entrepreneurship: A Content Analysis', *Journal of Strategic Innovation and Sustainability*, 7 (1) (2011): 99–119; B. Doherty, Haugh and Lyon (2014); M. L. Granados, V. Hlupic, E. Coakes and S. Mohamed, 'Social Enterprise and Social Entrepreneurship Research and Theory: A Bibliometric Analysis from 1991 to 2010', *Social Enterprise Journal*, 7 (3) (2011): 198–218; J. C. Short, T. W. Moss and G. Lumpkin, 'Research in Social Entrepreneurship: Past Contributions and Future Opportunities', *Strategic Entrepreneurship Journal*, 3 (2) (2009): 161–94; S. U. M. Tobi, D. Amaratunga and N. M. Noor, 'Social Enterprise Applications in an Urban Facilities Management Setting', *Facilities*, 31 (5) (2013): 238–54; C. Trivedi, 'A Social Entrepreneurship Bibliography', *Journal of Entrepreneurship*, 19 (1) (2010): 81–5.

4

1960s–1980s regeneration

Social enterprise and the third sector during the 1970s and 1980s

This chapter describes the emergence of indigenous community structures in the UK, many of which still exist as today's social enterprises. Though Harold Wilson's 1964 to 1970 Labour Government introduced urban policy measures for specific local communities in 1968, it took another 30 years for many organisations during this period to gain recognition as local support and regeneration structures in their own right and to receive their own funding under government policies and programmes. Many were formed despite rather than as a result of government policies. Though many of these represent the true antecedents of today's social enterprises, these are seldom reported in most UK academic contributions.

Some under-reporting and lack of recognition of these community activities and structures during the 1970s and 1980s may result from their not having been either a Labour or Conservative government policy priority. Though central government direct community support did not emerge until New Labour Governments from 1997 onwards, some community policy absorption into Westminster, Whitehall and regional portfolios may have been easier because some senior civil servants had previously worked on policy-making and setting up similar structures in the 1970s and 1980s. One interviewee made this relevant point (Former Senior Civil Servant II 2015):

> [I]t would be a falsehood to fail to acknowledge that most of that sector was funded by the Tory Government that preceded Labour's arrival. Actually, if I'm candid, I worked on every significant economic development policy and programme in the UK between 1989 and 2014 and, in essence, there was a sharing of purpose, but a difference of nomenclature and some difference of tonality and emphasis.

Overview – from market failure to government failure

The institutionalisation of urban problems forms a context for the growth of indigenous local organisations in the 1960s and 1970s. They were created during a post-Fordist period of market failure and massive job losses, and were very different from their later counterparts which accepted market discipline within a new role created by government (Carmel and Harlock 2008; Dowling and Harvie 2014; Fecher and Lévesque 2008; Prior and Clark 2014; Whitehead 2015). So while the current policy predisposition and institutional location is for social enterprises and third sector structures as public service deliverers, this later role was not shaped by 1970s and 1980s antecedents or origins (Southcombe 2014). This new role also means that during the author's own personal experience the conceptual framework for TSOs has moved politically from left to right – with local agencies seeking public funding for job creation and community support becoming market-driven service delivery vehicles, in many cases as an interim step to privatisation.

Mounting problems of urban deprivation in the 1960s and 1970s drove Labour and Conservative governments towards "two related but discrete periods: an era of experimentation between about 1967 and 1975 and a subsequent period of more permanent inner urban policy" (Lawless and Brown 1986, 220). Though throughout this period there was a possibility for growth of local social economies, community participation in regeneration was not prioritised. The sections below discuss these two periods.

As is emphasised throughout Chapter 3, there is no reason why many of these community structures should not have become the basis of a mainland European social economy. But this development was not helped by UK academics' failure to respond to invitations to join in discussions on a social economy in mainland Europe during this period.

Laville et al. underline the importance of European discussions about the social economy (Laville, Lévesque and Mendell 2005, 13, 14):

> In France, the first social economy forum was set up in 1977 by Henri Desroche at the Colloque du Comité National de Liaison des Activités Mutualistes, Coopératives et Associatives. In November 1978, a pre-colloquium held on the social economy in Brussels made it the subject of a Europe-wide debate (Desroche 1983, 198).

> Moreover, it is possible that certain organizations experience similar complexity without having any one of the three identified legal forms (co-operative, non-profit or mutual society). That is why Henri Desroche added the concept of "uncertain characteristics" reflected in community enterprises, trade union enterprises, communal enterprises and public enterprises controlled by a democratic body (Desroche 1983, 205).

Throughout this chapter, using a Critical Realist analysis, the author traces causal mechanisms, based on a series of common experiences or developments, including influences by other actors and clients (Fletcher 2020, 181), which have resisted a more broad-based social economy and instead moved towards marketised developments.

First period – urban policies 1967 to 1975

There was little direct support for communities under Labour's initial urban policies. "Harold Wilson's 1964 election victory was founded on a (Fordist) platform to boost Britain's accumulation regime through 'active' state policies for industry, training, science and technology, and regional development (Martin, 1989)" (MacLeod and Jones 1999, 591). The motivation for Labour's first urban policies during the 1960s was race and immigration. The first Urban Programme (UP) in 1968 was a response to the anti-immigration speeches of Enoch Powell and others (Stewart 1987, 132). A retrospective paper describes the origins of Labour's first urban policy (Former Senior Civil Servant I 2016, 6–7):

> On 22 July 1968, however, James Callaghan, as Home Secretary, announced a programme of £20-£25mn over the next four years. The money was to be made available to 34 authorities selected on the basis of the proportion of immigrant children on the school roll and the proportion of households having more than 1½ persons per room.

The dominant contemporary view was that poverty was limited and localised to small areas, which could be targeted through localised initiatives. The object of urban policy was conceptualised in terms of the social pathology of particular groups of people in small areas of Britain's cities (Atkinson 2000, 217). But some alternative analyses also appeared. Those working on the twelve local CDPs created in deprived areas under the new 1968 UP were among the first to recognise the inadequacies of this approach. But, despite their protests, the government resisted community participation under CDPs (Former Senior Civil Servant I 2016, 8):

> The teams, led initially by Coventry, became increasingly radical. They concluded that the problems of their areas lay in deep rooted inequalities which required wholesale structural change in British society and industry to eradicate…. This culminated in a strike and the subsequent resignation of four of the Batley team in July 1974. The Home Office reaction to the growing unrest was to institute a Management Review in June 1974 and to close the initiative in 1976.

The brief given to local CDP teams assumed that deprived people themselves were the main cause of the problem, to be solved through overcoming apathy and promoting self-help and that local research into problems would bring about policy changes (CDP Inter Project Editorial Team 1977, 4). "To quote Miss Cooper of the Home Office, they were 'gilding the ghetto or buying time'" (CDP Inter Project Editorial Team 1977, 55). "The new dimension was the participation by the local community in the regeneration process. This may have been imperfect but, prior to 1990, it did not exist as a significant feature of urban policy" (Former Senior Civil Servant I 2016, sec. 6.3).

Following Labour's UP and CDPs, Edward Heath's Conservative government, elected in 1970, introduced Inner Area Studies in Liverpool, Lambeth and Birmingham in 1972 and 1973, areas in which tensions from lack of funding under UP interventions were already beginning to show a need for community involvement.[1] The overall conclusion from three Inner Area Studies was that the uniformity of the basic processes of government denied the real needs of the inner city (Stewart 1978, 208). Later conclusions about these early Labour and Conservative approaches to community development were no more complimentary. "As Murray Stewart put it: 'Government ... was eventually forced to accept an interpretation which recognised that the failure of programmes to reach disadvantaged communities was structural rather than pathological'" (Fordham 1995, 6).

Scale of 1970s and 1980s deindustrialisation

The growth of local mechanisms for community self-defence, including many earlier social enterprises, is better understood against a background of unprecedented 1970s and 1980s job losses and deindustrialisation.

Not all of the UK benefitted from "Thirty Golden Years" of Fordism (Lipietz et al. 1990). During the transformation of economic and social life in the "old industrial regions", those spaces which formed the "cradles" of industrial capitalism, were "at best a pale shadow of what Fordism was meant to be about (Hudson, 1989, p. 21)" (MacLeod and Jones 1999, 576). The national decline in manufacturing employment (a loss of over 1,900 000 jobs between 1971 and 1981) disproportionately affected the large urban areas where it had been concentrated (Hausner 1987, 5). "By the end of 1980, the UK's total output of manufactures had fallen back to the level achieved in 1967 and the volume of production of many individual industries was back to the 1950s. Employment in most was back to the level of the 1940s and some to levels not experienced since before the Second World War" (Cripps 1981).

In 1976, the Pound Sterling was still an International Reserve Currency, with more than half the world's trade conducted in sterling. The conditions attached to a 1976 IMF loan involved "credibility as the cornerstone of government economic strategy, and the centrality of macroeconomic stability to securing it" (Clift and Tomlinson 2008, 550, 561, 566). Following the 1967 devaluation of sterling (Godley, May 1977), the collapse of manufacturing (Rowthorn and Ramaswamy 1997) and the need to reduce public expenditure (Robinson and Wilkinson 1977), the collapse of the Keynesian welfare state was followed by the onset of a "Schumpeterian Workfare Postnational Regime" (Jessop 2002). Some contemporary contributors found it difficult to recognise the scale of the change from the pre-1970 Golden Age (Lipietz et al. 1990). Those who made "most consistent efforts towards flexibilisation" "suffered simultaneous deindustrialization and a deepening deficit in the balance of payments for manufactured goods" (Lipietz 1997, 4).

Despite the scale of deindustrialisation, community involvement in regeneration rarely featured in national economic policies during the 1970s. The grand narrative for the Labour Governments of 1974 and 1976 was a policy framework of the National Plan, the National Economic Development Council and the National Economic Development Office, replicated by Regional Economic Planning Councils and Boards. Albeit with a very narrow majority, the Labour Government of 1976, in which the author was a Minister, ushered aircraft and shipbuilding into public ownership and injected substantial funding into British Steel and British Telecom and through the National Enterprise Board into British Leyland. But alongside these major interventions, a Private Member's Bill from David Watkins MP became the 1976 Industrial Common Ownership Act and was followed by the 1978 Co-operative Development Agency Act. Though rarely noted by current academic contributions, as shown later in this chapter, these two Acts became the basis for doubling the size of the co-operative economy during the 1970s and 1980s.[2]

Second period – Labour's 1977 White Paper and 1978 Inner Urban Areas Act

Though Peter Shore's 1977 White Paper "Policy for the Inner Cities" did not highlight race, "there is no doubt that one of the basic justifications for the policy was the fear of racial tension and a consequent loss of social control" (Stewart 1987, 132). There was little learning from the stream of previous initiatives (133). The diagnosis was largely unchanged (Former Senior Civil Servant I 2016, 9):

> In spite of the change of government the analysis of the inner area studies fed directly into Peter Shore's 1977 White Paper "Policy for the Inner Cities".

The nature of the problem had not changed significantly from that identified in 1968 ... Greater emphasis, however, is laid on the impact of economic run-down "the decline in the economic fortunes of the inner areas often lie at the heart of the problem".

For a limited number of areas the government sought a formal agreement with other public and voluntary organisations to produce programmes to assist the regeneration of the urban cores concerned (Lawless and Brown 1986, 226). But community participation was ill equipped and outnumbered. Though the 1977 White Paper purported to move away from a small area focus to a corporate approach, it bore striking resemblances to policy instruments which had been recently considered (Fordham and Victor Hausner and Associates 1991, 3).[3]

The White Paper increased urban provision in England and Wales from £30m a year to £125mn a year in 1979–1980 for Partnerships receiving priority. The Inner Urban Areas Act 1978 enabled designation of three tiers of authorities – Partnerships, Programme Authorities and Other Designated Districts. "The voluntary sector in particular felt excluded" (Former Senior Civil Servant I 2016, 11, 12). During this period, the author was designated as "Minister for Merseyside" but cannot recall any significant discussions on any role for local communities.

Despite these limitations, some community groups were drawn into the implementation of inner cities policy through their limited access to available funding – though this did not directly target communities. In 1985–1986 there were over 4,500 voluntary projects receiving UP support, with £76mn of spend. The inner cities policy meant incorporation of the non-statutory sector "at worst as a replacement for cut-back local government services, at best dependent on Urban Programme funding for continuity" (Stewart 1987, 141). Though later 1981 Inner Urban Areas Act Ministerial Guidelines to Partnership and Programme Authorities did not prioritise voluntary and community sector development, there was, however, £1000 for new workers' co-operatives in designated areas (JURUE Division of ECOTEC Research and Consulting 1986, 4). But funding more directly relevant to communities was reduced. Between 1980–1981 and 1982–1983, rate-support grant assistance to highest-priority Partnership authorities fell by 10.3% (Hausner 1987, 28). Funding voluntary projects had allowed the government to get away with the myth that communities were involved in tackling urban deprivation (Richardson 1986, 81).

Apart from difficulties in accessing the UP, neither the new Youth Opportunities Programme nor the Special Temporary Employment Programme in April 1978 could directly fund community enterprises. "The MSC has recently made known that in certain special circumstances it will consider applications from Enterprise Workshops ... It is understood that the funds available for such projects is strictly limited" (Pearce 1979, 6).

But though the voluntary or third sector per se failed to penetrate the public policy mainstream (Kendall 2000, 545), small-scale community activity continued to emerge. Knight described changes in a London Borough: "The 1980s saw a radical change in the borough's voluntary sector, spurred by the supply of additional funding (Urban Programme, Greater London Council, European Social Fund, European Poverty Programme, Church Urban Fund), and a new wave of self-help activity, particularly among black and women's groups, and often inspired by religious leaders" (Knight 1993, 119).

Conservative regeneration programmes

Under Conservative governments' further implementation of the UP and other initiatives for inner city areas, there was still little funding for local communities. The 1978 Act's Inner Urban Areas Act partnerships were short lived. "The most obvious nail in the coffin in 1981 occurred when, in responding to the Toxteth riots, Heseltine bypassed entirely the mechanism established to deal with urban problems. In creating the Task Force he explicitly rejected the partnership structure" (Stewart 1987, 139). Over a five-year period Urban Development Corporations, Enterprise Zones, Task Forces (Merseyside), Urban Development Grant, City Action Teams, and Task Forces (Employment) came into being. But these initiatives were mostly capital related and risked damaging any developing relationship with community organisations (Stewart 1987, 141).

In August 1981 in his "It Took a Riot" report to Prime Minister Thatcher, Michael Heseltine wrote that 120,000 out of a Merseyside workforce of 720,000 were unemployed, for which he advocated "substantial additional resources" (Heseltine 1981, 1, 21). He introduced the Urban Development Grant (UDG) as a "one-off" response to the 1981 Merseyside riots. UDG was property-related, "to lever significant private sector investment into the inner cities ... to act as a stimulus to the economic regeneration of our urban areas" (Department of Environment 1984, cited in Johnson 1988, 1). There were eight local Task Forces, with a further eight in April 1987 to "contribute towards the economic regeneration of the most deprived inner city communities" (Victor Hausner and Associates 1989, 1). A Programme Paper for Inner City Task Forces, written 20 years after the 1968 UP, showed Task Force leaders complaining on their appointment of a lack of familiarity with issues for inner city regeneration (Hausner 1988, 17).[4]

Through these initiatives, funding was becoming more centralised with increasingly difficulty for access by communities. By 1988–1989, £255mn of the £530mn in the "urban block" went to Urban Development Corporations (UDCs) (Former Senior Civil Servant I 2016, 18). Employment was only later grafted on to UDC aims and objectives and community development was initiated following woeful attempts at local liaison by London Docklands. The UDCs' "substantial preoccupation" was shifting local populations rather than redistributing transfer payments, with economic rather than social policy imperatives (Imre and Thomas 1993, cited in O'Toole 1996, 19).

Introduced in May 1991, "City Challenge was one of those rare initiatives which represent a sea change in policy development. It broke the pattern established over the previous two decades, of regeneration projects being developed largely in isolation of each other" (Former Senior Civil Servant I 2016, 28). But while local communities might have a role in partnerships, "it has generally not been a high priority of government policy to develop such community participation in the 1980s" (Robson et al. 1994, 51).

In November 1993, the government set up Government Offices in the regions and the Single Regeneration Budget (SRB) "bringing together a range of programmes which support local regeneration, economic development and industrial competitiveness" (Permanent Secretary to Department of Environment 1993). Throughout this period, as External Funding Manager at Wirral Metropolitan College, the author was involved in key discussions with the Government Office for Merseyside leading to the SRB Wirral City Lands Pacemaker Project. He does not recall or recognise this extent of community involvement described in many evaluations (Department of the Environment 1997, 32).

For City Challenge and SRB "Community leaders have requested training and support in specific areas, such as running committees, managing community facilities, recruiting new members, dealing with conflict, handling equal opportunities, developing strategy, policy and marketing" (Purdue et al. 2000, 52). But Department of Environment and other government responses were disappointing.[5] From 373 approved SRB schemes in rounds one and two only eight were led by community groups and fourteen by voluntary sector organisations. (Department of Land Economy 2002, 47).

The case for community involvement

Forty years of smaller area-based initiatives followed Harold Wilson's first 1968 UP (Matthews 2012). The Department of Environment, Transport and the Region (DETRS)'s own Report on Area-Based Initiatives showed that the voluntary sector was often co-opted for the bidding process and then abandoned. Community leaders felt excluded from professional networks and resources for "representativeness and accountability" were not available for the voluntary and community sector (Department of Environment, Transport and the Regions and Stewart 2000, 66, 67). Hausner[6] wrote that conventional market-oriented economic development programmes were difficult to implement in distressed communities which lacked development opportunities (Hausner 1987, 35). Many in government departments had little knowledge of community issues (Former Government Advisor I 2015):

> Kenneth Clarke had a meeting of the Taskforce, Kenneth Clarke was the Paymaster General in the eighties, asking a group of people who had just been sent out to Government Task Forces and had been in their jobs about a week. And it just showed the lack of any real understanding, how long things take to turn around, where you had got Hendon in Sunderland or Aston in Birmingham, long term economic decline, are you going to create jobs in a year, what planet are you on?

Later evaluations confirmed how little had been achieved for communities through various urban policies. Following interviews with managers from Inner City Task Forces, Task Force "successor bodies", City Challenge, UDCs, Estate Based Initiatives and Scottish New Life Partnership estates, Fordham concluded "writing more than 10 years ago, Professor Joan Higgins wondered why the same questions were being asked to which the answers were largely known in the sixties" (Fordham 1995, 30). Twenty-four years after Harold Wilson's 1968 UP the main emphasis of government policy was still on small targeted areas. "Critical Social and Welfare Issues" – a Report on Small Area-Based Urban Initiatives" in April 1991 – was based on forty-two case studies. Its conclusion on the Comprehensive Community Programme (the successor to the 1968 CDPs) was that "increased emphasis on spatial targeting with UP, the UDCs, Task Forces, and in Scotland the New Life Partnerships, all represent further examples of a somewhat discontinuous tradition" (Fordham and Victor Hausner and Associates 1991, 3).[7]

Capacity building

Throughout this period, though there was little consensus among policy makers or practitioners on the interpretation of terms like "community consultation", "empowerment" and "capacity building", community-based organisations "may often be the only way to get to otherwise 'hard-to-reach' groups". The case for community involvement and capacity building activity lies precisely in the transience of the short-life initiative (Fordham 1995, 32). The policy framework must explicitly recognise that an integral component of small area initiatives is tackling poverty, and not just through the promotion of economic activity but by concentration on welfare provision and benefits, and the provision of quality education which will underpin future employment and enterprise opportunities (Fordham and Victor Hausner and Associates 1991, 61).

Many involved recognised the need to broaden the community base (Former Government Advisor II 2016):

> I wanted to broaden the community base because I was open to any institutional capacities that could ... So in that sense I was institutionally catholic in my view about how this could approach and particularly community organisations.

"Most community organisations took the pragmatic view that if they do not cooperate they will not get the money" (Colenutt and Cutten 1994, 238). Evaluations show that the operation of the SRB Challenge Fund was top down, competitive and centralised in the belief that improvements would eventually stimulate wider change through a process of "trickle down". But the concept of trickle down is now largely discredited (Fordham, Hutchinson and Foley 1999, 13). "Bottom up community involvement needed funding support – technical assistance, management development and additional staff resources and rigorous assessment of long-term funding options" (Fordham 1993, 304). Acknowledgement of these support needs for capacity building came from those developing programmes (Former Government Advisor II 2016):

> "Where is your institutional capacity?" If they were community organisations that were involved, that could be fine ... I recommended was institutional capacity and I recommended what I call ... "capacity building" and it was fundamentally important to have an institutional ability to devise and deliver an effective policy and without that the policy wasn't worth the paper it was written on.

As shown in Chapter 5, after thirty years of Labour and Conservative urban policies, it was left to New Labour's SEU and Policy Action Teams to advocate capacity building. Immediately preceding this, the NCVO's Deakin Commission in 1996 recommended compacts to become the "core component of community governance", "to develop the skills of local groups and individuals further. This is true capacity building" (Osborne 2000, 42). But all this still took time to move forward.

Pressure for community and third sector activity

Despite little government prioritisation, there was growing pressure for community involvement and enterprise, with many initiatives funded by the

Calouste Gulbenkian and German Marshall Foundations. "During the 1970s and 1980s community development initiatives also fed a growing concern that communities should lead efforts at regeneration through acquiring assets and enterprise" (Woodin, Crook and Carpentier 2010, 28).

"Community Work and Social Change" (the Younghusband Report) in 1968 "reviewed the value and purposes of community work, and made recommendations on the kinds of training that were available and which should be further developed" (Thomas 1996, 14). The Community Work Group "Current Issues in Community Work" (Boyle et al. 1973) "reviewed the major features of community work at the time, and suggested, inter alia, the need to establish area resource centres, a national resource centre for community work, national forums and a national fund for community work projects" (Thomas 1996, 14). Though direct employment of community workers by community groups might offer an attractive solution, Boyle was wary that this could lead to conflicts of loyalty and responsibility (Boyle et al. 1973, 94).

Four committees, supported by the Calouste Gulbenkian Foundation[8] (Younghusband, Boyle, Serota and Jones) sought, by the end of the 1980s, to "extend the normative side of community development by addressing the issue of wellbeing, and rights, of children and young people" (Thomas 1996, 99). The Wolfenden Committee on the Future of Voluntary Organisations, which was set up to examine and review the role and function of voluntary organisations in the UK over the next 25 years (Wolfenden 1978), mentioned that "a Community Work Group under the chairmanship of Lord Boyle which suggested that Area Resource Centres should set up Local Intermediary Bodies within existing organisations to serve the needs of community groups within their area" (Wolfenden 1978, 13). But it was not until twenty years later, with New Labour's Policy Action Team Reports, that recommendations for increased community support were taken seriously forward.

Emergence of voluntary and community structures

Despite government reluctance to provide direct funding for community organisations, many indigenous local structures were formed. Many of them were early social enterprises. The Wolfenden Committee reported that charities registered with the Charity Commission had grown to 123,000 by 1976. In 1970 only 3% had an annual income of more than £10,000. The Committee estimated that the total income in 1975 was £1000 million (House of Lords Parliamentary Report 1978). Wolfenden did not advocate direct funding for community structures, but instead recommended funding intermediary bodies in 32 London Boroughs, 36 Metropolitan Districts and

16 Non Metropolitan Districts with a population of over 150,000. "If resources were included for special projects and administration, the cost would still not exceed £2.5mn" (Wolfenden 1978, 179).

These recommendations would not be easy to implement. "Whether the statutory system can change its direction and make substantially greater use of voluntary organisations and the informal sector, as recommended by the Wolfenden Report, is questionable" (Webb, Day and Weller 1976, 56). Lewis later wrote "[A]lthough their critique does have some purchase, it crucially fails to acknowledge the extent to which Deakin (later) tackled head-on the wider context of the changing nature of the voluntary-statutory relationship, albeit by "preaching" to government about its role" (Lewis 1999, 257).

By 1979/80 total grants for various purposes to voluntary organisations had risen to £93mn and by 1987/88 they amounted to £293mn. Between 1979/80 and 1987/88 government support in the form of direct grants increased in real terms by 91.6% (Nathan 1989, 68). During the 1970s and 1980s, though there were also community development trusts and similar structures, these had less access to funds. "Hart in 1997 estimated that members from urban areas held assets worth £29mn, which dwarfed the £92,000 held in rural settings ...The assets were areas of land or buildings that were used mainly for managed workspace, offices or community centres" (Aiken, Cairns and Thake 2008). Despite this apparently significant funding, most was not provided for initiatives from communities themselves. The context for community organisation around social reproductive issues was predominantly subordinated to the negotiation between the state and the market via trade unions and representative democratic institutions (Carley, Jenkins and Smith 2001).

A detailed and wide-ranging survey of 1970s structures across the UK described "community companies (limited by guarantee or by shares), community cooperatives, workers cooperatives, neighbourhood cooperatives, and a variety of 'purpose-built' models".[9] Many of these were very similar to today's social enterprises (Gostyn et al. 1981, 3):

> These new enterprises are community business ventures: they have been initiated by local people working together through existing community organisations or through new ad hoc committees. Control of the enterprise remains within the community; profits are recycled into it, or into other projects of community benefit. Typically, the enterprises are companies limited by guarantee and some have charitable status.

The report went against the grain of government policies (Thomas 1996, 93):

> Its report was published in 1981 as "Whose Business is Business?" and it played a major part in stimulating thinking and experimentation about local

economic development ... The Foundation pressed ahead with the publication of the report despite the opposition of the Manpower Services Commission (MSC) and the Department of Employment, whose attitude to supporting and funding community enterprise changed to hostility as Norman Tebbit replaced James Prior as Secretary of State for Employment.

These community enterprises placed less emphasis on distribution of profits or gains to the membership. Indeed, these may be excluded (Stares 1982, 14).

There were other surveys of structures emerging without direct government support. London Voluntary Service Council knew of thirty-one similar voluntary sector projects in London in December 1980. The Greater London Council located some fifty producer co-operatives in London in 1980 (Knight and Hayes 1982, 10). There were developments in Scotland too, except that most social enterprises were originally labelled community businesses. A contemporary description was "a trading organisation which is set up, owned and controlled by the local community and which aims to create ultimately self-supporting jobs for local people" (Buchanan 1986, 19). "Community employment initiatives predate central government's renewed interest in involving 'the community' ... by 1993 it was estimated there were 329 community businesses and enterprises in England and Wales (Pearce, 1993)" (Hayton 1996, 2).

In 1985 the Local Development Agency Development Fund was established in partnership with the National Council for Voluntary Organisations (NCVO). The aim of the Fund was "to improve the quality of local voluntary action by providing Central Government grants to local government development agencies in England". Seventy Local Development Agencies developed voluntary action, organised support services and resources; 388 new voluntary groups had been started (Murphy 1990, 1). But in total these local funding improvements still did augment the role of communities in regeneration.

ICOM and co-operatives

This section focuses on the rapid growth in local common ownership structures, many of which would today be called social enterprises. The UK common ownership movement grew after the formation of the Scott Bader Commonwealth in 1951. In 1971 the ICOM was "born out of the ashes of Democratic Integration in Industry (DEMINTRY), a society which had been campaigning for twelve years for owners of businesses to convert their firms into Common Ownerships" (Campbell 1983, 1). In 1971, an ICOM Working Party recommended a Revolving Loan Fund since "the orthodox method of a financial backer who becomes a major shareholder is inappropriate by definition of common ownership. Thus loan capital is needed, so that no ownership is necessarily attached to the provider of money" (ICOM Working Party 1971, 1). In 1973, with a grant from Rowntree Social Service Trust, ICOM opened a London office with a full-time organiser. ICOM model rules were introduced (Campbell 1983, 1).

Using the Conservative 1972 Industrial Development Act, in 1974 a new Labour government injected funds into worker co-operatives at Triumph Motorcycles at Meriden in the West Midlands, Kirkby Manufacturing Enterprises on Merseyside and the Scottish Daily News, formed in occupations by workers in 1973 during the previous Heath Conservative government. The author was one of the leaders of the Meriden occupation to form a co-operative. Other shop steward combines, including at British Leyland, British Aircraft Corporation, Dunlop, Chrysler, Lucas Aerospace and Vickers Engineering, developed plans for "socially useful ideals for demystifying new technology (with a view to empowered democratic participation)" (Smith 2014, 6). The Industrial Common Ownership Act 1976 (Watkins 1976), introduced while the author was a Minister in the Department of Industry, provided a legal definition of a common ownership enterprise, a £20,000 per annum (for five years) grant for ICOM and a £250,000 grant for on-lending to common ownerships via Industrial and Common Ownership Finance (ICOF) (Campbell 1983, 1). Section Two of the Act limited membership to those employed in the organisation and limited transfer of assets, especially on dissolution (Labour Government 1976). Before the Act, most of these structures had been registered as private companies limited by shares (Social Enterprise Advisor 2017):

> [S]o, that process was going on and then the relationship with ICOM was that people started to say, "Well, we need to register our business," because they basically weren't, they were an unregistered, they were, you know, just private people.

Paul Derrick emphasised democratic control by those working in these organisations and not by shareholders (Derrick 1981, 2):

> [W]e are using the term "common ownership" in the sense of the common ownership of productive resources by the group of people using those resources. This means that the enterprise is democratically controlled by those working in it and not by any outside shareholders or by retired members or by any other agency.

However, the examples below show that ICOM's application of this definition was soon applied to a very wide range of organisations.

This was followed by the Co-operative Development Agency Act in 1978. ICOM lobbied for provision in the Inner Urban Areas Act for grant aid availability specifically for common ownership and for changes in the Finance Act to enable conversion of conventional firms into co-operatives without attracting capital gains tax (Campbell 1983, 2). As a result, the Inner Urban Areas Act 1978 provided designated district authorities with powers to make loans or grants to groups of people intending to set up co-operatives, provided they meet the definitions in the 1976 Act (Pearce 1979, 5). ICOM was soon registering more than 200 new co-operatives each year (Sawtell 2009b):

> The first Directory published by the CDA in 1980 listed 330 worker cooperatives and the third Directory in 1984 showed 911 … A directory published by the Cooperative Research Unit (CRU. Open University) in 1989, listed 1400 worker cooperatives, probably the highest figure recorded.

60 local Co-operative Development Agencies supported by local authorities provided start-up assistance. Over ten years, this triggered the creation of 1,176 co-ops employing 6,900 people – an average of six staff per co-op (Cornforth et al. 1988). After 1976 ICOM registered over 2,700 co-operatives (Co-operative Commission 2001, 73). Many accounts of the development of co-operatives during the 1980s showed up to 1500 of these organisations (Sawtell 2009a; 2009b; Cornforth et al. 1988; Cornforth 1983; Ridley-Duff 2009). Worker co-ops were a widely recognised form of social enterprise (Spear 2006). The CENTRIS Report shows that in 1991 there were 150 community businesses and co-operatives with about 8,400 members and shareholders, and an annual turnover of more than £15mn (Knight 1993, 181).

There was a similar expansion in Scotland. "January 1997 CBS Network – 110 community businesses in Scotland, 1,095 full-time employees, 68 part-time, combined turnover £13.67mn" (Kay, Community Business Scotland Network 2003). Though covering a wider range of TSOs in Scotland, a 1997 University of Glasgow Training and Employment Research Unit (TERU) Census reported 3,700 local organisations employing 42,000, with 60,000 volunteers (McGregor et al. 1997). This increased to 70,000–90,000 employees in a further TERU 2003 Census (McGregor et al. 2003). SENSCOT, of which the author was until recently a director, and social enterprise organisations in Scotland regard these as the first social enterprise censi. Before this, in 1987 the Strathclyde Community Business Annual Report was already describing structures in similar terms (Pearce 1987):

> A community business is a trading organisation which is set up, owned and controlled by the local community, and which aims to create self supporting jobs for local people and to be a focus for local development. Any profits from its business activities go whether to create more employment of to provide locals services, or to assist other schemes of community benefit.

Spear has a different interpretation of these origins. "[T]he Highland and Islands Development Board created a major innovation – community businesses – to help stem rural depopulation, by providing community services and employment; after 20 years as a rural strategy, it was transplanted with considerable success to inner city areas, firstly in Glasgow, then in other parts of the UK (400 community businesses with 3500 jobs in 1995) and Europe" (Spear 2000, 60). A more coherent exposition, which supports the author's interpretation, is by Pearce,[10] who traces social enterprises from 1970s Job Creation Programmes, with a focus on community development and co-operative and community business structures (Pearce 2003).

Social enterprise at Beechwood College

Because of the emerging structures described above, during the 1970s some contributors were already describing a new "third sector economy". "Third sector enterprises are defined as those which release the talents and energy of the community to build its own future; pursue social objectives ... a broadening of the intrinsically important common ownership concept beyond worker cooperatives alone, to include a range of 'social' enterprises generically described as Community Business Ventures (CBVs)" (Murgatroyd and Smith 1985, 9). The role of Beechwood College was significant, since much of its activity was at least twenty years before New Labour, though in many cases this was not called "social enterprise" (Former Senior Civil Servant IV 2015):

> I don't think the 1990s was when they were invented at all. There was a lot of that sort of activity going on before that.

> There was a lot of going from the 1960s, the late '60s there was a big burgeoning with the Community Development Unit in the Home Office ... In the early '70s a lot of idealism at the time, the same sort of thing ... You had the antecedents in the '60s, late '60s, '70s, and it struggled on into the '80s, but it was the harnessing of it and the focusing of it on specific government targets.

This view was echoed by a contemporary (Former Senior Civil Servant II 2015):

> I worked on every significant economic development policy and programme in the UK between 1989 and 2014 ... the Right would claim to have funded much of the cooperative development movement through the nineties, pre-Blair.

> ... the way that people do a, sort of, post-hoc rationalisation that says, this is all Socialist or emerging from Labour and that it started in the Blair years, just isn't borne out by the facts because, not only was all this supported by

Labour-leaning local government, it was also entertained, maybe using differ-ent language, in the Major, Thatcher years.

Beechwood College was founded in 1977 (Social Enterprise Advisor 2017):

> Beechwood was just a derelict mansion and we got a job creation programme from EU, the EU and we got about £170,000 to renovate the building for the purpose of running it as ICOM's college basically and centre.

In 1981 Beechwood published its "Social Audit Toolkit (A Management Tool for Cooperative Working)" (Spreckley 1981) as a considerably more radical and rounded manifesto than Leadbeater's welfare reform proposals sixteen years later (Leadbeater 1997). Freer Spreckley, as a key figure in founding Beechwood, summarised its significance (Spreckley 2017):

> [W]e were running training courses on social accounting and auditing…when we got to the latter part of 1970s, we started talking about social enterprise as opposed to workers' co-ops.

> We sold 2,000 copies of that booklet ('Social Audit: A Management Tool for Cooperative Working') … 2,000 of those little pamphlets was quite powerful really and all the CDAs were, you know, most of the CDA's became social enterprises based on that, that was before Mr Leadbeater.

Spreckley listed "criteria which can measure social performance in terms of benefit or loss to the working members, the local community and the wider community" and wrote that the co-operative definition was becoming too limiting (Spreckley 1981, 2, 3, 11). As early as 1981, there was a recognition that ICOM needed to demonstrate flexibility to accommodate emerging structures.

In 1976 for the Industrial Common Ownership Act ICOM had written and registered a set of model rules which were to become widely used by groups wishing to set up worker controlled enterprises (Spreckley 1981, 9). By 1981 social enterprise had a definition of good practice in co-operatives and commercial organisations that adopted social accounting and audit as part of their normative annual measurement (Spreckley 2015, 2). Spreckley emphasised that the concept and structure of social enterprise were firmly established and defined (Spreckley 2015, 16). It is the central contention of this book that organisations supported by Beechwood College and local co-operative development agencies were the real antecedents of current social enterprise in the UK, rather than Leadbeater and various Demos pub-lications in the 1990s, which, as shown later, pursued entirely different motives. A former advisor amplified the significance of social enterprise training at Beechwood College (Co-operatives Advisor II 2016):

One of the problems of cooperation was that it was a reaction to capitalism but it was a single stakeholder reaction ... What he (Freer Spreckley) was trying to articulate in that is that it should be a social enterprise, not a single stakeholder enterprise which was a key vision, can I say.

Though there were other contributions on indigenous community structures during the 1970s and 1980s (Ridley-Duff 2009; Cornforth et al. 1988; Ridley-Duff 2011; Spear 1999; 2006), not all of these recognised the significance of their not being registered as co-operatives under Industrial Provident Society legislation. Because they were companies limited by guarantee, they were the legitimate predecessors of today's social enterprises. If they had been formed and promoted 20 or 30 years later, they would have been "social enterprises" (Southcombe 2014):

> [T]he Co-operative Movement not being able to give us the models or tools to work with – and so we had turned to creating Companies Ltd by Guarantee and holding companies to increase the democratic nature of our enterprises.

These developments show clearly the details of social enterprises twenty years before New Labour. Charlie Cattell, at that time ICOM's lead on registration, who is still a social economy consultant, emphasised this continuity in an interview which supports the main contention of this book (Cattell 2015):

> The evolution of client social enterprises nearly always follows the same pattern ...

> In 1985, the support agency would have been a CDA and the client group would have been registered as a company limited by guarantee using ICOM model rules for a common ownership worker cooperative, with limited powers to distribute trading profits, and no power to distribute residual assets on a solvent dissolution. Once in a while a group would register a company limited by shares, with co-operative features. Either way, we'd have marked that up as one more co-op created.

> Now the support agency won't have "cooperative" in its title. The client group will be registered as either a community interest company or as a simple company limited by guarantee, with limited powers to distribute trading profits, and no power to distribute residual assets on a solvent dissolution. Once in a while a group will register a company limited by shares, with social enterprise features. Either way, it will be marked up as one more social enterprise created.

> The end result of either process will look more or less identical.

Registering organisations as companies limited by guarantee was easier and cheaper than as an IPS co-operative (Senior Management, London Co-operative Development Agency 2015):

> [P]eople that were coming from community businesses angles and from regeneration initiatives, were able to implement bigger things with greater impact than the one we were doing.

Well at the time we became very knowledgeable, or more knowledgeable, on the flexibility of the structures created by Co-operatives UK in terms of companies because they were relatively cheap to set up and also Co-ops UK had a differential in terms of the charges they were doing.

… And even now you can still see people that every time they talk about a co-op, they say okay we'll set up a company. We can do it online easily.

The wide variety of structures being registered by ICOM were similar to those today. In 1987, the ICOM Journal reported (ICOM 1987, 2) "ICOM also processed registrations for four voluntary sector bodies: an unemployment project, two arts/media projects, and a Credit Union Development Agency Work is also underway on registering two new local CDAs, two women's centres, a sheltered workshop for the mentally ill, a lesbian and gay centre, and other community, employment and arts projects". As testimony to the flexibility of ICOM rules, the report concluded (ICOM 1987, 2):

Anyone interested in non model rules registration of any type should phone or write to Charlie Cattell at ICOM Central Office. Charlie will send you general information on the service and a questionnaire to fill in about the structure required.

ICOM continued to broaden its range of company registrations. The ICOM 1985 Annual Report states "ICOM is improving its legal services and has received a steady flow of requests for 'one-off' constitutions, such as cooperative development agencies and community groups." The report includes ICOM 1982 White Rules for a common ownership co-operative registered under the Industrial and Provident Societies Act, 1982 Blue Rules for a common ownership company registered under the Companies Act, "Leicester" 1984 Yellow Rules for a common ownership co-operative registered under the Companies Act and ICOM 1984 Green Rules for a common ownership co-operative registered under the Industrial and Provident Societies Act (ICOM 1985, 4). "This version of the voluntary sector – with its emphasis on the more radical elements of its development, mutual aid and pressure group functions, as opposed to its more traditional service-provision role – chimed with political goals, was to be the grass-roots mechanism which some left-wing Labour local authorities, and most prominently of all, the Greater London Council" (Salamon and Anheier 1997b, 266).

Ten years after Beechwood's Social Audit, in 1991 Keltie and Meteyard in "Community Business News" were describing[11] "organisations in the social economy" as "social enterprises" (Keltie and Meteyard 1991), with features closely resembling those of most social enterprises today (Knight and Hayes 1981, 302). Ten years before social enterprise was defined by New Labour, similar definitions were available. But there was already a move away from calling these "co-operatives" (Former Government Advisor I 2015):

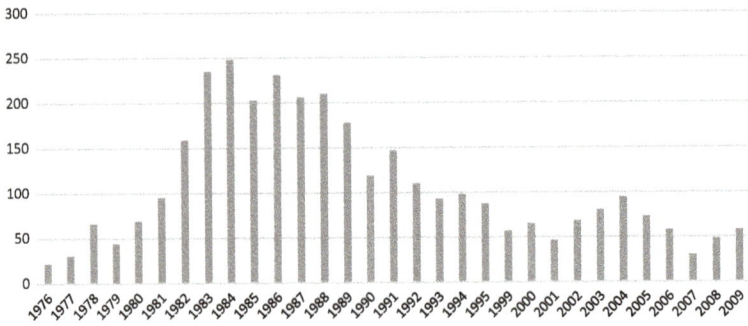

Figure 4.1 ICOM registrations

I remember meeting with the ICOF board … I was presenting them a marketing report which basically said that their labelling, their branding we call it now, was out of kilter with what people wanted and that the term co-op was associated with the 1960s, it was associated with Old Labour, it was associated with trade unions, it was associated with failure because a lot of co-ops were management buy outs and then the underlying business model wasn't working. And that they needed to modernise.

What you do is you change the label and modernise it and be a bit wider in what you will support, so you will go outside co-ops, but you keep the ideology the same.

ICOM *and registrations*

Few UK contributions acknowledge ICOM's role as the "'union', or trade association of producers' or workers' co-ops, divided from the Coop Union" (Yeo 2002, 32). During 2001 the two organisations moved into closer association. Registrations increased rapidly (Figures 4.1 and 4.2).

All these represented substantial growth (Co-operatives Advisor III 2016):

[W]hat we saw in the eighties after the support that the Co-operative Movement had been given by the GLC and this is talking about London, but also there's a national side to this. … There had been very, very massive support for cooperatives, small cooperatives, small worker cooperatives going on … you know where the Co-operative Movement looked, as though it was on a massive growth curve.

There was a wide variety of indigenous structures. Those which emerged for community involvement comprised two distinct strands – co-operatives of

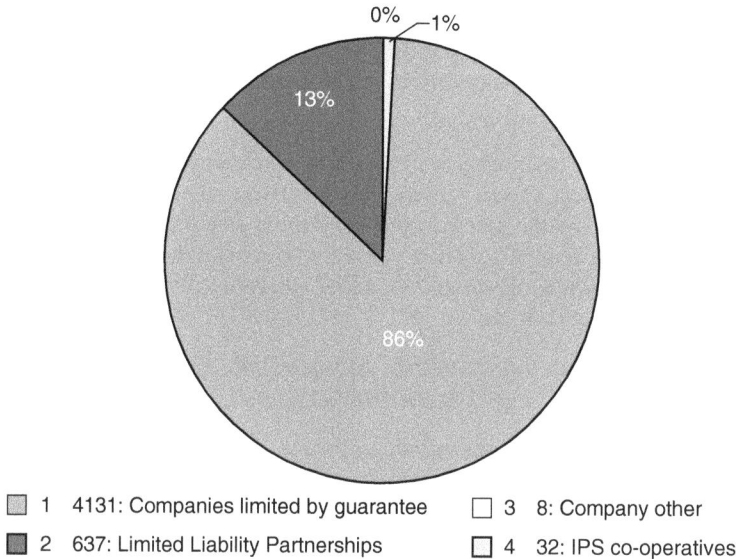

Figure 4.2 ICOM registrations continued

- 1   4131: Companies limited by guarantee
- 2   637: Limited Liability Partnerships
- 3   8: Company other
- 4   32: IPS co-operatives

various legal forms, especially following Labour's 1976 Industrial Common Ownership Act (Watkins 1976), and local community regeneration agencies, of which Local Development Information Service (LEDIS) examples are shown below (IDOX Group from Planning Exchange 2017). Many contributors described these structures as "social enterprises" (Lawless 1989, 126). "Social enterprise emerged from the community enterprise movement that had rejected capitalist, state and charitable solutions to problems caused by the collapse of traditional industries chiefly in the north of England and Scotland" (Southcombe 2014).

These evolving structures were complemented in Labour's General Election Manifesto of May 1983,[12] which included the following commitments:

- give generous encouragement and help to worker cooperatives and local enterprise boards
- establish a Cooperative Investment Bank
- development agencies and local authorities will be empowered to support and to help establish cooperatives and local enterprise boards
- new rights to workers to convert their firms to cooperatives. (Labour Party 1983).

David Owen as new leader of the Social Democrat Party (renamed from the Social Democratic Alliance after its 1981 Limehouse Declaration) was uncharitable about new workers' co-operatives, which he described as "financially unsound" (Owen 1980, 13). However, Owen continued to be active in promoting co-operatives as forerunners for social enterprise (Co-operatives Advisor II 2016):

> 1979 it must have been, when he was still Minister in the Labour Callaghan government, talking about, painting this great scenario of the future of the coop movement; by the year two thousand there would be twenty thousand coops across the country … There was a lot of activity that then has a direct historic connection to the origins of social enterprise. Its precedent is absolutely cast in those early days.

Kenneth Clarke as Conservative Minister of Employment was also supportive in his own way (Clarke 1987, 1):

> Cooperatives are built round a group of people who own their own company, whose rewards are based on the success of their enterprise, and who have no need of trade unions to represent the interests of the workers against those of capital.

Though these initiatives were not prioritised by government, policies for supporting social enterprise were echoed in progressive Conservative circles (Former Senior Civil Servant II 2015):

> I would have found a ready ally in both conventional civil servants and reasonably right-wing Tory ministers, for initiatives that were about creating economic ventures in inner city areas, that might have been called co-ops but it might have been easier if you said that these were community-based business ventures.

ICOM continued to expand, introducing rules for smaller co-operatives. "The rules are in the form of a Memorandum & Articles of Association for a Company Limited by Guarantee, which allow for a minimum of two members, as opposed to the seven required by the Industrial & Provident Societies Acts" (*The New Cooperator* 1985, 3). Most common ownership co-operative were companies limited by guarantee[13] (Former Senior ICOM/ICOF Management II 2015).

There was also growth in mutuals, including a range of Hospital Contributory Schemes (Gorsky, Mohan and Willis 2005). Alongside the NHS, these operated convalescent homes and offered supplementary sick pay and cash contributions towards spectacles, dental and other care, together with the Manor Hospital in North London. Their trade union-based mutual structures, now under the British Health Care Association, still include significant schemes in Leeds, Sheffield, Birmingham, Coventry, Bolton, Bristol and Wolverhampton. Though there was little practical government support for these organisations, in the 1950s they listed 3.4mn contributors, including

2mn in London's Hospital Saving Scheme. Leeds retained between 160,000 to 200,000 members (Gorsky, Mohan and Willis 2005).[14]

All this shows that though many UK academic contributions describe most third sector activity before New Labour as co-operatives, there was a much wider range of registrations and structures. A Company Limited by Guarantee, similar to most social enterprises today, was the dominant form of registration.

US influence

In contrast to the UK in the 1960s and 1970s, in the United States Sherry Arnstein's "Ladder of Participation" became a standard reference work for citizen and community involvement, based on a widening gap between rich and poor in modern society. Consultation was the preserve of the articulate. "In short, it is the means by which they (public) can induce significant social reform which enables them to share in the benefits of the affluent society" (Arnstein 1969, 2). But the message of President Johnson's "Great Society" had not yet arrived in the UK. In the mid-1960s in the United States, poverty became a central policy issue. The "Great Society" prompted a wider range of community activity. The fact that the national government openly financed an organisation of America's poor that was harassing local welfare departments is evidence of the federal role in the late 1960s (Fischer 2003, 27). In a reflection on earlier American influence, in 1988 Kenneth Clarke as Home Secretary commented that "the US is the only country in the world from which Britain has anything to learn about tackling inner city problems" (The Independent, 4/1/88) (Carley, Jenkins, and Smith 2001, 32). In the 1980s British governments turned to the United States for inspiration once again (Parkinson 1989, 423), based on the ascendancy of the community sector in North America (J. Henderson 2015, 3):

> The US Government's "war on poverty" in the 1960s led on to a growing role for non-profit community development corporations (CDCs) across the 1970s, 1980s and 1990s. (Atkinson and Moon 1994; Cochrane 2007)

The UK community anchor model was influenced by North American Community Development Corporations – "often sizeable non-profit community-based organisations leading local economic and social development (Cochrane, 2007; Pearce, 1993; Thake, 2006)" (J. Henderson 2015, 6). Many structures were based on American experience, imported and developed in the UK with support from the Calouste Gulbenkian Foundation (Thomas 1996; Boyle et al. 1973), the German Marshall Fund and European funding. Much of this derived from lack of political representation, racial discrimination, and poor service and welfare delivery mechanisms (Hausner 1988, 24). But the UK model relied on a commitment from external private and public representation and funding – the antithesis of the American model. Differences between North American and UK approaches were clear[15] (Victor Hausner and Associates 1989, 6).

Influence of the European Commission

For the author as a Member of the European Parliament, the significance of the European Commission's 1983 paper on Local Economic Initiatives (LEIs) was clear. The Commission worked in close collaboration with the OECD Co-operative Action Programme on LEIs in which a majority of European Community governments had participated since its inception in 1982 (European Commission 1983, 2). The Commission's description of initiatives which "seek to operate by commercial criteria and be operationally viable" and which "operate without any continuing public subsidy and the objective of achieving or maintaining financial independence" referred to contemporary social enterprises, including worker co-operatives, non-profits and voluntary organisations (European Commission 1983, 5,6). Though worker co-operatives had increased from 6,500 to 13,900, with an increase in employment from 298,000 to 540,000, "it would seem likely, on the basis of the Commission's consultations, that a considerably larger number of people are involved in other enterprises which could be categorised as LEIs"[16] (European Commission 1983, 9).

The Commission saw "local employment initiatives (LEIs) as a valuable contribution to combating mass unemployment, with 136 new initiatives in London which provide 3,000 jobs" (Salisch 1984, 19). This was followed by a Local Employment Development Action[17] (LEDA) programme, an action learning programme, started in 1986, involving twelve areas. Many UK initiatives, which would today be described as social enterprises, were funded following this EEC/OECD LEI initiative. The author below lists a small sample, which were funded by local authorities, foundations including Calouste Gulbenkian, German Marshall Fund and Barrow Cadbury, MSC programmes, ESF and the private sector[18] (IDOX Group from Planning Exchange 2017):

- Aston Reinvestment Trust in 1989
- Community Enterprise in Strathclyde in 1984
- Community Businesses in Scotland throughout the 1980s (following the Local Enterprise Advisory Project and Local Action Resource Centre)
- Local Co-operative Support Organisations throughout the 1980s
- Eldonians Development Trust in Liverpool in 1987

- London Co-operative Training
- Radical Roots in the West Midlands in the 1980s
- Sheffield Co-operative Development Group in 1981
- Unemployed Workers' Centres from 1980 to 1985 under the auspices of the TUC
- Tyneside Economic Development Company in 1983.

Many of these organisations were described in "Whose Business is Business?" (Gostyn et al. 1981) described above.

A unified voluntary, community and social enterprise sector

Many other contributions do not synchronise developments in the voluntary and community sector with social enterprise. By 1993 references to co-operatives and "social enterprises" were becoming interchangeable. Savio and Righetti provide an example. "The cooperative on which this research was conducted is a representative example of the evolution that took place in the sector. This social enterprise was created under the initiative of the psychiatric services, and service professionals and clients are currently part of its management committee" (Savio and Righetti 1993, 239). In 1993, the CENTRIS Report also sought to define the characteristics of these organisations, including non-distribution of profits, no benefits to shareholders and the attainment of a worthwhile or moral purpose (Knight 1993, 74).

Many contributions overlook close connection between policy developments across voluntary, community and social enterprise structures. Social enterprise "is not a new organisational form, but a product of the evolutionary development of non profit or voluntary organisations (Kerlin 2010; Peattie and Morley 2008), co-operatives and mutual organisations (Nyssens 2006)" (Doherty, Haugh and Lyon 2014, 421).

The elevated status of voluntary organisations became a "core political principle", including renaming of the Home Office Voluntary and Community Unit as the Active Community Unit (Ross and Osborne 1999, 50). "The VCS could be treated as a single entity, and it even had identifiable interlocutors in the form of the National Council for Voluntary Organisations (NCVO) and other national bodies". The entity had effectively been created after the 1978 Wolfenden Report. Social enterprisess were included, though, until that point, they were institutionally dealt with as businesses, and part of the market, rather than the third sector (Carmel and Harlock 2008, 156, 159, 160). Westall echoes this. "The origins and thinking behind social enterprise can be dated back to a magazine called New Sector which arose from the community business movement in 1979. This journal asserted that there was a new terrain that was market-oriented but distinctly social in nature, existing to "'promote the principles of collective enterprise and common ownership'" (Westall 2001a, 23).

Though many contributors recognised "contexts that restricted the well-being in several regions of the world starting from the 1980s such as the reduction in the financing of the public social programs, the bad functioning of the government and the increase of unemployment they did not describe these as social enterprises (Defourny and Nyssens 2010b; Kerlin 2010)" (Gonçalves, Carrara and Schmittel 2015, 1595).

Voluntary, government or mainstream businesses illustrate the range of models incorporating different stakeholder involvement or ownership and also the lack of clear distinctions between sectors. The government OTS uses it in relation to organisations that fall under different, but often overlapping and well-known, categories – namely those of voluntary and community organisations, charities, social enterprises, co-operatives and mutuals (Westall 2009, 3, 9).

Marketisation

Conservative governments' policies for 1980s' marketisation of public service delivery and the willing response of voluntary organisations later resulted in New Labour policies for social enterprise.[19] Ongoing pressure for public service marketisation therefore appears as a necessary factor in New Labour policies for voluntary, community and social enterprise sectors.

Under the Conservative government, there was little public debate about the welfare state until 1986 (Young 2013):

> A coherent radical momentum would be … cautiously unveiled at the 1986 party conference. The Next Move Forward … and if resurgent Thatcherism had a theme it would be connected to the institutions … Now it was the turn of that impenetrable tundra called the Welfare State.

"The Thatcher government sought to degovernmentalise the social services and other state enterprises (Le Grand and Robinson, 1984; Johnson, 1989), replacing collective provision with more emphasis on market competition." Instead of representing Wolfenden's supplement to statutory provision they would be a preferred alternative (Kramer 1992, 41). These market concepts developing in the 1980s in the voluntary and community sector were pilots for New Labour's social enterprise policies. Though in Germany and the Netherlands the third sector has historically played a larger role in the construction and delivery of the welfare state, in the UK "it took shape in the context of outsourcing in the 1990s and in New Public Management"

(Brandsen and Pestoff 2006, 494). Le Grand and Estrin (1989, pt. preface) and others describe meeting to discuss many of these ideas immediately following Labour's 1983 General Election defeat, showing that the Party was already changing its policy direction during the 1980s. The preface to "Market Socialism" called this "nothing less than a rethink of socialism: a revaluation" (Le Grand and Estrin 1989, pt. preface). "What is needed is a model of society where power is more evenly distributed between these groups: where the interest of the owners of capital, of workers and of consumers are all taken into account, with none taking automatic priority" (Le Grand and Estrin 1989, 23).

The Conservatives' 1981 Financial Management Initiative brought a new emphasis on management, promoted by funders and practitioners, to ensure more efficient delivery of clear, jointly agreed objectives. The 1987 Woodfield Efficiency Scrutiny of Charities was followed by a Charities Framework White Paper in 1989 and the Making a Difference programme to support volunteering, building on existing, small-scale schemes (Smith 2001). The Efficiency Scrutiny of the Funding of the Voluntary Sector (1990) and the Charities Act (1992) used "a carrot and stick approach to turn voluntary organisations into a 'third force' – delivering state objectives through voluntary means" (Knight 1993, xi). The 1990 report defined "the interests of the state narrowly in terms of the interests of the commissioning government departments, it sought to establish the grounds on which funding for voluntary organisations could be justified on a purely instrumental basis" (Lewis 1999, 261). "These organisations would then accept the dictates of the government, becoming nonprofits and part of the social market economy" (262). John Major's 1990 Conservative government further developed choice through its Citizen's Charter (Deakin 1996). Despite these initiatives, and over ten years after the Conservative administration had assumed power, there was still relative lack of interest in the sector itself (Kendall 2000, 549, 550). But, alongside these policies, NCVO's own pressures continued to actualise causal mechanisms[20] in pointing to a direction later to be endorsed by the NCVO's own Deakin Commission in 1996, as described below.

Le Grand describes 1988 and 1999 legislation as a "big bang". Schools could "opt out" of local authority control, FE and HE would bid for funds from their Funding Councils, Health Authorities would receive devolved budgets and GPs would become fundholders (Le Grand 1991, 1260). The invitation to enter contracts with the statutory authorities may result in the voluntary organisation looking increasingly towards the authorities rather than towards other branches of its own organisation, or towards other local voluntary organisations (Lewis 1993, 190). The 1988 Education Reform Act, the 1988 Housing Act, the 1988 Griffiths Report on personal social services, the 1989 White Paper on the reorganisation of the NHS and the 1989 Local Government Act provided a basis for "quasi market" activity in the voluntary and community sector. The role of the state changed from being funder and provider, so that for social policy initiatives, voluntary initiatives and grants were being replaced with contracts. "If these reforms are carried through to their conclusion, the welfare state in the 1990s will be a very different animal from the welfare state of the previous 45 years" (Le Grand 1991, 1257). Voluntary organisations faced an emerging "contracts economy" with legislation such as the National Health and Community Care Act (1990). "The more the voluntary sector became an instrument of the state, the more it was cast as a 'reactive shadow' tracking the behaviour of the state, rather than pursuing its own agenda of reform" (Knight 1993, xi).

Replacing the public sector with non-governmental activity was a key Thatcher government policy, which continued under John Major from 1990 till 1997. Measures were also introduced to facilitate charitable giving, promote "quasi-markets" and "encourage contracting-out in fields where voluntary sector providers co-exist with other sectors (Le Grand, 1991; Wistow et al., 1994)" (Salamon and Anheier 1997b, 267).

Voluntary organisations' response

Alongside moves towards Le Grand's "big bang" as above, NCVO published "Working Together" by the Bedford Press, recommending a partnership between public bodies and voluntary organisations. "Extension of the market principles to funding soon meant the end of the 'arms-length' relationship between government and voluntary sector" (Knight 1993, 43). By 1981 an NCVO working party on "Improving Effectiveness in Voluntary Organisation", chaired by Charles Handy, pointed to a need for the sector to embrace the management practices of business and led to NCVO's establishment of a Management Development Unit (Rochester 2013, 49). Handy advocated that the traditional notion of a job might be replaced by "a portfolio of activities that everyone manages for themselves". This might include "voluntary work, performed for charitable organisations, the community, friends, family, or neighbours; educational work, which makes it possible to learn, to develop skills, to read, and to educate oneself (Aubrey, 1994)" (Boltanski and Chiapello 2005, 109). In his 1978 "Gods of Management" Handy wrote (Fischer 2003):

> The most talented people and the highest-value work will flow to and from villages of like-minded individuals, bound by a common purpose and managed by reciprocal trust. Villages will shrink and grow as market needs dictate, and

no single village is likely to support a lifelong career based on a single pursuit. Outsourcing and subcontracting will abound.

Some voluntary organisations were already operating what Handy termed "Shamrock" organisations – a small core and network of associates, operating outside the traditional grants economy and charging fees for particular training or consultancies (Knight 1993, 48). Handy's "shamrock" organisation displayed three integrated levels: a core of employees, a group of contractors and a group of temporary workers (Handy 1989, 65). He championed the notion of a "portfolio life" – workers who would pursue "a multi-faceted, multi-client freelance career in which individuals take responsibility for their for their own earning potential, personal development and general well-being". Workers are thereby independent to an extent never yet approached in organisations, moving about among a portfolio of jobs, employers and types of work (Crainer 2013).

"It is this recognition of the indispensability of the community that makes yeoman democracy – a form of collective individualism – the political analogue of the cooperative competition of craft production" (Piore and Sabel 1984, 305). Because Piore and Sabel's "flexible specialisation" is based on increased competition and a negation of traditional collective values, Harvey argues that much of this was at the expense of traditional mutual aid systems and arising social hierarchies within the communities themselves. This growth of informalisation was tolerated and was thoroughly consistent with the new regime of flexible accumulation" (Harvey 1987, 263). In opposition to Handy, Piore and Sabel, Harvey argued for alternative and more collective and social forms of control (Harvey 1987, 269, 270).

NCVO continued its promotional work during the 1980s. In 1984 it published a pamphlet entitled "The Management and Effectiveness of Voluntary Organisations". In 1989 NCVO established the working party chaired by Lord Nathan to look into effectiveness in the voluntary sector. Another report from NCVO looked at the prospects for voluntary organisations in the new environment of contracts, monitoring, evaluation and case management (Johnson 1992, 101). NCVO's Management Development Unit joined with Brunel University to pioneer a master's degree for the sector. However, a proposed National Development Centre for Community Development, funded by Calouste Gulbenkian, foundered because it was regarded as elitist. A framework was emerging, in which many third sector structures not only began to accept new economic frameworks but also a new role created through government rather than market failure (Carmel and Harlock 2008; Dowling and Harvie 2014; Fecher and Lévesque 2008; Prior and Clark 2014; Whitehead 2015). For the author, all these developments provided more conditions for the actualisation of causal mechanisms for New Labour policy developments.

Five years before New Labour, the Knight CENTRIS Report was already recommending eligibility conditions for funding these organisations. He described a "first and third force". The latter, which included many social enterprises, "acts philanthropically on sub-contract from the state. It is organised through not-for-profit companies that must conform to agreed criteria of operation"[21] (Knight 1993, xvii). Membership of a "third sector economy", based on social enterprise characteristics from Keltie and Meteyard (1991), would be a condition of public money being placed in the organisation and for involvement in public sector contracts (Knight 1993, 303). Echoing Knight's "first and third forces", Labour's approach recognised an increasing division between grassroots voluntary groups and "a new breed of professionalised, well-funded and well-organised voluntary organisations" (Morison 2000, p. 103)" (Fyfe 2005, 552). McLaughlin (2004) later suggested that the report anticipated a "third force" of voluntary organisations which would make a "Faustian Pact" with the state as financier. Though Thatcher and Major Governments sought to build on this "third force", Knight's suggestion that an appropriate quid quo pro from the state for the sector's "altruistic" contributions must be an entitlement or right to tax relief fell down on grounds of "technical feasibility" (Kendall 2003, 51).

Dahrendorf's forward to "The Voluntary Sector: Comparative Perspectives in the UK" supported Knight's analysis of a first and third force (Kendall 2003, xiv):

> Increasingly it appears that "the sector" is in fact two sectors: one genuinely voluntary, happily remote from government, hard-pressed to meet the charity tests of social usefulness – and the other linked to government as well as business, defined by its social objectives, subject to all sorts of controls and rules, and voluntary only in name.

Though the findings of the CENTRIS Report were largely discarded because Knight's "very pertinent questions" did not fit the government's agenda (Centre for Civil Society and NCVO 2001, 5), they represented another example of steps towards marketisation and featured among the author's demi-regularities as examples of a continuing change in structures. But despite hostility to Knight's report, others were already writing in similar terms about the voluntary sector and contracts in a market economy. "Having made their 'Faustian pact' with the state as financier, these organisations would accept the dictates of government, becoming non profits and part of the social market economy" (Lewis 1999, 262). There was a "'new public management agenda' (Hood 1991; Ferlie et al. 1996), with its 'ability to introduce service providers, especially the VCO sector, to the discipline of the market (Mackintosh 1992)'" (Ross and Osborne 1999, 51).

The government sought to bring voluntary and community organisations into a more direct relationship. "Ministers made numerous speeches extolling the values of partnership with voluntary bodies ... This was formalised in 1995 with the 'Partnership Declaration'". The newly formed "Voluntary Service Agency" (formerly the Home Office Voluntary Services Unit) used discretion under the National Health and Community Care Amendment Act of 1994 to allow charities to compete for contracts under more favourable terms than other organisations (Knight 1993, 292). A "voluntary code of good practice management" was introduced in 1994 under the Management and Evaluation Institute, including funding for accredited courses in management, finance, and evaluation techniques. Though most of this was supported by NCVO and welcomed by the voluntary sector, there was also concern about undermining the autonomy of these organisations, since all of this represented the gradual contractualisation and commercialisation of the third sector, especially social enterprises as part of Knight's "third force". All this was later echoed by Carmel and Harlock (Carmel and Harlock 2008, 156).

Kendall and Deakin

For the author's analysis, the culmination of NCVO's policy entrepreneurship and further actualisation of underlying causal mechanisms were represented by its setting up a Commission on the Future of the Voluntary Sector under Nicholas Deakin (Deakin 1996), which was funded by the Joseph Rowntree Foundation. The Committee reported that there were 200,000 to 240,000 voluntary bodies under a "narrow definition", with a possible 1.3mn bodies under a "wider definition". Their total operating expenditure was estimated at £13.5bn in 1995. Deakin's key recommendation was a Concordat between the voluntary and community sector and government, which later formed a basis for New Labour's channelling increased funding into the sector "by recommending that partnership could actually be operationalised through a Concordat between the third sector and the state" (Kendall and Knapp 1995). New Labour's approach was incorporated in its 1997 New Commitment for Regeneration initiative, developed in partnership with the Local Government Association (Ross and Osborne 1999, 53, 54):

> This approach has been taken forward by a consortium of national voluntary organisations, which produced a draft Compact early in 1998 (Working Group on Government Relations 1998). The Labour Party also gave a firm

commitment to take forward this approach in both its Election Manifesto and the subsequent policy paper on the VCO sector. (Labour Party 1997)

Deakin's report urged government to take a more positive and "higher voltage" interest in the sector's well-being (Lewis 1999, 263). NCVO followed Deakin by setting up a Quality Standards Task Group in 1997 but this was overtaken by the performance hub set up as part of ChangeUp, New Labour's capacity building programme (Rochester 2013, 118).

Though Kendall describes Deakin's report as going beyond Wolfenden by recommending "that partnership could actually be operationalised through a Concordat between the third sector and the state" (Kendall 2004, 53) his assertion that "the original idea of packaging the third sector-state relationship as a Compact effectively came from nowhere to occupy a significant position within the new government's policy in just over two years" is puzzling (Kendall 2000, 544). For the author, the Compact did not "come from nowhere", but represented the logical continuity of NCVO's previous managerial and marketisation preparations. Kendall's assertion that there was "little or no awareness among voluntary organisations of being part of a coherent 'sector'" despite the sector's being actively promoted by NCVO and the Charities Aid Foundation is equally puzzling (Kendall 2000, 545). As shown in Chapter 1, a developing coherent voluntary sector was already echoed by other academic contributors (6 and Leat 1997, 39; Alcock and Kendall 2010; Rochester 2013, 77).

The role of Demos: social enterprise as welfare reform

Kendall's failure to recognise the logical emergence of the Concordat and the development of a coherent voluntary sector is compounded by his misunderstanding of the role of the think tank Demos. He writes that though Demos had a long association with the political left, with its ideas more readily absorbed by New Labour, when Mulgan joined the Downing Street Policy Unit, some Demos recommendations failed to find their way into New Labour's policy (Kendall 2000, 552).

But Kendall's interpretation completely overlooks Demos and Mulgan's role in shaping New Labour's policies for social enterprise and the Downing Street Strategy Unit's recommendations in 2002 as described in Chapter 5 (Kendall 2003, 57). For the author, Kendall thus fails to recognise deep-seated causal mechanisms, with examples of demi-regularities, from the NCVO's 1980s managerialism inspired by Charles Handy, echoes of "flexible specialisation" (Piore and Sabel 1984) and through a succession of Demos contributions.

Before the election of New Labour, in a 1995 Demos pamphlet "The Other Invisible Hand: Remaking Charity for the 21st Century", Mulgan and Landry suggested an examination of legal structures. Anyone wanting to set up mission driven organisations should not be required to "have a board" if these were non-profit. They should not be constrained in their ability to raise capital when there was no evidence that provision of a public good must involve the state. An expanded notion of the public good could be made more publicly visible with indicators and measurements (Mulgan and Landry 1995, 58, 62, 90, 92). Future public services funding could be based on outputs of "quality of social life and relationships" (Mulgan and Landry 1995, 94). Leadbeater's "Rise of the Social Entrepreneur" two years later (Leadbeater 1997) opened the door further for dilution and outsourcing of the welfare state and private finance to solve social problems, with indicators and measurement for payment by results. There should be a return "to the voluntaristic tradition of welfare innovation", of which the eighteenth and nineteenth century was the heyday. "A professionalised, innovative and entrepreneurial sector of social organisations will be a vital ingredient in a modern welfare system" (Leadbeater 1997, 20). In anticipation of opposition "through use of unpaid labour", there should be private sector growth finance (Leadbeater 1997, 81).

Despite the role of Beechwood College from 1978 as described above and its various publications (Spreckley 2015; 1981), Leadbeater's "The Rise of the Social Entrepreneur" is frequently hailed as a "founding document" for UK social enterprise. But, as shown above, its origins were very different from Beechwood, since it premised an argument for welfare reform (Leadbeater and Christie 1999, 9):

> In the post-war era the growth of the welfare state was seen by most people as a symbol of social progress. No more. The welfare state is widely criticised for being inflexible, slowing moving, bureaucratic, dehumanising and disempowering.

These welfare arguments led to policy and institutional developments between 1998 and 2002 (Former Senior Civil Servant IV 2015):

> There was the Demos Publications on social enterprise and civic enterprise. People were talking about civic entrepreneurs and so, entrepreneurialism in its civic and social guises were seen to be very much a part of the Blair reforming approach.

Kendall failed to recognise that it was policies from these Demos publications which came to fruition in Mulgan's policies from the Cabinet Office Performance and Innovation Unit (PIU) and Downing Street Strategy Unit. These developments were supported by others, including Westall, who suggested a review of legislative models to determine how existing legal frameworks might need to change in order to accommodate diverse social enterprises, equity or user involvement (Westall 2001a, 19).

For the author, these are all connected happenings and events. The Millennium Commission's distribution of funds and Leadbeater's framing his contribution as a critique of the welfare state to outsource public service delivery are real manifestations of ongoing causal mechanisms described throughout this book. The social entrepreneur would become an effective and cheap alternative to the welfare state, though this argument was not supported by research or evidence (Hulgård 2010, 296). Leadbeater opposed a "megastate". The "welfare state was more of a barrier to than a source of sustainable solutions to social problems". "According to the social enterprise (SE) perspective, the modern state was devised to respond to the social problems that developed throughout the twentieth century and continues to do so." Several early writers, including management writer Peter Drucker, endorsed Leadbeater's view (Hulgård 2010, 296).

But Hulgård also saw possibilities for a policy entrepreneur role – "a new platform for civil society and creates more room for collectives and solidarity movements to influence welfare society's evolution in future" (Hulgård 2010, 299). The pervasive reach of neoliberalism throughout the economy and its organisation of governance and the social is not merely the result of leakage from the economic to other spheres but rather of the explicit imposition of a particular form of market rationality on these spheres (Brown 2006, 693). "(T)he economy is tailored to it, citizenship is organized by it, the media are dominated by it, and the political rationality of neoliberalism frames and endorses it" (Brown 2006, 704).

As further evidence of the author's earlier "causal mechanisms" others warned of a forthcoming shift towards a marketised interpretation and problems in individual cases where enterprises in the public and free social economy sectors modify their objectives with a view to seeking profit in a private sector fashion (Thiemayer 1982, 358). "The transition from radically antistatist neoliberalisms of Reagan and Thatcher in the 1980s to the more socially moderate neoliberalisms of Blair, Clinton, and Schröeder during the 1990s may therefore be understood as a path-dependent adjustment and reconstitution of neoliberal strategies in response to their own disruptive, dysfunctional sociopolitical effects" (Brenner and Theodore 2002, 359). Rose summarises this direction of travel: "The objects, instruments and tasks of rule must be reformulated with reference to these domains of market, civil society and citizenship, with the aim of ensuring that they function to the benefit of the nation as a whole" (Rose 1996, 44).

In Kendall's analysis there seems little understanding of the purpose of the Commission on Social Justice (Commission on Social Justice 1994) or Le Grand's Quasi-markets described above. As the new leader of the Labour Party, John Smith launched the Commission in 1992. This recommended "a greater emphasis on responsibilities as well as rights', improving opportunities available, increasing incentives for work and decreasing the barriers, as well as enhancing employability and human capital through education and training". The state was "not just as a passive provider of benefit, but as an enabler" (Haddon 2012, 5). Patricia Hewitt, at that time with the Institute for Public Policy Research, was a key figure throughout the Smith Commission (Haddon 2012, 6). In 2001 Hewitt set up the Social Enterprise Unit in the DTI and in 2006 the Social Enterprise Unit in the Department of Health.

For the author these ongoing structural changes provide further evidence of a pattern of demi-regularities and a strong and underlying pattern of events from NCVO's entrepreneurialism through to the role of Demos to Blair's promotion of social enterprise via Patricia Hewitt.

Blair continued to develop NCVO's themes above in his 1997 Fabian Society pamphlet "The Third Way: New Politics for the New Century" which recognised the need for government partnerships with the voluntary sector, strengthening civil society and helping communities to improve their own performance (Blair 1998, 14) (Kendall 2000, 551). Kendall's contention that promotional activities of policy entrepreneurs with a stake in the sector "had really only recently gathered momentum after mainstreaming had already taken place" (Kendall 2003, 216) completely neglects National Council for Voluntary Organisations', (NVCO) previous role in promoting managerialism and marketisation. He is more accurate in describing Blair's policies after 1994 with a communitarian hue, but in a more pro-market and less traditional pro-state position with recognition of the third sector (Kendall 2000, 550).

Throughout the 1990s, policy discourses were increasingly dominated by references to the strengths of the market and the weaknesses of the state. After New Labour's coming into office in 1997, the rapid adoption of a "Compact', the allocation of additional resources to foster development and the initiation of and following through to major Treasury reviews have all been symptomatic of this step change" (Kendall 2003, 216). But when Kendall contrasts Deakin with Knight's CENTRIS Report, he fails to mention that Deakin's recommendations fitted closely with those already being made by NCVO and Charities Aid Foundation (CAF) in their view of a Concordat as an intermediary stage towards marketisation.

"In vogue in the past few years in several countries (in particular with the popularity of the dominant managerial current of New Public Management and the fashion for public private partnerships), the state is encouraged to construct public policy by cooperating with the private sector – that is, with the dominant socio economic agents in the market economy" (Vaillancourt, LeClerc and Bouchard 2013, 137). "This quasi-market opens up the construction and production of policy to participation by organisations from the public, private, and third sectors, while inviting those organisations to compete with one another for contracts (Bartlett and Le Grand 1993; Means and Smith 1994; Lewis 1999, 2004)" (Vaillancourt, LeClerc and Bouchard 2013, 137). Stoker describes this as "entrepreneurial welfarism" – "a politics of redistribution not simply of income but rather of life chances or opportunities ... There is no assumption that the state will pay but rather the state uses its fits legal authority to ensure that someone takes responsibility for meeting welfare needs (White 1998)" (Stoker 2004, 51). The UK approach is for a marketoriented welfare sector, with TSOs focusing on conventional business practices, and with social economy values and approaches competing with the private sector (Spear 2000, 62).

"There was a shift away from government towards the 'discovery' of NGOs as flexible, creative non-state actors with an assumed range of comparative advantages over government agencies" (Lewis 2010, 334). "The roll-out phase reconstitutes neoliberalism in 'more socially interventionist and ameliorative forms, in order to regulate, discipline and contain those marginalized or dispossessed by the neoliberalisation of the 1980s'" (Graefe 2005, 3). After Reagan, Thatcher and Bush, the neoliberal project "gradually metamorphosed into more socially interventionist and ameliorative forms, epitomized by the Third-Way contortions of the Clinton and Blair administrations" (Peck and Tickell 2002, 389).

This period saw "the introduction of the market (and the creation of a 'market proxy' where no market exists) into the funding and the delivery of local state services" and the "creation of new institutions, combining business representatives with state officials to oversee and to deliver all forms of economic and social policy" (Jones and Ward 2002, 485). Labour's "subordination of the "social' to the market represents not merely a by product of the neoliberal project but the intention and consequence of the restoration of the power of the economic elite, it is unrealistic to expect anything else" (Fuller and Geddes 2008, 275).

Carmel and Harlock later described an overall process where the government was already "creating a governable terrain via the mechanisms of procurement and performance" (Carmel and Harlock 2008, 157). Harris confirms Lewis' description of a continuing government partnership with the voluntary sector which had always existed. Lewis argues that "the most important question is not, therefore, to establish whether such a partnership exists but, rather, to understand how it has changed over time" (Harris 2010, 36) Lewis argues that the voluntary sector had always sought a "partnership" with the state, but its nature, in terms of funding, terms and conditions and the associated expectations of each party have changed significantly over time (Lewis 1999, 256).

For the author all this represents a series of demi-regularities which actualise causal mechanisms, which, as shown in Chapter 5, continued throughout New Labour's social enterprise policies from 1998 to 2002 and culminated in legislation for community interest companies (CICs) in 2004, which had been encouraged by Mulgan in the Policy and Innovation Unit and Downing Street Policy Unit for further outsourcing and third sector flexible delivery. This represents Bhaskar's conceptualisation "in the experience of the social agents concerned, to the essential relations that necessitate them" – that is, the movement from empirical to structural/causal (Bhaskar 2015, 26).

New Labour's approach represented a "significance of building the capacity of VCOs to engage in the policy formulation and implementation process" (Ross and Osborne 1999, 53). New Labour's Compacts with the voluntary and community sectors in 1998 began the process of their commercialisation: "the Compacts provide a mechanism whereby the more 'managerially minded' parts of the voluntary sector are being encouraged by the state to pursue their interests through a framework of 'good practice' which emphasises and reinforces an economic rationality rather than a traditional volunteering ethos" (Fyfe 2005, 545).

An Active Community Unit was established in the Home Office in 1999. The voluntary and community sector thus rapidly became institutionalised in the Compact. "Remarkably, this idea (the Compact) was introduced into the policy and politics bloodstream afresh, and had become a significant element of government policy by November 1998 – just 28 months after the idea was initially floated by Deakin at the Commission report's launch" (Kendall 2000, 555). These ideas only really entered the UK political lexicon relatively recently, some time after commitments were already being made by Labour towards the third sector (when in opposition), and vice versa (Kendall 2000, 555). Again, Kendall fails to recognise that all this represented continuity from NCVO's 1980s policies, with continuing organisational changes as demi-regularities. He is more accurate in describing this as a pragmatic endorsement of the advantages of markets in the economic sphere (Kendall 2000, 550). Though McKay et al. portray considerable growth in charitable voluntary and community sectors through commercial revenue between 2003 and 2007, this growth was evident before the early years of New Labour in 1997 (McKay et al. 2011, 343). More accurately, Lewis describes policies emerging in similar terms to WISEs and the EMES (Lewis 1999, 265), as shown in chapters 3 and 6:

> There remains the issue of how far the voluntary sector is being harnessed to New Labour's project "for itself," and how far it is still a matter of it serving government's ends … Nevertheless, the central pillar of New Labour's social

policy – the welfare-to-work program – may eye the possibilities offered by voluntary-sector employment for its own purposes.

Local government

Despite a lack of central government encouragement, as shown above, from the 1970s onwards many indigenous organisations continued to receive support at a local level. Centres against unemployment, women's employment projects, industry-wide campaigns against closures, trade union and community resource centres, welfare rights campaigns and training projects for young people, women and ethnic minorities, "mushroomed over the past 4 years, and have altered the pattern of non-governmental activity in several cities" (Benington 1986, 16).

A 1998 Local Government Management Board Survey reported 889 enterprises supported by 74 authorities, including furniture recycling and community credits (Westall 2001a, 33). Using data from Leadbeater and Christie (Leadbeater and Christie 1999, 12, 13), Westall writes that in 1999 there were 1500 worker co-operatives, 544 co-operatives or jointly controlled farm businesses, 300 community well-being and health centres and 293 friendly societies (Westall 2001a, 34).

The scale of their activity, "including their district authorities, preserved or created well over 10,000 jobs" (Benington 1986, 19). Sheffield set up an Employment Committee, an Employment Department and a Sheffield Co-operative Development Group, with co-operatives as an "alternative to 'capitalist-oriented economic development policies" (Cochrane, Allan 1991, 362). Many encouraged co-operative and community enterprise to provide permanent local jobs in socially useful products for people marginalised by market forces" (M. Parkinson 1989, 430). This resulted in increasing levels of central intervention in the local government during the 1980s, through legislation, minimal consultation, targeted funding, the by-passing of local government and a major reorganisation of local government (O'Toole 1996, 63). As shown above by reports from the Community Ventures Business (Gostyn et al. 1981) and from the Local Economic Development Information Service (IDOX Group from Planning Exchange 2017), many of these organisations had continued from the 1970s and many would today be labelled "social enterprises".

Conclusion

Isolated from the development of a social economy in mainland Europe, Labour and Conservative governments resorted to top down localised solutions to counter 1970s and 1980s large-scale deindustrialisation and massive job losses. Despite numerous evaluations of these initiatives (Fordham and Victor Hausner and Associates 1991; Fordham 1993; 1995; Fordham, Hutchinson and Foley 1999), which clearly demonstrated the need for more direct community involvement, it was not until New Labour came to power in 1997 with its Neighbourhood Renewal Programme, SEU and Policy Action Teams, that more direct funding for community capacity and involvement appeared.

In the meantime, apart from the Industrial Common Ownership Act 1976 and the Co-operative Development Agency Act 1978, with co-operatives encouraged and funded by the ICOM and local authorities, direct funding for community structures was promoted by foundations like Calouste Gulbenkian (Thomas 1996), the German Marshall Fund and European Commission (European Commission 1983). Supporting these developments, the role of Beechwood College (Spreckley 1981), with its social enterprise "manifesto", is overlooked in most other academic contributions. Despite different nomenclature, especially as shown above from the interview with Charlie Cattell (2015) as ICOM's registration specialist, many of these emerging local community structures were identical with contemporary social enterprises and other third sector structures.

Following the 1978 Wolfenden Report, this period of earlier development for the voluntary and community sector, promoted by Charles Handy's brand of managerialism for NCVO, and publications from the think tank Demos, culminated in the Deakin Commission (Deakin 1996) and New Labour's Compact with the third sector. All this led to the full marketisation of social enterprise and the third sector shown in Chapter 5.

Notes

1 For further details about these Inner Area Studies, please see F. J. C. Amos, 'Change or Decay: Final Report of the Liverpool Inner Area Study', *Town Planning Review*, 49 (2) (1978): 196–8; G. M. Lomas, 'Inner London: Policies for Dispersal and Balance: Final Report of the Lambeth Inner Area Study', *Town Planning Review*. 49 (2) (1978): 203–6; B. M. D. Smith, 'Unequal City: Final Report of Birmingham Inner Area Study', *Town Planning Review*, 49 (2) (1978): 199–202.

2 In 2018 and 2019, the author was a member of the Shadow Chancellor's Implementation Group to carry forward Labour's manifesto commitment to "double the size of the cooperative economy". He has written elsewhere of his surprise on learning that many involved in Implementation Group discussions had no understanding that "doubling the cooperative economy" had already happened in the 1970s and 1980s.

3   As a leading consultant who worked with Victor Hausner in role as the Govern-
    ment's regeneration advisor, Geoff Fordham played a key role in most of
    Hausner's work. He completed a range of evaluations with Hausner and others,
    most of which did not appear in mainstream academic journals, but which are
    cited in this chapter. The author is very grateful for these documents from Geoff
    and Rachael Fordham.
4   Evaluations were conducted by the Department of Environment and other
    departments involved in Inner Cities Programmes and the UP. For further details
    about Department of Environment evaluations, the UP and community involve-
    ment please see *DoE Inner City Programmes 1987–1988. A Report on Achieve-
    ments and Developments* (London: Department of the Environment 1989);
    Renewing the Cities: A Report on the DoE Inner City Programmes in 1988–1989
    (London: Department of the Environment 1990): 1–44; *The Urban Programme
    1985. A Report on Its Achievements in England* (London: Department of the
    Environment 1986).
5   For further details about Department of Environment and other Government
    responses, please see Department of Land Economy, University of Cambridge
    (2002); 'Government Response to the Environment Committee First Report into
    the Single Regeneration Budget' (Secretary of State for Environment, 1996):
    1–25.
6   After working for the US Carter Administration, Victor Hausner arrived in the
    UK to work for the Policy Studies Institute. From 1982, he led an ESRC 5 Volume
    Research Project on urban programmes and their implementation and had access
    to senior civil servants and ministers.
7   These conclusions are significant, since they are based on Fordham's detailed
    series of interviews with local project managers throughout most Labour and
    Conservative Government area based and national regeneration schemes from
    the 1970s to the 1990s. Throughout all of this, he worked closely with Victor
    Hausner.
8   Data and interviews throughout this chapter show that in the 1970s and
    1980s, rather than central government, a combination of funding from the
    Calouste Gulbenkian Foundation, German Marshall Fund, European
    Programmes and private companies provided funding for much initial com-
    munity development.
9   The Community Business Ventures Unit was funded by government, Calouste
    Gulbenkian Foundation, Shell UK, NatWest Bank and others. The government
    later established the Community Enterprise Programme. By the early 1980s, as
    shown later, the EEC (later the EU) and OECD had established new programmes
    and initiatives. The Centre for Employment Initiatives, with EU and other fund-
    ing, was formed to support and advise on developments. Much of this was
    inspired by a three-week USA study team visit, invited by the German Marshall
    Fund of the United States, which included John Pearce and Colin Ball   both of
    which are featured in this book. The Unit's 1981 report was among the first
    which described community structures in detail and showed that many of these
    had similar structures to today's social enterprises.

10 In 2003, based on his personal experience in Cumbria and Community Business in Strathclyde, John Pearce later wrote 'Social Enterprise in Anytown' (Pearce 2003), essentially a 'social enterprise manual', whose tone and contents contrast with those of Social Enterprise London. Pearce was already aware of a London policy thrust towards a social enterprise market economy. Contributions from Pearce were based on considerable practical experience.

11 Keltie and Meteyard in 1991 were already describing today's social enterprises:

1   Quality employment: a concern with equal opportunities; staff involvement in management; commitment to training; opportunity for staff to have capital or tangible stake in business.

2   Wider accountability: Social enterprises ensure that the community of interest or geographic community have their interests looked after in commercial decisions.

3   Learning organisations: a commitment to indigenous recruitment to develop native talent and skills; education an integral feature of the work.

6   Collective Ownership: worker, community or social ownership. Any external equity would be 'ethically sourced'.

7   Trading not aided: The organisations provide goods and services in return for payments. The organisations are not primarily grant-aided either from public funds or charitable sources; they may work on contracts.

9   Co-operation not competition: Enterprises in the social economy thrive in an atmosphere of co-operation, by hiving off new businesses, or inter-trading between businesses.

12 In 1980 the author was Chair of the Labour Party National Executive Committee Working Party, which produced a document on workers' co-operatives, which was followed by a 1981 National Executive Committee Statement from which these election manifesto commitments derive.

13 A detailed description of the differences between companies limited by guarantee and co-operatives is shown in Appendix 2.

14 For further details of the growth of mutuals, see Birchall (2008); Gorsky, Mohan and Willis (2005).

15 After working for the Carter Administration in the United States, Victor Hausner's role and conclusions are significant. He worked with other consultants to produce reports for government departments, many of which have not been previously accessed. Their findings on community development are quoted in detail in this chapter.

16 Much of the LEI initiative and the Commission's Communication to the Council of Ministers was inspired by Michael Young, who in 1997 created the School for Social Entrepreneurs in London, and by Chris Brooks of OECD, who had previously set up Youth Aid in London. The Commission continued working alongside OECD in support of LEIs. The fact that "high level" bodies like the European Commission endorsed local initiatives, considered them to be useful and cost-effective and even organised events in specific localities of different member wtates and regions, served to convince local and regional authorities of the

potential value of bottom up approaches rather than their more instinctive top down responses. Simultaneously, this gave credibility to local activists, "many of whom had been toiling in the wilderness for years, even decades" (Morley 2017).

17 The LEDA programme funded organisational costs in the different areas and associated publicity within and between member states. In order to attract funding, localities needed practical ideas, which the LEDA programme sought to provide, drawing on successful experiences from across the EEC. This later included production of a Handbook on Local Initiatives, some of which is still being used in the European Commission's promotion of recent 'Community Led Local Development', funded with Structural Fund programmes.

18 The IDOX Group in Glasgow housed a large collection of former Planning Exchange papers, which the author recalls as a unique repository of 1970s and 1980s regeneration documents. He is grateful to IDOX staff for his retention of many of these documents, since many others have now been destroyed.

19 For the author, the willing response of voluntary organisations brought about the actualisation of causal mechanisms, which later resulted in New Labour policies for social enterprise. For his Critical Realist approach, this represents one of the author's examples of retroduction. Following Fletcher's interpretation, continued regulation and pressure for state provision of public services would have produced a different manifestation of capitalism and neoliberalism as mechanisms (Fletcher 2016, 191).

20 As described in Chapter 2, in explaining the author's Critical Realist approach.

21 For this study and the CENTRIS Report, Barry Knight obtained funding from 23 different funding bodies, for extensive research he carried out between 1989 and 1993. Page viii of the (Knight, 1993) report describes how "when the project described here was begun in 1989, it was sold to funders on the basis that it would be the "new Beveridge". But the Report upset many in Government Departments and NCVO.

5

New Labour, co-ops and social enterprise

New Labour approach – an overview

While Ferlie et al. in their overview of New Public Management describe "quasi markets" and "Next Steps agencies" in the 1980s and early 1990s (Ferlie et al. 1996, chapter 1), New Labour policies for social enterprise and third sector delivery of public services had not yet arrived. However, as shown above, and later in this chapter, some demi-regularities and underlying causal mechanisms could already be observed.

The New Labour Governments of 1997 and 2001 presided over a major political rupture with the wider Co-operative Movement, which is not described elsewhere. Labour sought to discard democratic, co-operative and mutual structures in favour of individually controlled and more malleable social enterprises which could be used for flexible, low-cost public service delivery.[1] Because the democratic accountability of earlier co-operative, mutual and community structures would have limited their acceptance of repositioning and changed roles, New Labour encouraged new legal structures with reduced accountability. Interviews in this chapter with key players show these tensions laid bare in ways which other commentators seem to have missed. While some academic contributors have described these developments as an almost seamless shift from a third sector based on co-operatives to social enterprises, there was a major political difference between the Labour and Co-operative Movements, with progress often propelled through interventions by Prime Minster Blair himself. Many political alliances did not survive during this period of major political rupture.

In engineering a shift to looser definitions for the third sector, New Labour sought a shift as politically significant as its abandonment of Clause IV of the Party's Constitution in 1995. Other contributions have underestimated the significance of this shift away from the ICOM – "in significant ways the 'union', or trade association of producers' or workers' coops" (Yeo 2002, 32).

New Labour rejected Keynesian demand management and redistributive fiscal policy and replaced these with "supply-side measures to integrate disadvantaged individuals into the mainstream economy and society via the labour market" (Hall 2003, 266). Promoting social enterprise was a key component in this political strategy.

Many contributions also overlook the significance of the party's Commission on Social Justice in 1994, established by John Smith MP as leader following Labour's defeat by John Major in the 1992 General Election. The Commission's Report represented a final break with Labour's 1980s taxation and public spending strategies and prescribed an economic and social framework for the New Labour Governments of 1997, 2001 and 2005. In future, many types of social expenditure would be an investment in society which enhances growth potential by providing services help underpin the efficient operation of the market economy (Commission on Social Justice 1994, 52). Labour's emerging policies for social enterprise fitted this political shift.

Expectations of the Co-operative Movement

Before the 1997 General Election, the Co-operative Movement anticipated policies more favourable to co-operative development. Numbers of new co-operatives were still growing. The 1993 London ICOM Worker Co-operatives Directory included 178 co-operatives trading in London (London ICOM 1993). ICOM's "Creating a Social Economy" 1996, included "Why a Labour Government should support the development of cooperative enterprises"[2] (ICOM 1996): "We believe that the Labour Party should commit itself to supporting the growth of a strong social economy once it is in power." Helen Seymour's Report on ICOM's 25th Anniversary in the London ICOM 14th Annual Report 1996 included promotional activity for co-ops[3] (London ICOM 1996):

> 1996 was ICOM's twenty fifth anniversary, and was marked by the launch of the two ICOM/ICOF campaigns: "Towards a Stakeholder Economy", a lobbying campaign aimed at gaining support for worker co-ops from the major political parties and the trade unions in the run up to the general election, and in tandem to this, "Co-operative Opportunity for All", a campaign to develop proposals for supporting a national cooperative development strategy, a national co-operative development strategy.

In the campaign "Cooperative Opportunity for All: A National Strategy for Cooperative Development, October 1996"[1] (campaign by ICOM and ICOF), ICOM and ICOF (Industrial Common Ownership Finance, which provided funding for many co-ops) anticipated continuing support from the Labour Party (ICOM/ICOF 1996):

The Labour Party and Co-operatives:

- The indications are that there will be greater support for cooperative enterprise from central government if the Labour Party should have a majority after the next general election.

There were other, similar campaigns. Peter Kellner wrote a pamphlet about "new mutualism" in 1998, seeking a "big idea" for New Labour to replace the old idea of socialism. A further pamphlet on mutuals argued that "the Co-operative Movement could contribute to combating social exclusion (Hargreaves, 1999)" (Birchall 2008, 8). Ahead of the 1997 General Election, the Labour Party's new constitution mentioned co-operatives in a more positive light – with its amended Clause IV – in words still retained today (Labour Party 2018, 4):

> Labour will work in pursuit of these aims with trade unions, co-operative societies and other affiliated organisations, and also with voluntary organisations, consumer groups and other representative bodies.

Carried forward by this optimism, the Co-operative Party in its 1997 General Election Manifesto looked forward to a new Co-operatives Act, as a recognition and promotion of the social economy so that this third sector could take its rightful place in the economic thinking of modern government, greater emphasis on worker co-operatives and promotion of co-operation to empower communities (Co-operative Party 1997, 3, 4).

But this mood of co-operative optimism soon changed. After Labour's 1997 Election victory, senior representatives from the Co-operative Movement began to see difficulties on the horizon through New Labour endeavours to outsource delivery of public services (Former Senior Co-operative Movement representative 2016):

> They didn't see us as part of the future ... they believed community organisations to take on some of the roles that they were keen not to privatise as the Thatcher Government had done, but to externalise some of these businesses, particularly social businesses, and social care, whatever and they hit on the term social enterprise.

The Co-operative Party continued to focus on a new Co-operatives Act (Former Senior Co-operative Movement Representative II 2016):

> In 1998, so a year into it we were miles behind the curve. We did not have, in the Coop Party, meaningful policy proposals that we could, say, take off the shelf that we could share with Labour ...There was a couple of years at the beginning of all of this where there was quite a lot of confusion in the cooperative sector about whether it saw itself as part of this new social enterprise thing or whether it wanted to sit on the outside and argue about different governance structures. ...

> I think that coops were seen as old fashioned, a bit dodgy-lefty, and social
> enterprise was seen as something, hey, this is new, this is interesting and so the
> two were not seen by the government as being connected at all.

But the Labour Party itself was changing. Apart from proposals from Demos, described in Chapter 4, to reform the welfare state, moves towards community empowerment with a business approach were being championed, following Blair's speech at the Aylesbury Estate Southwark in 1997. A key element in making this vision a reality, he argued, was the "backing of thousands of 'social entrepreneurs'" (Zadek and Thake 1997). Elsewhere they commented (Thake and Zadek 1997, 6):

> The weight of social responsibility is being returned to the community. In
> order to carry this weight, the social fabric that has been eroded over decades
> needs to be revitalised and repaired. This will not be achieved through public-
> sector-led programmes alone.

The "community sector" gained "increasing usage in the UK under the 'New Labour' UK government (1997–2010), given the latter's emphasis on communitarian thinking and a 'Third Way' (Haugh and Kitson, 2007)" (Henderson and McWilliams 2017, 2).

New Labour Neighbourhood Strategy

New Labour's social enterprise policy fitted alongside it transition to other ad hoc and less accountable structures, the trajectory towards which had already started before Blair and New Labour. John Major's Conservative's legacy was a fragmented public domain with decentralisation of key civil service functions to "Next Steps" agencies and the transfer of certain responsibilities from elected local authorities to new appointed executive agencies". Based on Rhodes (2000), Hall estimates a Conservative legacy of 5,521 such bodies, spending £39bn per annum and involving 70,000 patronage-based appointments. New Labour sought to improve on this (Hall 2003, 274):

> The past five years have witnessed a proliferation of new regeneration funding
> regimes. These include traditional generic area-based initiatives (for example,
> New Deal for Communities), thematic area-based initiatives (for example,
> Education Action Zones, Employment Zones, Health Action Zones, Sport
> Action Zones) and client-focused initiatives (for example, the New Deals for
> Young People, Long Term Unemployed and other vulnerable groups).

But this proliferation of area-based initiatives and bureaucratic regulatory frameworks for neighbourhood renewal inhibited rather than facilitated partnership and participation (Hall 2003, 275). Because the Neighbourhood Renewal Fund was highly focused, it was highly appropriate for New

Programme	Dates	Approximate Annual Cost (£million)	Number and Scale of Areas included
SRB	1995/6 to 2006/7	520	1028 schemes ranging from local authority ward to combinations of Local Authorities
NDC	1999/00 to 2009/10	200	39 neighbourhoods
NRF/WNF	2001/02 to 2010/11	500	95 local authorities at peak
HMR	2003/4 to 2010/11	275	12 subregional housing markets comprising parts of 28 local authorities
Local Enterprise Growth Initiative (LEGI)	2005/06 to 2010/11	70	30 local authorities

Figure 5.1 Size of New Labour's Neighbourhood Renewal Programme

Labour to promote social enterprise, not only as a public service delivery vehicle, but as a political process through which organisations might raise more of their own funds. "It is not going too far to say the success of the New Labour project itself turns on whether social entrepreneurs can be effective within "the community" and across the broader national policy arena" (Thake and Zadek 1997). The sharp focus of the Neighbourhood Renewal approach represented a significant departure from previous Conservative approaches (Former Senior Civil Servant IV 2015):

> I was responsible for the New Deal for Communities Programme which was £50mn in 39 neighbourhoods" ... And we were deemed not to be spending the money quickly enough. Now that's because you were trying to get community groups to decide what they wanted to do with £50mn and you don't do that in five minutes. I mean, these people were just dazzled in the headlights.

Social enterprise fitted neatly the New Labour policy discourses of "reform", "modernisation" and professionalisation of both the voluntary and the public sectors (Bastow and Martin 2003). A community-based social entrepreneur represented initiative and self-reliance at the local level (Grenier 2009, 59) (Figure 5.1).

New Labour vocalisation of social enterprise

SEU and Policy Action Teams

In the forward to the SEU's initial "Bringing Britain Together" policy, Prime Minister Blair highlighted the failure of previous policies for poor areas from the 1960s onwards, including the UP, UDCs and Task Forces in the

1980s and SRB in the 1990s. "But none really succeeded in setting in motion a 'virtuous circle of regeneration'" (Social Exclusion Unit 1998, 9).

Among tasks set for the SEU's new Policy Action Teams (PATs) there is no mention of social enterprise. The closest is "how access to capital for small firms can be improved, especially for start-ups, including innovative approaches such as 'microcredit'" (Social Exclusion Unit 1998, 62). The mention of "microcredit" is significant since this concept was already making headway elsewhere as part of a major political shift from welfare to entrepreneurialism, sometimes labelled "banking on the poor". "(M)icrocredit has been instrumentalized to both facilitate and sustain neoliberal restructuring. In this context, the 'poor' have been assigned what has been referred to as 'minimal' consumption needs" (Weber 2004, 377).

The PAT3 (Business) Draft Report highlighted "social economy initiatives at national level and those engaged in aspects of community economic development, such as intermediate labour markets (ILMs), social firms (for production by people with disabilities), or social housing". Though the report mentions a lack of support services, lack of demand for social economy goods and services, complex legal structures, the problems of sustainability and grant dependency, it only offers a possible "social labelling scheme" and recommends that the "Small Business Service should be responsible for this agenda" (Policy Action Team 3 1999, 75, 76, 78, 80). There appeared some confusion[5] around social enterprise and the social economy.

More impetus was afforded to social enterprise policy and development in "Enterprise and Social Exclusion, the Treasury Report for the National Strategy for Neighbourhood Renewal". "The PAT (Policy Action Team) believes that the starting point must be to recognise social enterprise as a group of businesses deserving support, capable of making a contribution to economic and social renewal" (HM Treasury 1999, 14).

The PAT3 Report did not advocate a social enterprise role in public service delivery but focused on social enterprises engaged in community economic development[6] (Policy Action Team 3 and Timms 1999, 101). The report also warned about undue dependency on grants rather than loans, "to ensure that a "grant-dependent" culture does not exist" (Policy Action Team 3 and Timms 1999, 111). PAT3 recommended for further development by Small Business Services, Regional Development Agencies and referred to EU policy. Social enterprise "became a new focus for political and policy concern within the UK at the turn of the new century, in part because of the expectation (or hope) that they could play a critical role in economic regeneration by promoting business and social development (see Peattie and Morley 2008)" (Alcock and Kendall 2010, 7).

The PAT 16 "Learning Lessons" Report favoured a different approach, with a social enterprise emphasis on individual entrepreneurship closer to

Leadbeater and others (Leadbeater 1997; Thake and Zadek 1997; Zadek and Thake 1997). "Social entrepreneurship has been defined as 'new ways of combining resources and people (both public and private) to deliver social outcomes, higher social value and more social capital'" (Policy Action Team 16 2000, 25). Its recommendations included a development fund to support social entrepreneurial activity and social enterprise appointments to Regional Development Agency boards (Policy Action Team 16 2000, 32,34). There should be an awareness raising programme "for politicians and public agencies on the benefits of social enterprise and the conditions necessary for its success" (Social Exclusion Unit 2001a, 217).

The most striking departure from previous policy came from the Policy Action Team on Community Self Help (PAT9) which reported that "community self-help is crucially dependent on support from outside the community", including existing support structures – statutory and voluntary – and the role of specialist community development workers, and that of specialist or generalist voluntary organisations based in poor neighbourhoods (Policy Action Team 9 and Active Community Unit 1999, vi). In its comprehensive list of recommendations, this report recommended development grants, small-scale consultancy support; training in accessible surroundings, enabling groups to purchase their own training through "technical assistance vouchers", with approved providers, "facilitating maximum use of existing community buildings", "providing or facilitating infrastructure support for community organisations, including office space, equipment and meeting rooms" and "establishing a 'community chest', over which local residents have decision making responsibility" (Policy Action Team 9 and Active Community Unit 1999, 18,19). PAT9's tone and substantial detail effectively overturned almost thirty years of top down 1970s and 1980s policies for communities, not only recommending an enhanced role for communities but in emphasising that this required funding.

But within the April 2000 recommendations for the "National Strategy for Neighbourhood Renewal: a Framework for Consultation" (Social Exclusion Unit 2000), the summary of PAT Reports still included little on social enterprise. "Social businesses should be recognised as legitimate businesses to support. These organisations exist for their communities, rather than just for-profit. Consultation question 5.6 asks what more the government can do to ensure social enterprises get the support they need" (Social Exclusion Unit 2000, 51). However, there was for the first time a mention of public service delivery. "Which public services can voluntary and community sector organisations help deliver and in what circumstances?" (Social Exclusion Unit 2000, 63). Since the SEU was closer to government than some of the PATs, it reflected government policy more directly.

However, social entrepreneurship did feature more prominently in the 2001 Neighbourhood Renewal Strategy progress report on recommendations made by PATs (Grenier 2009, 43) with specific policy recommendations for social entrepreneurship (Social Exclusion Unit 2001a, 28):

- To support community groups and social entrepreneurs the government will be introducing a fund of £50mn over 3 years to set up local "Community Chests" to provide small grants for community organisations in deprived areas.
- Social entrepreneurs would also be eligible for help from the Community Development Venture Fund.

However, in Consultation Responses to the National Strategy Action Plan, the Social Investment Task Force (see later) features more prominently than social enterprise itself, with a commitment of £10mn in matched funding to the Community Development Venture Fund (Social Exclusion Unit 2001b, 33). "(S)ocial entrepreneurs would be eligible to apply for the Community Development Venture Fund" (Social Exclusion Unit 2001b, 91).

Since none of the PATs viewed social enterprise as a business model or in terms of local economic or community democracy, SEL and the SEC soon took on a leading role as policy entrepreneurs.

Transition from co-ops to social enterprise

Two academic schools of social enterprise are described below. The first describes the change of emphasis from co-operatives to social enterprise as almost seamless and natural. The second describes social enterprise as a New Labour construct so that no transition is either necessary or described.

As part of the first school, Haugh and Kitson describe how "prior to the election, a review of the Labour Party's relations with the third sector led to the publication of 'Building the Future Together' (Labour Party 1997) in which a compact between the party and the third sector was proposed" (Haugh and Kitson 2007, 982). Largely ignoring any historic difficulties, Haugh et Kitson offer their own interpretation of this relationship (982):

> The historic roots of the Labour party in the Co-operative Movement, however, and the remnants of its commitment to social justice, fed into a declared proactive stance in favour of recognising the benefits and potential contribution of a vibrant, active and engaged third sector.

But this interpretation of almost seamless transition is contradicted strongly by interviews and data later in this chapter. Brown, who lectured at Beechwood College from 1978, is more accurate when he describes the challenge to the Co-operative Movement and its intensive lobbying to be included under the "social enterprise umbrella". Initial definitions of social enterprise "challenged the Co-operative Movement's right to be included under the social enterprise umbrella" (Brown 2003).

The first signs of the second school appeared during the 1990s. "In 1994 and 1995 the first signs of change were apparent to a more strategic and focused approach. In 1994 and 1995 the 'social entrepreneur' featured in two left of centre think-tank reports" (Atkinson and Moon 1994; Thake 1995, cited in Grenier 2009, 38). The reports sparked debate and a growing excitement that social entrepreneurship was something significant. "A second report was published by New Economics Foundation (NEF) in 1997, 'Practical People, Noble Causes', by Stephen Thake and Simon Zadek. These reports provided publicity, credibility and media friendly stories of social entrepreneurs and their achievements" (Grenier 2009, 40). For the author these developments represent a further appearance of demi-regularities – early signs of framing public service policy in a marketised setting, "revealing a more comprehensive understanding of the theoretical frame, while pursuing quality empirical outputs" (Meyer and Lunnay 2013, 2).

The institutionalisation of social enterprise was already beginning. In June 2000, the Millennium Commission launched a competition for "innovative proposals" from organisations or consortia which would continue to distribute funds "to individual people with a bright idea to help themselves and their communities" (Millennium Commission 2000). The opportunity to bid for the £100mn endowment inspired a proposal for the support of "social entrepreneurs" by UnLtd, a collaboration between the main social entrepreneur support organisations (Ashoka UK, the SSE, CAN, the Scarman Trust, Comic Relief, Changemakers, and SENSCOT, cited in Grenier 2009, 39, 42). Nicholls also refers to similar "paradigm building actors", such as the Ashoka, Skoll and Schwab Foundations, Community Action Network (CAN) and the SEC (Nicholls 2010, 618, 619):

> [T]here are foundations, such as UnLtd (Nicholls, 2006b) and the Skoll Foundation (Lounsbury & Strang, 2009). Third, there are fellowship organizations, such as Ashoka (Bornstein, 2004) and the Schwab Foundation for Social Entrepreneurship (Elkington & Hartigan, 2008). Finally, there are network organizations (Grenier, 2006): in the United Kingdom, these include the Social Enterprise Alliance, the Community Action Network (CAN), and the Social Enterprise Coalition (SEC).

Nicholls' contribution is echoed by a former civil servant, who also believed that social enterprise was a New Labour development (Former Senior Civil Servant V 2017):

> Michael Young was probably the key figure in the UK, and he had set up the
> School for Social Entrepreneurs in the mid '90s. Adele Blakebrough set up the
> Community Action Network ... I commissioned Charlie (Leadbeater) then to
> write a pamphlet on it which, again, was sort of mid '90s or something ... They
> didn't really enter the sort of Labour bloodstream before '97.

Nicholls' social enterprise origins all date from the New Labour period rather than from antecedents of the 1970s and 1980s. "The reflexive isomorphism here suggests that social entrepreneurship is a field dominated by social purpose businesses, many delivering public welfare contracts" (Nicholls 2010, 618). Grenier offers a similar contribution describing social entrepreneurship as "emergent in that the few organisations working explicitly on social entrepreneurship tend to be relatively young, established mainly in the late 1990s and early 2000s". The term "social entrepreneur", rather than "community leader, social activist, voluntary sector pioneer", was "relevant to the current climate and situation" (Grenier 2002, 3). Andrea Westall[7] describes a strong North American influence. "The current conceptualisation of the third sector in the UK is informed partly by the US-influenced non-profit space or 'sector' which is usually seen as being predicated on organisations that respond to market and government failure (Westall 2009, 2).

In contrast to Haugh and Kitson and others above, these interpretations enable Teasdale, Defourny, Nyssens and others to assume no connection to any previous structures, and therefore miss any policy shift which was taking place. "While many of these organisational forms have been in existence for centuries, the language now used to describe them is new, and emerged around 1990 in the US and mainland Europe (Defourny and Nyssens, 2010)" (Teasdale 2012, 100). This view is not supported by any interviews and data which form the basis of this book, with a wide range of data collection described in Chapter 2.

The Labour Party and the Co-operative Movement

In describing co-operatives and social enterprises, many academic contributions fail to mention the difficult historical relationship between the Labour Party and the wider Co-operative Movement. After the Great War, because it was unclear whether the Labour Party would dominate working-class politics at the expense of organised consumers, many thought that the Co-operative Party could better serve the interests of workers as consumers, just as the trade unions represented the interests of workers as producers. The Cheltenham Agreement of 1927 sought to restore good relations and allowed local Co-operative Parties to affiliate to Labour parties. But this was only voluntary (Gurney 2015, 1487).

Both the Gaitskell Co-operative Commission in 1956 and the Monks Report after the 2001 Co-operative Commission were dominated by co-operative retail matters. Little changed in the relationship with the Labour Party, with only one page on the social economy (Co-operative Commission 2001, 78), none of which was seriously taken forward. The arrangement today is that the two parties do not stand candidates against each other and still publish separate election manifestos. The author represented Co-operative Political Committees on the Labour Party National Executive Committee from 1976 to 1982. Many in New Labour saw these Political Committees as mainly left dominated and politically unyielding. Many academic contributors have seriously misinterpreted these political relationships, which deteriorated seriously during this period. After their demise, the main relationship between Co-operative and Labour Parties today is through the Co-operative Party's financial support to Labour and Co-operative MPs and Councillors, Co-operative Party votes in some Labour Party elections and fraternal representatives speaking at each other's conferences.

Spear et al. describe New Labour social enterprise as "a marriage between cooperative and community enterprise discourses helped position social enterprise close to the heart of the 'third way project' in 1999" (Spear, Cornforth and Aiken 2014, 22). He also describes a second stage, influenced by a "social business discourse" following the DTI Social Enterprise Unit and a third stage, promoting voluntary organisations as vehicles for public service delivery. From interviews, the author has found no evidence to support these interpretations. Instead, as shown below, Labour policies for a marketised version of social enterprise faced continuing opposition from the Co-operative Party and the wider Co-operative Movement.

As shown from events and interviews below, to the author the interpretation of Ridley-Duff, who was a founding signatory of SEL in 1998 is equally puzzling (Ridley-Duff and Southcombe 2012, 183):

> [T]he influence of the Co-operative Movement and New Labour is evident, and terminology remains linked to the goal of socialisation (eg. participatory democracy, cooperatives, cooperative solutions). This reflects the orientation of the cooperative development agencies and worker cooperatives that collaborated in its creation.

Teasdale's interpretation is similar (Teasdale 2012, 108):

> The label social enterprise was initially used in England to reposition co-operatives and mutuals as new models for public and private ownership. An early alliance of co-operative and community enterprise practitioners utilising

the language of New Labour helped embed social enterprise on the policy landscape in 1999.

Teasdale continues that social enterprise "was primarily a way of designing new (mutual) structures for public services and private businesses" which would permit "radically altered ways of behaving whose values might be inherent to the processes of the business itself" (Westall 2009, 6; Teasdale 2012, 109). Apart from omitting the significance of Beechwood College and Spreckley's publications (Spreckley 2015; Spreckley 1981) these interpretations are unsupported by interviews and data collection throughout this chapter.

As shown below, the reality is that under the Labour Governments of 1997 and 201, the Co-operative Movement had to fight hard to maintain co-operatives within New Labour's social enterprise strategy. A more accurate description is from Martinelli et al. (2003, 224):

> Cooperativism has been taken over by the "Third Way" agenda, as part of their "stakeholder society" and "partnership" concepts. Described as a middle way between "Old Leftism" (social democracy) and "New Right" (neoliberalism), the "Third Way" has been used to describe a new way of doing politics, characteristic to the "New Labour" government in Britain since 1997.

There was an ideological continuation from Thatcherism to New Labour and Third Way thinking, so that social entrepreneurship is closely identified with the government as "pretty pure Third Way Blairism" (Grenier 2002, 10). This supports the author's Critical Realist interpretation, with all these events representing a similar direction of travel through underlying causal mechanisms.

Rather than any smooth transition, the interviews and data below show fundamental differences of approach between ICOM, London Cooperative Training (LCT), the wider Co-operative Movement and rapidly developing New Labour policies. Initial actions of the first New Labour government (1997–2001) were not sympathetic to existing mutual businesses and failed to find time for a new bill promoted by the co-operative sector to modernise co-operative law and provide clearer criteria for what constituted a co-operative (Birchall 2008, 5, 9).These tensions have been misinterpreted in other descriptions of New Labour's policy shift, as "opportunities for different delivery mechanisms for firms in competition with one another, and signalled the way for third sector organisations to work in partnership with the government, or other providers, to deliver public services" (Haugh and Kitson 2007, 983). Some have interpreted this as a move away from the individualism of the 1980s (Teasdale 2012; Hazenberg et al 2016, 208, 209). Though Hazenberg draws on Teasdale's reference to "individualistic social entrepreneurs" (Teasdale 2012, 102), he misinterprets that the overall policy direction of SEL and New Labour was designed to move in the opposite direction – towards individualism and away from co-operative and mutual approaches.

There are similar academic misunderstandings of developments in Scotland. "In Scotland, the Scottish Executive did not diverge greatly from English policy partly due to the fact that both governments were Labour-led" (Hazenberg et al. 2016, 209). The reality is that, especially with the introduction of Futurebuilders in 2003 as the UK government's main social enterprise loan programme, the Scottish Executive made clear its different position in adopting a broad definition of the "social economy" for Future-builders Scotland (EKOS Consulting Ltd and Scottish Government Social Research 2008, 17). It was not until April 2007 that a Labour Liberal Democrat Scottish Government produced is own separate strategy for social enterprise, following an amendment by Green MSP Mark Ballard in the Scottish Parliament in May 2005.

Meanwhile in London from 1997 onwards there was a rapid shift from co-operatives to a much looser definition of "social enterprise", which was challenged and resisted by London ICOM members (Former London ICOM Members 2016):

> I think those of us who were really committed to the cooperative structures – in those days you had to have seven people to set up a cooperative, and that was always very difficult, to find seven people ... But obviously with a social enterprise, you could be just that one person ... But those of us who are cooperative and felt that it is a sort of a pulling together and working on that structure, however difficult it is, we were committed to sort of expanding the cooperative thing. But social enterprise was reducing it.

The author is also concerned about other interpretations of this New Labour policy shift. As an example, Ridley-Duff and Bull contend that "the government consultation of 2002 signalled a shift to US model of social entrepreneurship to satisfy funders of the voluntary and charity sector ... multi stakeholder SE models did not stop developing, but were marginalised by a government initiated discourse" (Ridley-Duff and Bull 2014, 19). The author had access to consultation documents before the DTI "Strategy for Success" document in July 2002 (Department of Trade and Industry 2002) and found no evidence to support this view. Instead, his own interpretation was supported (Former Senior Civil Servant V 2017):

> It depends, I guess, how pluralistic an economic system you want, and I think probably the people around me wanted a more diverse ecology of types of organisation which would mean growth of coops but also of other entities like equity-taking social enterprise; we weren't fixated on one organisational form

being the answer to everything, we wanted a wider variety to choose from, so you didn't have to be either a, you know, PLC or a coop.

Formation of SEL

The real drive for New Labour policy came with the formation of SEL in January 1998 and the SEC in July 2002, which throughout this period both acted as high-profile policy entrepreneurs. Though ironically both organisations were initiated from within the Co-operative Movement, their activities promoted a dramatic shift away from co-operatives. In February 1997, an initial Steering Group of LCT, London ICOM (LICOM) and London Boroughs Grants Unit endorsed a "strategy for close integration of all available resources for worker cooperatives, common ownerships and social economic development in London". An initial Strategy Day on "The Merger of all London Cooperative Support Organisations" took place on Saturday 8 February 1997. At an Extra Ordinary General Meeting to discuss the Future of London ICOM on Thursday 3 April 1997, four resolutions proposed a range of merger options for LICOM and LCT. All of these prioritised the promotion of co-operatives. (London ICOM 1997c). A further LICOM Strategy Day was held on 11 July 1997, with an "Aims of Research" brief[8] (London ICOM 1997b, 3). LCOM and LCT joined together to produce "A New Strategy for London Cooperative Support Organisations" (London ICOM 1997a, 3) which continued to prioritise co-operatives. Consultants were appointed with funding from London Boroughs Grants Unit. A Steering Group of LCT, LICOM and LBGU (London Borough Grants Unit) commissioned this project[9] (London ICOM 1997a):

> The consensus that emerged that day generally sought some ring-fencing for worker cooperative support and development in the capital. This was despite the strong case put by the consultants for change to be set in the context of a community economic development environment.

There was opposition to these developments within ICOM (Former Senior ICOM/ICOF Management II 2015):

> We were saddened by the fact that the people involved were mainly from the coop sector and I understood the reasons for it, because their own careers, their own jobs were in jeopardy ... That the coop name hadn't survived the past problems even going back to the '70s, but certainly in the '80s when it was seen to be panacea for unemployment, creating jobs through deindustrialisation ... So we never kind of rebounded from the problems of the '70s.

> The survivors of that period wanted to retain their interest in the coop sector, but they thought the way to do that was to expand into what was becoming

the thing, the flavour of social enterprise … It was interpreted as a business in a community without really any kind of structural or any cooperative about it and social enterprise just seemed to be the term that encaptures what funders and the politicians at the time, what they intended. The word social and enterprise.

London ICOM and LCT joint commissioning of a consultants' report was to be followed by setting up a Steering Group for SEL, described in an October 1997 member's letter (London Cooperative Training Secretary 1997):

> It has been agreed that LCT and LICOM will wind up and together will promote the launch of a new organisation in February 1998. The new organisation will promote throughout London, cooperative and other social enterprise including community businesses, credit unions and LETs.

> A steering committee was set up to take on the development of the new body and has met regularly along with the working groups formed at the first meeting. These cover the constitution for the new body, staffing, promotion and marketing, and premises. The main proposal is to establish the new body, which has been named Social Enterprise London (SEL), in March 1998 with LCT and London ICOM winding down in the meantime.

When it emerged, the consultants' Strategy Report for LCT and LICOM continued to prioritise co-operatives.[10] The report referred to an "integrated and unified London wide service for the support and development of cooperative and democratically managed businesses" with a post "specifically for the support and development of the worker cooperative sector" (CAG Consultants 1997, 1):

> We propose that this focus on cooperative development is a priority task for the new body, and whilst a whole range of organisations should be involved in the delivery of cooperative development support, the new body takes on the role of its co-ordination and response on a London wide basis. (CAG Consultants 1997, 8)

The purpose of the report for LCT and London ICOM was clear (Co-operatives Advisor I 2015):

> [T]he thrust of the report was saying – as there was no London strategic development body at that time, it hadn't yet arrived – so the thrust of the report was saying to the coop sector, things are changing, you've got to get your act together, here is an opportunity to be the coop regional body that works with that regional development body and pulls funding down, represents the sector.

Though the report presented a strong focus on co-operative development, there were soon tensions about the direction of travel, with a resignation by one director, who sought a continued emphasis on co-operatives[11] (Director of London ICOM 1997):

> [I] feel that London ICOM has dragged its feet unnecessarily through a process in which it should have been taking a lead, but despite this there is now an opportunity to get what we are all working for: an effective and influential regional development agency with a remit and resources committed to worker cooperative development and an active and relevant federation of workers' cooperatives.

The need for a regional lead body for co-operatives was also expressed during a September 1997 London ICOM Emergency Staff Sub-Committee Meeting (London ICOM 1997d):

> A strong LICOM representation on the (Social Enterprise London) Steering Committee was felt necessary to examine ways of further influencing the forthcoming organisation towards the promotion and development of worker cooperation in London and to embody this and a dominant LICOM and a representative worker coop influence in the constitution, Board and management of the new organisation.

Despite these reservations, an initial meeting of the new SEL Steering Committee on Friday 10 October 1997 decided on its aims and objectives and a name for new organisation (Social Enterprise London Steering Group 1997, 3). The Steering Group also took initial decisions on its structure, with its composition first described in a letter of September 1997 (London Cooperative Training Secretary 1997). There was agreement on a title – "Social Enterprise London: for Cooperative Solutions" – the first time that "social enterprise" had featured in the title of any London organisation (Former Social Enterprise London Board Member II 2015):

> So we had a meeting where we had to consider the change of the name and recognition that we needed to be wider than just coops and find some kind of umbrella term which would mean that the new organisation could seem to be representing others including credit unions ... So we had endless wrangles about it and in the end came up with the proposal of social enterprise because we'd had the social entrepreneurship stuff, because it was about being enterprising, it wasn't about being a charity.

This was echoed by other board members (Former Social Enterprise Board Member IV 2015):

> [T]wo, four, five, six of us and we as a little group coined the name "social enterprise" we thought that is what we should call this new organisation ... Now I am not saying that it is possible that someone in that room had read an article that you just referred to or a publication or anything (Charlie Leadbeater pamphlet) but it seemed to come out of the ether in that meeting.

Other board members thought that this new title would suit New Labour (Former Social Enterprise London Board Member II 2015):

> They loved it, it fitted New Labour completely, New Labour also liked this idea of widening it as wide as you can … So basically, social enterprise could be charities doing good things in an enterprising way – then that excluding democracy completely … and as far as Labour was concerned they didn't care and the people who were leading the Labour Party at the time had no sort of commitment to the Co-operative Movement.

A Focus Group member echoed this view of the new politics (Focus Group Voice 1 2016):

> New Labour hated the Co-operative Movement or the word cooperative because it reminded them of Old Labour. And they wanted to be new, that's why they called themselves New Labour and that's why they preferred the expression "social enterprise", because it's so much looser, you can't say what's a social enterprise.

This was echoed elsewhere in the Co-operative Movement (Focus Group Voice 2 2016):

> So that, you see, all this really manifestly shows that that went down a storm when, you know, Tony Blair got elected. The thing about the political relationship and the political will is that there wasn't political will in the Coop Movement, and as [Anon] pointed out, there was really no Coop Movement.

Views on New Labour and the Co-operative Movement were expressed elsewhere, in response to a question about co-ops not moving fast enough (Former Senior Civil Servant IV 2015):

> Well, remember Blair did want to, there was a touch of near zero. There was New Labour, the Coop Movement would have been associated very much with Old Labour and if someone had come to him and said the Coop Movement is going to spear your reform he just wouldn't, it wouldn't have had any affect at all.

The Annual Report to the LICOM AGM on 2 December 1997 reported on the steering committee that "the main proposal is to establish the new body, which has been named Social Enterprise London (SEL), in March 1998 with LCT and LICOM winding down in the meantime" (London ICOM 1997a, 4). SEL was registered as a Company Limited by Guarantee in February 1998, which prioritised co-operatives its Objects[12] (Social Enterprise London Ltd 1998).

Despite these differences which are clearly recorded, Spear still interpreted SEL as "established in 1997 by cooperative practitioners aiming to modernise the Co-operative Movement and capture public and political interest in the work of cooperative development agencies (Ridley-Duff and Bull 2011; Teasdale 2012) without alienating people through the language of common ownership". Spear also wrote that among SEL's objects were (Spear et al. 2017, 17)

> [T]o promote cooperative solutions for economic and community development [and] to promote social enterprises, in particular cooperatives and common ownerships, social firms, and other organisations and businesses which put into practice the principles of participative democracy, equal opportunities and social justice.

But the author contends the Spear's interpretation, based on this partial extract from the Objects of Social Enterprise London, failed to recognise its direction of travel (Co-operatives Advisor I 2015):

> When SEL was established it developed in a different direction, so the gap between finishing the report and Social Enterprise London is the moment when the idea of a social enterprise sector in its own right crystallized … there's no mention of social enterprise in the (consultant's) report, nor a real social enterprise strategy … it's all about coops and CDB's and they formed the initial board.

Funding scene changing

On Friday 24 April 1998, London Boroughs Grants recipients heard from its Operational Services announcing a significant policy change: "over time, to move to a situation where no organisation receives more than 60% of its revenue income from the LBGC". This was to be an incremental approach, to affect "organisations that have been LBGC funded for 5 or more years" (Campbell and London Borough Grants 1998). London Boroughs Grants Committee produced a ten year view of funding (Former Senior Management, Grant Awarding Body 2015):

> My feeling six months in was as wonderful as £30mn was, its real value was going down year by year. We were behaving as though we were a parish council when in fact, we were the biggest investor before the Lottery came in, in the country.

> I was beginning to see that there was a development in London of social enterprises and social businesses … They didn't distribute profits and given our poverty driven remit meant the best social enterprises would end up employing their clients and all that kind of stuff. One of the more controversial aspects of the Next 10 Years report was the recommended new focus on social enterprises – the Committee needed some convincing on this.

One of the new things was to open the door to investing in social enterprises. And I think one of the main conduits for that and one of my main areas of learning ... was growing Greater London Enterprise.

SEL board members responded to this (Former Social Enterprise London Board Member II 2015):

But it was this whole thing of shifting from grants to contracts ... I can see that this idea of having more contractual relationships with all these organisations that we were dealing with suited the local authorities much better ... There was definitely a view of making things more business like everywhere.

A similar view was expressed in the Focus Group (Focus Group Voice 1 2016):

I remember going to see a local authority official and explaining what social enterprise was because I was quite enthusiastic about it in the early days before I'd got a bit disappointed by it, you know, and worried about it. And as I explained it to her you could see, you could practically see the pound signs going around in her eyes as she recognised, we could turn voluntary sector organisations into social enterprises, we won't have to fund them.

Despite the strong initial focus on co-operatives from LICOM and LCT and from the consultant's report, during his interview for the position as the first SEL director, Jonathan Bland's presentation on Wednesday 08 April 1998 made little mention of co-operatives and instead focused on management and administration (Social Enterprise London Meeting 1998). Following the board meeting, some concern was expressed (Former Social Enterprise London Board Member VI 2016):

I was there during the recruitment of its first Executive Director... which was an eye opener for me. I had been so immersed in the day to day work ... that I had not fully realised that there was already a world out there of people making a career out of things we held dear. They operated with varying degrees of cynicism, with the rhetoric of cooperation increasingly being used in programmes which distort basic cooperative principles.

SEL Steering Group minutes for May and June 1998 show the first meetings at which Bland, as its new director, was present (Social Enterprise London 1998a). At the May 1998 meeting of the Steering Group, he gave an "Assessment of Immediate Priorities (including a Provisional Revised Budget)". "In general I believe that we should use projects to develop SEL, adding to our core funding base for promotional activities and financing service development" (Social Enterprise London 1998a, 3, item 3). Item 4 shows that he sought a complete review of the SEL structure, including the Roles of Committees and Officers (Draft) and Standing Orders (Greenwich Example).

Minutes from these early SEL meetings were already showing a departure from support for co-operatives. At the June 1998 SEL Steering Group meeting, there was a major disagreement over broadening the role of a "Cooperative Officer" (Social Enterprise London 1998a, 3 item 3). Bland sought to "broaden the role of the Cooperative Officer to cover other kinds of social enterprise promotion as well as cooperative development … Both the consultants and our core funder LBG have made it very clear that we cannot restrict our focus solely to cooperatives". Minutes of the Steering Group Meeting on Thursday 09 June 1998 (Social Enterprise London 1998b) show a close vote on the "Enterprise/Coop Officer", which was carried by one vote after a second vote, following a dispute over the Chair's casting vote. There was also discussion over the budget, with a suggestion that "language should be changed, to avoid an impression that the coops role might be diminished".

The significance of this change of direction has been highlighted (Former Social Enterprise London Board Member 2015):

> [I]t was a directional meeting to some extent, so we voted on his direction, I can't remember the details but I remember one particular vote, and that was as to whether the defined full-time post for development in there was going to be a cooperative development worker or a social enterprise development worker. And I remember (Bland) lobbying heavily for that to be the social enterprise worker, and it was to do with, "Oh, we won't be able to achieve what we're setting out to do."

Despite its difficult inauguration, from its beginning SEL was well funded (Social Enterprise London 1998a, 7 item 3), including "general income of £224,000, including core LBGU of £207,000 and Project Income of £603,006 including £32,000 from LBGU and £624,000 ESF". Projected total expenditure for 1998 was £917,000 (Social Enterprise London 1998a, 10 item 3): "Having taken over activities previously carried out by or contracted *to* LCT, including significant ESF Projects", totalling £740,000, most of which was ESF. Bland's April 1998 interview presentation included "A Vision for Social Enterprise London 2001" with mention of a "£1mn a year organisation" (Social Enterprise London Meeting 1998).

At the final Steering Group Meeting on Tuesday 15 September before the first full AGM in 1998, in his recommendations for the future board's composition, Bland suggested names for possible co-options from external organisations, including *The Big Issue*, Body Shop, trading arms of charities, Greater London Enterprise, the London Training and Enterprise (TEC) Council and Business Links (Social Enterprise London Steering Group 1998, 2, 3, item 5). For LCT and LICOM cooperators who had set up SEL, these new suggestions represented a major change in policy. Before any structure and management decisions for SEL had been taken, before a management structure was in place, before the inaugural AGM, and even before the Steering Group Meeting, Bland had already written to these potential new members. His introductory letter said that "membership applications will be considered at the next board meeting to be held on the 15th of September" (Social Enterprise London Steering Group 1998).

Bland's invitations to potential new members were accompanied by a background paper on social enterprise, including definitions for eligible structures which might become members,[13] with no mention of co-operatives (Social Enterprise London 1998c). The minutes give no indication of the extent to which this was either discussed or approved at the Steering Group. But these minutes show that the aims and objectives of SEL had moved dramatically since joint meetings of LICOM and LCT had decided to set up SEL a year previously. Despite all this, the Inaugural General Meeting of SEL on Thursday 15 October 1998 to consider these important issues – with eighteen in attendance – lasted only one hour (Social Enterprise London 1998d). So, in one year, with Bland a new director in post for six months, the focus and direction of travel of SEL had already changed fundamentally from its original purpose.

The justification for departing from the direction of the initial CAG Report was explained by a supporter of these changes (Former Senior Social Enterprise Representative 2016):

> The context was that there were two organisations that were funded by London Borough Grants that were failing effectively. One was called London Cooperative Training and one was called London ICOM … Whatever your question, the answer was a worker cooperative, and for some local communities they needed other things – social firms that could work with disabled people, credit unions, other kinds of things that would innovate to meet local needs.

Seeking a wider audience for this new direction, the SEL Launch Conference "Social Enterprise and Social Inclusion" on Wednesday 27 January 1999 included an even wider range of external speakers, including Patricia Hewitt, Polly Toynbee, Ed Mayo, Peter Kellner, Trevor Phillips and John Edmonds (GMB) (Social Enterprise London 1999a). Apart from providing their general endorsement, most speakers had little direct relevance for the Co-operative Movement. After this, SEL's "Strategic Objectives and Operational Principles" in March 1999 show further travel in this direction. Only a small number of people were involved in its preparation (Social Enterprise London 1999b, 3):

> This document draws together a set of strategic objectives and operating principles for Social Enterprise London. It is the product of work carried out by

SEL's Board and Staff Team over the period from November 1998 to February 1999. This process also included input from SEL's main funder (London Boroughs Grants) and other key London organisations working in the field, such as the London Development Partnership (the shadow London Development Agency).

For social enterprise, a wider definition was adopted (Social Enterprise London 1999b, 4):

> SEL adopts a broad inclusive definition of social enterprises as:

> "Economic entities that trade in a market in order to fulfil social aims". Such aims include: the creation of employment, stable jobs, access to work for disadvantaged groups, the provision locally based services (often linked directly to the needs of the local community such as care, education and leisure) and training and personal development opportunities.

"Possible Social Enterprise Solutions – Potential included" referred to private sector corporate social responsibility and public service outsourcing (Social Enterprise London 1999b, 7):

> – Working with the private sector in the context of growing recognition of importance of relationship between long-term corporate interest and corporate social responsibility
> – Privatisation of a range of public services by Local Authorities and national initiatives provide opportunities for new forms of management particularly in the areas childcare, education, homecare and services to the elderly.

This Strategic Objectives and Operating Principles paper showed that the scope for social enterprise was growing ever wider[14] (Social Enterprise London 1999b, 4). SEL was already in dialogue with the government and beginning to influence its policy agenda. ICOM/ICOF Policy and Promotion Committee Minutes for 17 March 1999 show (ICOM/ICOF Policy and Promotion Committee 1999):

> Social Enterprise London has submitted a note to the Treasury on the role which social enterprises can play in combating Social Exclusion which drew heavily on a briefing paper which Charlie provided on behalf of P&PC.

Some board members expressed increasing concern (Former Social Enterprise London Board Member 2015):

> [A]ctually, the idea of social enterprise speaks to the need to look more carefully at the relationship between stakeholders within a particular business operation and, to socialise it, in the right kind of way for the most effective outcome. Now, for me, that would be a coop, but it's where is the coop, where does the power lie and what are the particular stakeholder exchanges that you're trying to achieve with that coop? ... So, social enterprise to me is a thing

through which I question the best type of structure to achieve the best exchange of values.

A summary of SEL's major change of direction was expressed succinctly by one former Board Member (Former Social Enterprise Board Member IV 2015):

> The founding board of Social Enterprise London was almost exclusively from the coop sector and the first Chief Executive … had worked at Lambeth Coop Development Agency. However, he took the stance that the image of cooperatives was not positive therefore he did everything to distance his organisation from cooperatives and the organisation never promoted cooperatives despite the board being in the majority.

This was echoed in the Focus Group (Focus Group Voice 5 2016):

> We lost that fight with SEL comes in, if we become Social Enterprise London they said, "We take this money and then they can establish also a new link with the New Labour and that more money will come in." … That is the beginning of SEL, London's Social Enterprise.

But other Board members took a different view (Former Social Enterprise London Board Member III 2015):

> There was a lot of tension about the coop people. It used to irritate me because the board had people from coop development agencies on it, from Southeast London Coop, obviously … was a strong coop person.

> Coops were seen to be very rule driven organisations from the past … the alternative third sector organisation, then rebranding it under social enterprise was considered quite a high priority.

This description of DTI policy was echoed elsewhere (Former Senior Social Enterprise Representative 2016):

> I think that DTI equated that with a kind of socialism type of approach, ownership of the means of production and from their point of view thought it could exclude things, but I think they just didn't like it.

At the SEL second Annual General Meeting in November 1999, the Chair's 14-page report of the first year's activities mentioned credit union development but nothing else on co-operatives (Corbett, Malcolm 1999). Others saw this differently (Co-operatives Advisor I 2015):

> [O]n the one hand the work was brilliant and successful – got the message into Government, got the funding to develop Social Enterprise London, and then exactly the same thing with the Social Enterprise Coalition (see below) … There was little interest in effective delivery partnerships, with local bodies, and no interest in coop development, only social enterprise.

This view was supported elsewhere (Co-operatives Advisor III 2016):

I'm on record and I think you've seen the letters that I was writing to (Bland) saying, look, you're supposed to be bringing resources to the ground and they ... and you're not doing that.

You know, what they were interested in was bigging up social enterprise. It didn't really seem to have any moral or ideological moorings.

This was echoed in the Focus Group (Focus Group Voice 4 2016):

But the whole political ethos was the little entrepreneur, and the seven people to make a cooperative was complex and heavy and difficult for people to do. So one man and his dog suddenly become a company, but that was easier and that social entrepreneurial stuff, right wing entrepreneurial stuff, suddenly took over.

Others took a different view (Former Social Enterprise London Board Member III 2015):

Yes, but we ... the people that actually were social enterprise rather than coop, were quite clear that it wasn't to be a super cooperative development agency for London. Quite the opposite, we were saying basically that we wanted the board skewed towards active social enterprise businesses and not advisors and coop agencies.

Despite these major disagreements about its direction of travel, SEL continued to find a Ministerial audience (Former Social Enterprise Board Member V 2016):

[D]uring the whole of 1999–2000, we were very busy knocking on the doors of the national party, of government, and trying to influence ... So, with that act of faith, we were asking politicians like Patricia Hewitt and special advisors and all of those others that we were talking to. [Bland] spent all this time talking to people about social enterprise.

The PAT Audit in January 2001 shows that, even while policy was at a formative stage, SEL now wielded considerable influence (Social Exclusion Unit 2001a, 55):

Understanding Social Enterprise is a project jointly sponsored by the SBS, BBA and Social Enterprise London. The aim is to produce materials, for the three organisations' websites to help improve the understanding of Social Enterprise among business advisers and bank managers, alongside other organisations who can access these materials online.

The author was however surprised by one justification given for this major change of direction and gaining Ministerial influence – that it was approved by the Co-operative Party (Former Senior Social Enterprise London Representative 2016):

We worked very closely with The Co-operative Party in promoting this. They were 100% behind it. In fact, there was even somebody on the board from The Co-operative Party.

[Anon] and [Anon] went in to see her (Patricia Hewitt) when she was a junior minister and she had a light bulb moment ... Prior to the 2001 election, we were going to have a big conference ... It was in the purdah period and so we had two ministers drop out. Patricia Hewitt said she would still do it and I actually had a one-to-one phone call with her, because it was in the purdah period, to brief her and she listened very carefully and obviously she had her own ideas.

2001 General Election and the DTI Social Enterprise Unit

During the "purdah period" before the June 2001 General Election, Patricia Hewitt, as a Minister of State in the DTI, was already advocating social enterprise delivery of public services. Testimony to the influence of SEL was provided by a former Board Member (Former Social Enterprise London Board Member 2015):

> Well she came here actually within the first week of being Minister for DTI. And I went back up to London where she was speaking on Social Enterprise at a conference that day. She asked me what the government needs to do to get social enterprise moving? "What are you SE guys asking for?"

Interviews and ICOM/ICOF documents (ICOM/ICOF Policy and Promotion Committee 1999) show that three years after its registration and the installation of Jonathan Bland as its director, SEL was now a major social enterprise policy entrepreneur, with direct influence at Ministerial level in the DTI. Grenier thus wrote that social entrepreneurs were considered close to New Labour. "So there is influence beyond the size of the existing organisations" (Grenier 2002, 2).

After the June General Election, on Thursday 09 October 2001, a seminar was attended by interested organisations from across the UK at which Patricia Hewitt and Douglas Alexander, now Secretary and Minister of State at the DTI, launched a Social Enterprise Unit[15] (Kenyon and Crellin 2001, 1, 2). The Unit had been advocated by those involved in consultations including Westall (2001a, 16). Hewitt spoke on public sector reform. Alexander referred to the "complementarity of this agenda with corporate social responsibility" (Kenyon and Crellin 2001, 1–7). The seminar showed how far New Labour's policy ambitions had moved since the formation of SEL. Others described this change of direction (Former Senior Civil Servant III 2016):

> [I]t was made quite clear to me that whatever the antecedents, social enterprise was a new and separate from, although it might be the child of a cooperative parent ... So there is a sense in which social enterprise as the term is used loosely today did begin with the work that the Social Enterprise Unit did and the Strategy and that was preceded by the ground breaking, foundation laying work that Social Enterprise London and Social Enterprise Coalition did (although they came at it from the cooperative perspective)

> Because they ... would not have been able to do anything if Patricia Hewitt
> hadn't set up the Social Enterprise Unit because they were still very linked into
> the cooperative approach ... And it began in September 2001 and the strategy,
> which set the agenda for the next few years, was published less than a year
> later.

Andrea Westall, having attended the Social Enterprise Unit's launch, was
already preparing for further extension of the social enterprise territory
(Westall 2001a, 23):

> Social enterprise as a concept has been particularly promoted by organisations
> such as the New Economics Foundation and Social Enterprise London. Social
> Enterprise London adopts the definition that a social enterprise quite simply
> "trades in a market in order to achieve social aims".

Since she was aware of current DTI thinking, Westall felt able to write about
the need for reviewing social enterprise legal structures "to accommodate
diverse social enterprises". "The key issue is really to ask how different legislative models may be more or less able to realise particular social aims"
(Westall 2001a, 19, 30). While working for the London Foundation for
Entrepreneurial Management, she had been asked by DTI to lead a working
group on mapping social enterprises and wrote to participants: "We see
advantages in keeping the definition fairly broad." Introducing the mapping
exercise, her letter continued (Westall 2001b):

> We should not rule out a business because it has part shareholders, providing
> its primary purpose is not simply to deliver shareholder value, nor include a
> business just because it is run as a co-operative.

Outsourcing

Ministerial contributions above at the Social Enterprise Unit launch show
that a New Labour agenda for outsourcing and external funding was already
considerably developed. Further detail was spelt out in November in a
speech by the Financial Secretary to the Treasury below. Westall wrote on
the role of local authorities as market makers. "Lessons from the previous
poor performance of local authority assisted credit unions and community
businesses need to be learned before any more proactive agenda is set in
place" (Westall 2001a, 20). From longstanding experience of community
enterprise development and from his vantage point in Scotland, Pearce
expressed concern that "social enterprises are seen as a means of driving
down costs, this may be achieved only by reducing wages (or quality of service) ... or by substituting free labour (volunteers or New Deal trainees) for
properly paid labour" (Pearce 2003, 53). Progress towards outsourcing
raised concern (Former Senior Civil Servant III 2016):

[F]airly noble and well intentioned early ideas were subverted via a later agenda. I mean, for example, I'm now very concerned about the way it's been used to privatise parts of the National Health Service, that to me is wrong; it's been used to privatise part of the education system, that's wrong.

... as well as the agenda being skewed towards the sort of backdoor privatisation of these things, the other thing that worried me and it had started a bit before I left but it's gained momentum since, and that is that a lot of the organisations that we were working with in those days were doing things additional to the basic statutory services or the basic non-statutory services local authorities provided. Now they are doing the services that local services should provide and nobody else is doing them.

Pressure for social enterprises to become more involved public service delivery also from within SEL (Former Social Enterprise London Board Member V 2016):

[T]here were these contracts that were being given out by the Government, and by Local Government, and we were, we felt at a disadvantage, which we were, at a disadvantage, as social enterprises and social businesses. So that there was a push from our side to say you have to address the public procurement agenda, and that was always part of the policy agenda.

Because, don't forget, Blair was very interested in the reform of the part of the public sector and making it more sensitive and, you know, delivering better, delivering the services better.

After the 2001 General Election, the government's outsourcing policy was soon confirmed (Co-operatives Advisor II 2016):

It was actually his modernisation of public services agenda where he (Blair) lost the confidence of the trade union movement ... She (Patricia Hewitt) would say, "You misunderstand. It is about the Modernisation of Public Services. It is not all about the private sector. It is going to be the third sector. It is going to be social enterprises." It was complete boloney ... People like Bates, Wells and Braithwaite (BWB) were totally focused on a private business model. That is why they invented CIC.

The reference to BWB is explained later. Concern about this outsourcing agenda was echoed elsewhere (Co-operatives Advisor III 2016):

So, I think, in a way, the fact that social enterprise is being used by some as a backdoor to privatisation on a practical level is serious. But I think that what is more serious is that it's kind of dovetailed into a neoliberal ideology is that actually governments are unnecessary, market and private enterprise can do it all. And that's very ... and ... I mean history gets ... has been rewritten.

There was continuing resistance from London ICOM members (Former London ICOM Members 2016):

So maybe some people were tempted by saying, "Well, let's, sort of, have this little covering of social enterprise, but it's really sustaining the Co-operative Movement." Maybe they were lured in that way. But I mean, what we were really frightened of is the fact that you could see it was just completely eroding the whole, sort of, Co-operative Movement.

Social Investment Task Force

While these policy initiatives were being developed in the Downing Street Policy Unit and Department of Industry, Gordon Brown as Chancellor in April 2000 had approached Sir Ronald Cohen, Chairman of Apax Partners, who was prominent in venture capital and a notable philanthropist, to set up a Social Investment Task Force (SITF). Brown sought a re-assessment of the role of external private finance in community development and specifically asked the SITF to undertake (SITF 2000, 2):

> An urgent but considered assessment of the ways in which the UK can achieve a radical improvement in its capacity to create wealth, economic growth, employment and an improved social fabric in its most under-invested, that is to say its poorest, communities.

Cohen's first SITF's report in 2000 recommended increased external investment and increased pressure for a reduction of grant dependency (SITF 2000, 13):

> Grants from local authorities and other public sector bodies and from charitable sources play an essential role in providing the start-up funds and "social equity" needed to build organisations and support activities that cannot otherwise be funded. However, when they are the sole or primary source of funds, they have encouraged a culture of over-dependence, which can stifle enterprise and even crowd out other finance options.

This first SITF report also laid foundations for a role for social investment financial intermediaries (SITF 2000, 24):

> The funding that intermediaries could facilitate might include the following:
>
> – programme-related investment from charities and foundations
> – private sector investments
> – local and national government funding.

Following the first report, one of the first SITF initiatives was setting up Bridges Ventures as a Community Development Venture Fund in 2002, with £20mn matched investment from the government. As shown below, alongside Social Finance, another intermediary set up by Cohen, Bridges was destined to become an industry leader in social investment. But though colleagues made recommendations for increased private investment, current third sector governance structures such as companies limited by guarantee and IPS registered co-operatives were not adequately structured to receive external loans and equity holdings.

Pressure for new delivery structures

The final stage of the author's Critical Realist analysis, retroduction, focuses on causal mechanisms and conditions. "The goal of retroduction is to identify the necessary contextual conditions for a particular causal mechanism to take effect and to result in the empirical trends observed" (Fletcher 2016, 189). "Demi regularities" observed in Chapter 4 from NCVO pressure for third sector involvement in service delivery continued to be manifested in a New Labour agenda for more flexible social enterprise rather than the collectivism of co-operatives and mutuals. But underlying causal mechanisms continued to indicate more basic motivations of lower cost delivery of public services, including the use of private finance, which would be recommended by the SITF.

The role of the think tank Demos and Geoff Mulgan has already been discussed in Chapter 4. By June 2001 he was Director of the Cabinet Office PIU. The Unit issued a summary of current initiatives to change the shape and size of the third sector and began a consultation on further tax relief in the 2001 Budget (Cabinet Office 2001a, 3). For its proposed review, the Cabinet Office mentioned the NVCO launch of a consultation document, which recommended changes to the legal definition of charities[16] (Cabinet Office 2001a, 3):

> A growing number of organisations which are not charities are facing new challenges working in the grey area between charitable and commercial activity. Examples include mutual enterprises, and organisations concerned with social enterprise and job creation.

Cohen's first SITF report recommended increased external investment and a new class of social investment financial intermediaries. Continuing in its policy entrepreneur role from Chapter 4, NCVO had set up a "Charity Law Reform Advisory Group" to examine the definition of a charity. The Institute of Philanthropy at University College, London also proposed a "Commission on the Regulation of Charities". But before this body started work, immediately after the June 2001 General Election, Mulgan's PIU Unit had announced its "broad-ranging review of the legal and regulatory framework for charities and the voluntary sector" (Centre for Civil Society and NCVO 2001, 9, 24):

> [T]o enable existing and new not-for-profit organisations to thrive and grow; to encourage the development of new types of organisation; and to ensure

public confidence in the sector. This will help to secure a strong, independent and diverse sector, capable both of challenging Government and working with it where appropriate.

This continued as part of the government's intention of placing greater emphasis on the role of the voluntary and community sector in service delivery especially for reducing social exclusion (Centre for Civil Society and NCVO 2001, 7). Social investment from private sources (see below) was also being trailed (Centre for Civil Society and NCVO 2001, 16):

> There is growing interest in the contribution of "social entrepreneurs", who work for community objectives through a combination of commercial and non-commercial activities … while confusion about when community development finance is or is not "charitable" has reinforced trustees' inherent conservatism and has deterred them from supporting community development finance.

The PIU Review relied heavily on NCVO's Advisory Group Report, with its one main recommendation: "The main reform option we propose is that all charitable purposes should pass the same test for public benefit, this being the 'strong' test currently applicable to charities falling under the fourth head, 'other purposes beneficial to the community'." This would "limit change to the substantive law to a minimum" (Centre for Civil Society and NCVO 2001, 30). The PIU Review also argued for a new public interest company (PIC) structure, with public interest objects and a lock on assets used for that purpose in perpetuity, whether limited by shares or guarantee" (Cabinet Office 2001b, 19). The proposed PIC structure represented a fundamental challenge for the co-operative and common ownership movement, with its strong aspiration to protect collective and democratic decision-making (Cattell 1999, 6):

> This (common ownership) means that if the cooperative is wound up while it is still solvent, then its assets cannot be distributed amongst the members, but must be given to another common ownership enterprise or to a central body such as ICOM or ICOF. These assets represent profits which have not been distributed amongst the members.

> For this important cooperative feature to be ensured, it must be protected by the law by being included in an appropriate cooperative statute. In the UK, the principle of common ownership is not yet protected by law.

Opposition from the Co-operative Movement

Echoing earlier Demos contributions by Mulgan, Landry and Leadbeater (Leadbeater 1997; Mulgan and Landry 1995), Stephen Lloyd from London solicitors Bates, Wells and Braithwaite complained that a potential social entrepreneur who wanted to keep complete control of his or her own organisation should not be overridden by trustees. He boasted that he had a "mole" inside the Downing Street Strategy Office (Lloyd 2010, 33, 43):

> So the Public Interest Company (PIC) initials were stolen. In response, the government decided to call it the Community Interest Company, not the Public Interest Company. To make a long story short, I did not draft the statute but gave the government the idea. I gave the government the outline, and then government officials drafted it.

The Co-operative Union and ICOM were opposed to this structure[17] (Co-operative Union 2002, 1). Stressing the need for protection of assets, the Co-operative Union recognised that the origin of the proposed PIC structure was similar to that promoted by the Public Management Foundation and Stephen Lloyd (Co-operative Union 2001, 2, 3). Throughout November 2001 the Co-operative Union expressed concern about proposals to change IPS law (Co-operative Union 2001, 1). Throughout these discussions, the strong hand of the Number 10 Policy Unit was being felt throughout government (Former Senior Civil Servant IV 2015):

> Well, I can't remember the detail of where exactly where it came from, but it would have come from the Number 10 Policy Unit. Almost certainly I would suspect Geoff Mulgan has got his fingerprints on it and it does align with the goals I have just mentioned to improve the life chances of those at the bottom of the heap.

Throughout 2002 the Co-operative Union continued to resist these developments since it feared these would disadvantage existing enterprises (Co-operative Union 2002, 1). The Co-operative Union and ICOM were also keen to see an "asset lock" for public benefit. "We consider that the ability to entrench assets for public benefit in perpetuity is a good thing" (Co-operative Union 2002, 2). ICOM and ICOF especially were concerned about the real purpose of CICs and the weakness of the proposed asset lock (Former Senior ICOM/ICOF Management 2015):

> [T]he other thing we had a problem with, and criticism is because there were CICs and we weren't doing small membership CICs. They are nothing more than sole-traders with some kind of mask, social mask and the asset lock is rubbish if the asset is meaningless. If it's a notebook or a pen or a laptop or a phone system which nobody will gather up in the case of closure.

For the Co-operative Movement, Birchall wrote on "new mutualism", dissolution, rights of members to dissolve a co-operative and split the proceeds, and the need for an asset lock to prevent a public service mutual being broken up for the benefit of members (Birchall 2008, 6). The Co-operative

Movement's own work for public service mutuals, was reinforced in the Co-operative Party's "Making Healthcare Mutual", which the Secretary of the Party called "a significant turning point in the debate about the reform of public services" (Birchall 2008, 9). The Party sought to rejoin mainstream discourses (Former Senior Co-operative Movement Representative II 2016):

> [Anon] said to me, "The Coop Party's failed. It should be in this Agenda. It should be not just social enterprise; it should be influencing the Labour Party." [Anon] would like a coop think-tank that was a bit like the Fabian Society that could develop these ideas with credibility and the rest of it ... to set Mutuo up as a think-tank to develop these ideas but we were so far behind the curve, by now it was 2001.

After the defeat of financier Andrew Reagan's attempt to take over the Co-operative Wholesale Society in 1997, the Co-operative Movement sought to recover lost ground and achieved some success with two Private Members' Bills.[18] One from Gareth Thomas MP became law as the Industrial and Provident Societies Act 2002. This raised voting thresholds, though his proposals for an asset lock were withdrawn. Following the PIU "Private Action Public Benefit" (Cabinet Office 2002, 52), Mark Todd MP introduced another Private Members' Bill, with an asset lock, which became the Co-operative and Community Benefit Societies Act 2003 (Blair 2003, 30).

Boateng's speech and Blair's breakfast meeting

In a comprehensive insight into the government's thinking, in November 2001 Financial Secretary Paul Boateng spelt out overall policy to change the scope and purpose of the wider third sector. He spoke of reviews taking place – for the involvement of the voluntary sector in delivery of public services and for examination of structures[19] (Boateng 2001, 6). In his speech, Boateng was presenting an overview of social enterprise policy for the next two years. This showed evidence of considerable advance preparation for rapid policy development, including the SITF described below (Former Senior Civil Servant V 2017):

> I don't remember what that speech was (see Boateng speech above). I mean, I wrote a paper, certainly in '98, on social entrepreneurship/social enterprise strategy and I remember that quite well, which sent to Blair and Brown ... And it had an element on legal structures and enabling new company forms which would allow equity, etc., etc. –
>
> It had a stream on capacity and, you know, "How do we generalise those kinds of training or development programmes like SSE and CAN and so on?" And procurement was the other key strand, "How do we open up public procurement?" And, you know, that knocked around a bit, but it did then lead

into what because the Social Investment Taskforce, it did lead into eventually what became the PIU project on regulation and charity law and social economy law.

This overall policy direction was soon reinforced at a Downing Street breakfast for co-op leaders on February 26 2002 hosted by Prime Minister Blair (Former Senior Civil Servant III 2016):

> [H]e [Blair] then sort of told them very clearly in the nicest possible way that they … that social enterprise is going to be this way. … [Anon] took us off into another room and then she basically put her very pointed stiletto heels in and made it quite clear what was and what was not going to be counted within social enterprise.

> I knew that Patricia Hewitt was very much a supporter of the coop but didn't want the whole social enterprise agenda dominated by them. She said … there's a huge cooperative agenda here that we within the Labour Party have got to sort out … but don't let it overwhelm the work you're doing on social enterprise.

SEC

After SEL, a "Coalition for Social Enterprise" was also being formed to promote the government's policies beyond London. Spear et al. describe the setting up of the SEC (2017, 17):

> There was resistance from co-operatives and community enterprises to this encroachment of social business. The Social Enterprise Coalition (SEC) was established in 2002 by members of the co-operative movement, ostensibly to unify the competing interests (Bland 2010). However, SEC's definition of social enterprise differed from the DTI's as it explicitly excluded social businesses that paid out profits to shareholders.

But SEC meeting notes from Thursday 26 April 2001, prepared by one of the subscribing signatories of the coalition's future incorporation, are contrary to Spear's interpretation and showed strong antipathy to co-operative structures[20] (Whitehead 2001, 3):

- Lack of real commitment from the Co-operative Movement to engage with like-minded organisations. This is especially the case at regional level.
- Distrust of Co-operative Movement amongst other individuals and organisations because of this.
- Lack of belief that the Co-operative Movement is dynamic and inclusive enough to engage in this initiative.
- Strong resistance of the Co-operative Movement to accept the umbrella term "Social Enterprise".

By November 2001, the embryo of the proposed SEC was submitting a Development Plan and Proposal for funding a "Coalition for Social Enterprise" which included a definition of "social enterprise" even wider than that being used at that time by SEL (Mayo and Thornton 2001, 3, 7):

> We should not rule out a business because it has part shareholders, providing its primary purpose is not simply to deliver shareholder value, nor include a business just because it is run as a cooperative.

> They key to success here has been self-identification. Individuals have wanted to describe themselves as social entrepreneurs, seeing in this term, "brand values" of energy, future relevance and leadership.

The emphasis on individual entrepreneurs meant that the proposed coalition was moving much further beyond the founding purpose of SEL and in the direction of a CIC. This was reflected in the Memorandum and Articles of the Social Enterprise Coalition[21] (Financial Conduct Authority 2002, 1), registered on April 29 2002. Minutes of the coalition's Implementation Sub-Group on May 05 and June 07 2002 show attendance of five representatives and one consultant (Implementation SubGroup 2002). There was agreement to seek tenders "to make an initial assessment of the performance of Regional Development Agencies and devolved national administrations regarding social enterprise support and development in their respective areas", which would form a basis for further discussions with the government. The Implementation SubGroup also set out a timetable leading to the first Annual General Meeting in July 2002[22] (Social Enterprise Coalition 2002). A "founding AGM" would be followed by a "full AGM".

With this wider remit, enlarged composition and even wider ambitions above, the coalition was launched in July 2002, on the same day as the launch of the DTI's "Strategy for Success" document (see below). "Members include national umbrella bodies of social enterprises, regional networks of social enterprises, national social enterprises and partnership organisations. The Co-operative Group, the Royal Bank of Scotland, and the Social Enterprise Unit of the DTI have given money to support the work of the Coalition" (Implementation SubGroup 2002, 19).

"Social Enterprise: A Strategy for Success", Cross Cutting Review and "Private Action, Public Benefit"

At the same time as the launch of the SEC, during 2002 three important publications set out an agenda for public service by social enterprises. On the same day as the inauguration of the SEC, the DTI's first Social Enterprise Strategy paper "Social Enterprise: a Strategy for Success" attempted the first New Labour definition of social enterprise (Department of Trade and Industry 2002, 12):

> A social enterprise is a business with primarily social objectives whose sur-
> pluses are principally reinvested for that purpose in the business or in the
> community, rather than being driven by the need to maximise profit for share-
> holders and owners.

The insertion of "principally" was the only way in which co-operatives
could be accommodated within the strategy, since, as shown in Appendix
Two, co-operatives may distribute their surpluses to members. Secondly, the
document included a very wide-ranging social enterprise definition, which
included private companies limited by shares as well as co-operatives
(Department of Trade and Industry 2002, 7):

> Social enterprises are diverse. They include local community enterprises, social
> firms, mutual organisations such as co-operatives, and large-scale organisa-
> tions operating nationally or internationally. There is no single legal model for
> social enterprise. They include companies limited by guarantee, industrial and
> provident societies, and companies limited by shares; some organisations are
> unincorporated, and others are registered charities.

The Treasury's Cross Cutting Review of "The Role of the Voluntary and
Community Sector in Service Delivery" (HM Treasury 2002) – in effect an
embryonic technical guidance manual for TSOs – and "Private Action,
Public Benefit" from the Downing Street Strategy Unit in September 2002
(Cabinet Office 2002), though these were of equal significance to the DTI
strategy, have received less attention. The Cross Cutting Review allocated
£188mn to the Home Office Active Community Unit – half for implement-
ing the review, and a further £125mn for the creation of "Futurebuilders" –
"our new one-off investment fund to help voluntary ad community
organisations in their public service work" (HM Treasury 2002, 3). The
Treasury Review also promoted the concepts of "full cost recovery" and
advance payment as significant funding features for TSOs. In addition to
£0.5mn annually to the sector for implementation, the new Futurebuilders
programme would be directed at organisations for delivery of key services
in the areas of health and social care, crime and social cohesion, in education and for children and young people (HM Treasury 2002, 25, 26, 32).

"Private Acton, Public Benefit" proposed the CIC as a "new legal form
for social enterprise" and an updating of IPS legislation for co-operatives
(Cabinet Office 2002, 3). There was a recommendation to amend charity
law to allow charities to undertake trading within the charity, without the
need for a trading company (Cabinet Office 2002, 44). The report continued
that CICs would be able to issue preference shares, with payment of dividends and possible voting rights. CICs would also be able to access debt
markets, especially with ethical investment funds considering them attractive (Cabinet Office 2002, 54). Not only was this a different context and

interpretation to many academic interpretations described below, but it proposed a different form of social enterprise with external investors which was opposed by the Co-operative Movement.

Following "Private Action, Public Benefit" (Cabinet Office 2002), the Department of Industry introduced more detailed proposals for CICs (Department of Trade and Industry 2003). The document made clear throughout that the aim was to stimulate the development of the social enterprise market and to encourage external private investment, equity and debt finance (Department of Trade and Industry 2003, 15, 18, 19). Though dividends payable to external investors were initially capped at 20% of distributable profits, "investors will often expect to have an influence over the direction of the company" and there was an expectation that "substantial commercial investors may expect to appoint directors to protect their interests" (Department of Trade and Industry 2003, 21). This dividend limit was raised to 35% in 2014 and the amount of external investment eligible for Social Enterprise Tax Relief was increased to £1.5mn in April 2017. These 2002 proposals appeared after first report from the SITF, with its recommendations for external private investment.

In defining themselves as purchasers and regulators of services, the public and third sector allow the invasion of market logic, competition and price. CICs would be similar to Dees' "enterprising non profits" (Dees 1998a). They "become generally accepted as legitimate criteria to apply in devising the governance and assessing the performance of third sector organizations (Deakin 2001, p. 39)" (Evers and Laville 2005, 242). External investors meant that a "hollowed out" welfare state is advantageous to the extent that it promotes workfare policies that guarantee labour market flexibility and an attractive environment for business investment (Roberts and Devine 2003, 312).

While delivering his consultant's report in response to the SEC tender, Peter Lloyd made a presentation at the House of Lords on Tuesday 11 February 2003 which was to complement policy changes described above. His presentation projected a range of support mechanisms, including "breaking away from the grant-chasing culture and moving toward Framework Contracting and Public Service Agreements". He recommended "beginning to examine the legal and financial frameworks that unreasonably limit the forms that legitimate social enterprises can take and the accountancy regulations that fail to recognise their different needs", including equity and loan structures (Lloyd 2003b, 19). Above all, he set out the need for intermediary organisations – "regional agencies to invest in the creation of intermediary support structures and to champion the scaling up of the Social Economy/Third System and the expansion of local enterprise" (20). His report included a comprehensive review of problems in moving social enterprise into mainstream support through Regional Development Agencies (RDAs), including reducing grant dependency and difficulties of organisations taking on loans. There was a role for the SEC in all of this in making social enterprises better businesses (Lloyd 2003a, 34, 51). Alongside DTI, Treasury and Cabinet Office documents described above in July, September and October 2002, through prefacing a shift of policy to RDAs, his presentation and report effectively formed a basis for UK social enterprise policy and its mainstreaming for at least the next ten years.

To interpret and implement all these initiatives, locally based support strategies for social enterprise were already appearing. A Demos funded report for Hackney Co-operative Developments produced a local Social Enterprise Strategy "Community into Business: Growing Hackney through Social Enterprise". "Social enterprises can act as a powerful driver towards community economic development and financial inclusion. Research has proven that they can help "plug" the leaks within local economies and keep money circulating within a particular area for longer; they enable the money being spent by a community to remain within the community" (Howland et al. 2003, 6). The Oxford Mutuality Taskforce and the Heart of England TEC and Business Link set up a strategy for social enterprise support which is being locally delivered by Social Enterprise Oxfordshire, a partnership of Business Links, Enterprise Agencies, specialist advice agencies, social enterprises and the voluntary sector (Westall 2001a, 42).

Carmel and Harlock later confirmed the marketisation of the sector which had been projected in the Cross Cutting Review in 2002 and in Peter Lloyd's report and presentation in 2003. There would be a level playing field in competition for service delivery, with procurement contracts rather than grants for the voluntary and community sector. There would also be provision for the enhancement of Deakin's original Compact into Compact Plus, three year funding and "full cost recovery". The result would be contestability and competition in the government market for public services (Carmel and Harlock 2008, 161, 162). A "discourse of performance established the market model". The market was no longer a matter for public debate (Carmel and Harlock 2008, 166, 167). "By holding out the promise of a greater say in the shaping of government policy, New Labour has increasingly been able to contain the voice of critics fearful of losing their place at the table of government (Newman 2000)" (May, Cloke and Johnsen 2005, 710).

Opposition to the CIC

A "fightback" from the Co-operative Movement had met with some success[23] in the DTI Social Enterprise Strategy in July 2002. But, despite this, following "Private Action, Public Benefit", in 2004 New Labour introduced legislation for a CIC structure (Department of Trade and Industry 2004). While the Co-operative Movement sought to pursue its own direction, concern about the proposed CIC was echoed by others (Former Social Enterprise London Board Member II 2015):

> [B]ut it was New Labour thinking ... the whole lot, in agreeing the CIC model when there was no benefit from it whatsoever ... Braithwaite's were desperate to get in on the act and because they were all about charity they struggled and they all started saying and the CIC model was kind of their way in.

Representatives from across the Co-operative Movement maintained their opposition (Former Senior Co-operative Movement representative 2016):

> The whole establishment of the CIC regime which we opposed because of its ... but it seemed an irrelevance to us given that there was a community benefit strand of the Industrial Providence Society Act.

> It was a period where there was a very clear drive to take cooperatives out of the scene ... Our fear was that social enterprise, the sexy new social enterprise sector and the Community Interest Company would write cooperatives right out of the game.

There was continuing disquiet from within SEL (Former Social Enterprise London Board Member 2015):

> Well, even worse, Community Interest Companies, I think, sought to marry the two diagonally opposite ones, which are the private paradigm and the philanthropic, charitable paradigm, believing you can have those in the same enterprise ... Similarly, with private businesses, so all CICs are, are privately focussed organisations designed to think two things in two different paradigms, and constrained to do either effectively.

Academic misunderstandings about the CIC

Alongside the academic misunderstandings about the difficult relationship between the Co-operative Movement and Labour Party described earlier, there are equally serious misrepresentations about the CIC structure introduced in 2004. Most of these fail to recognise New Labour's objective of diluting accountability through promoting individual control of social enterprise and encouraging private investment.

Several contributions describe this as similar to a series of legal enabling measures for social enterprise across Europe. "In the UK, the Parliament approved a law creating the 'community interest company' in 2004 but two years earlier, the British government also put forward a definition of social enterprise as 'a business with primarily social objectives whose surpluses are principally reinvested for that purpose in the business or in the community rather than being driven by the need to maximise profit for shareholders and owners'" (Defourny and Nyssens 2010c, 37). The CIC represented a legal embodiment of the DTI Strategy for Success definition (Defourny and Nyssens 2006, 4), with the CIC "dedicated to its expressed community purposes" (Defourny and Nyssens 2010c, 44).

Though Defourny and Nyssens originally interpreted proposals for a CIC as part of a continuing progression from the DTI's 2002 social enterprise strategy document, they did not grasp its significance (Defourny and Nyssens 2006, 4):

> The Blair government launched the "Social Enterprise Coalition" and created a "Social Enterprise Unit" to improve the knowledge of social enterprises and, above all, to promote social enterprises throughout the country. Within the same framework, the Department of Trade and Industry, which supervises the Unit, has put forward its own definition of social enterprise and a new legal form, the "Community Interest Company", was voted by Parliament in 2004.

These academic misunderstandings and misinterpretations continued. The CIC is the "newest organizational form for social enterprise in Europe" introduced in the United Kingdom in 2005 (Kerlin 2006, 254). Others argue that CICs will make it easier to raise capital. "These new legal structures redress the previous costs associated with the requirement for SEs to create two legal structures to accommodate their dual mission – one to trade or access capital, and the other to secure the fiscal advantages of charitable status for receiving grants, donations and bequests" (Doherty, Haugh and Lyon 2014, 425). Following their description of legislation in France and Belgium, CICs have been conceived to complement government services at the community level in areas such as childcare provision, social housing, community transport or leisure (Galera and Borzaga 2009, 223). The CIC was described as anchored in the wider community, with the asset lock representing a new approach to the property relationship as a way of dealing with social needs: a foundation in common property (Peredo, Haugh and McLean 2018, 595).

As explained above, the thrust of the Department's consultation was that governance would be concentrated more in the hands of individual directors and further from local community accountability. Following Stephen Lloyd's Bates Wells and Braithwaite claims above (Lloyd 2010, 33, 43), the Department of Industry's own document provides examples of governance issues for which the diluted accountability of CICs would provide a remedy. One company, "where trainees put themselves forward for the management committee, had led to problems over accountability, discipline and grievance procedures". Another had "voluntary board members who have a say in project management and day-to-day recommendations but this can cause conflict between the board and the chief executive" (Department of Trade and Industry 2003, 10, 14).

In view of this Spear et al.'s description of the CIC legal structure as "particularly suitable for some types of community-based social enterprise – those that wish to work for community benefit within the relative freedom of the non-charitable company form, but with a clear commitment to a non-profit-distribution status" is surprising (2017, 35). As shown later, community-based social enterprise was not uppermost in the minds of those promoting the CIC (Former Senior Civil Servant V 2017):

> The CIC isn't particularly an individualistic model but it certainly gives some accountability to investors, if you take equity, and part of the reason was … This is a … you know, you're opening up a whole big issue about accountability.

The author is also puzzled by Ridley-Duff's interpretation of CICs. "For Haugh (2005, p. 3) 'social enterprises' are prevented from distributing their profits to those who exercise control over them. Certainly, this appears to be the wish of the UK government through the statutory requirement for an 'asset lock' if enterprises want to qualify as a CIC" (Ridley-Duff 2007, 388). These interpretations are the exact opposite of what was intended for CICs, especially those based on companies limited by shares, which was originally sought by the solicitor who originally promoted the concept (Lloyd 2010).

None of these academic interpretations seem to recognise that any organisation which seeks to become a CIC must first register as a company limited by guarantee or shares or whatever structure they chose, so that the CIC is simply an "add on" feature. The CIC is not a company registration in itself.

This once more shows the author's retroduction for "causal mechanisms". There is an unbroken link from Mulgan and Landry's original 1995 suggestions against directors' having to answer to their boards (58), through Mulgan's leadership of the PIU (Cabinet Office 2001b, 19), Stephen Lloyd's "mole in the Treasury" (2010, 33, 43), through the DTI definition above (Department of Trade and Industry 2002, 7) to the introduction of legislation for the CIC (Department of Trade and Industry 2004). Each Annual Report of the Registrar of Community Interest Companies shows CICs based on companies limited by shares as a fast-growing structure. The CIC Regulator's 2020/2021 Annual Report shows that 4,125 out of 23,887 (17%) CICs are companies limited by shares (Regulator of Community Interest Companies 2021, 24). The highest numbers of complaints concern director's conduct and governance (Community Interest Company Regulator 2019, 12, 15). This series of events is very different from the academic interpretations above.

Summary of New Labour and Conservative further events

The basis and framework for policies to transform the third sector into its procurement and public service delivery role, including provision for increased private investment, had thus been fashioned during this critical period between 1998 and 2002. Consequently, only a basic summary of further events is advanced in this next section.

Because of this swift transformation, the concept of social enterprise presented difficulties for potential lenders. Report for the Small Business Service (SBS) mentioned a preoccupation with definitional issues about the distinctive characteristics of social enterprise (Bank of England 2003, 10, 13; J. Brown 2003; Smallbone et al. 2001). The Bank of England reported that social enterprises had greater difficulties in borrowing than for-profit businesses and that there was little venture capital or business angel finance. There was a latent demand for patient capital, with almost 40% of social enterprises having a turnover of less than £100,000 and a preference for grant funding (Bank of England 2003, 49). A further SBS report on Lending to Social Enterprise in 2004 showed that while many social enterprises have little physical security and many have no clear understanding of commercial bank funding, this is a major barrier to their future growth and success (Small Business Service 2004, 9).

At the beginning of 2004, despite concern expressed from the SEC and others, the Social Enterprise Unit was moved from the DTI to become part of the SBS. In October, the DTI launched a public procurement toolkit in the new Social Enterprise Magazine. HM Treasury held four seminars on the role of the voluntary and community sector and a review was conducted on progress since the 2002 Cross Cutting Review. Business Links were becoming involved in start-up training. As part of Small Business Services, the Social Enterprise Unit undertook research with the Community Development Finance Association. Oversight of the Futurebuilders Fund, which originated from the 2002 Cross Cutting Review was transferred from the Treasury to the Home Office Though later in 2005 the Home Office Active Communities Unit pressed for more discipline in third sector delivery, as outlined in its "Compact Plus: Strengthening Partnerships: Next Steps for Compact", it later withdrew these proposals following opposition (Home Office 2005, 6). This brief summary of developments showed that social enterprise delivery was now being mainstreamed throughout government.

The Social Enterprise Unit commissioned two major social enterprise surveys in 2004 and 2005. The 2004 survey was based on organisations that generated a minimum of 25% of income from trading activities and were either companies limited by guarantee or IPS. The survey estimated that

there were 15,000 social enterprises employing 475,000 people with a combined annual turnover of £18bn, of which 82% was generated through
trading. The 2005 survey used a minimum of 75% of income from trading,
with not more than 50% of profits paid back to owners or shareholders.
Respondents were also asked whether they fitted the government's definition of social enterprise. The 2005 survey estimated that there were at least
55,000 social enterprises in the UK with a combined turnover of £27bn per
year, or 5% of all businesses with employees. But the majority of these businesses were sole proprietors, partnerships or limited companies with only
one executive director (Spear, Cornforth, and Aiken 2007, 24, 25). These
surveys showed that a wide range of structures now felt able to label themselves "social enterprises".

As Secretary of State, Patricia Hewitt's January 2006 White Paper "Our
Health, Our Care, Our Say: a new Direction for Community Services"
expanded NHS outsourcing to include the third sector, with extended NHS
delivery based on payment by results (Department of Health 2006, 19). Her
Department set up its own internal Social Enterprise Unit. "In essence, Social
Enterprises use business solutions to achieve public good" (Department of
Health Social Enterprise Unit 2007, 4). In 2006 the original DTI Social
Enterprise Unit moved to the OTS, with a Social Enterprise Action Plan
"Scaling New Heights", which moved social enterprise policy to RDAs.
Under "Ensure that the right information and advice are available to those
running social enterprises" (Cabinet Office and Office of the Third Sector
2006), the Action Plan announced £0.5mn for RDA social enterprise support, together with Futurebuilders and Phoenix Funds. The Action Plan recognised a poor situation "on the ground", including the complexity of the
support landscape and TSOs considering themselves unsupported by
Business Link. Mainstreaming of social enterprise into central government
delivery mechanisms was now complete.

New Labour introduced the "Right to Request" in June 2008 and "Transforming Community Services" in July 2008. The National Audit Office June
2011 Report summarised these developments in the "Establishing Social
Enterprises under the Right to Request Programme" including delivery
being provided under contract to the PCT by other bodies such as social
enterprises or Foundation Trusts" (National Audit Office 2011, 5).

Capacity building

For further involvement in procurement and public service delivery, after the
Futurebuilders programme, it was intended that the Capacitybuilder and
ChangeUp initiatives would provide support. With funding of £231mn,

from June 2004 onwards, the ChangeUp programme sought to improve infrastructure and front-line organisations. Capacitybuilders took over the management of ChangeUp in April 2006. The Capacitybuilders' programme management cost £3.3mn in 2007–2008. The National Audit Office concluded that delayed programme implementation meant that there was only twenty-one months to spend £80mn of available funding, with only £64mn spent in 2005–2006 (National Audit Office 2009, 21).

On the Futurebuilders programme the 2009 National Audit Office Report was similarly uncomplimentary (National Audit Office 2009). Futurebuilders as the main social enterprise loans programme was described as "experimental" (National Audit Office 2009, 5). The NAO commented on a low number of successful applications, long delays in processing, high fund management costs and high application costs for smaller applicants. A further evaluation of Futurebuilders was not generous. "Futurebuilders investee organisations have to date operated in the context of increasing public expenditure and greater opportunities for third sector delivery. Key challenges will be around continuing this development under conditions of public expenditure restraint and contraction" (Wells et al. 2010, 76).

The House of Commons Public Accounts Committee was also not impressed with these developments. In "Working with the Voluntary Sector" on February 15 2006, the Committee reported that only limited progress had been made in increasing the sector's involvement in delivering government programmes (House of Commons Public Accounts Committee 2006, 4) On both ChangeUp and Futurebuilders, the Committee was equally critical in its June 2009 Report on "Building the Capacity of the Third Sector". Its lack of planned evaluation was alarming in view of risks in the Programme (House of Commons Public Accounts Committee 2009, 5).

Despite this extended support, the Evaluation of the Social Enterprise Investment Fund (SEIF) reported that up till 31 March 2011 a total investment of £80,712,510 was made across 531 organisations. But the evaluation also found SEIF primarily operating as a grant fund with only 14% (£11,372,637) invested as loans, with a further £3,086,430 of repayable grants (Alcock, Millar and Hall 2012, 4).

Because of limited success in these programmes, to accommodate more TSOs within this process, the 2010 Coalition Government further widened the definition for those organisations which might be called a "social enterprise" to include a self-definition process. In "Social Enterprise: Market Trends", based on the BIS (Business, Innovation and Skills) Small Business Survey 2012, the Cabinet Office said that "the enterprise must consider itself to be a social enterprise – defined as having mainly social or environmental aims" (BMG Research 2013, 8). From its other "good fit criteria" (no more than 50% distribution and not less than 25% income from trading), the Cabinet Office projected 688,200 "good fit" social enterprises, including those with no employees. This self-definition process includes private sector organisations which consider themselves a "good fit". Social enterprise was beginning to lose its discrete meaning. The Baring Foundation's Independence Panel for the Voluntary Sector's Report "Independence under Threat" in January 2013 described social enterprise as a "convenient brand" (Panel on the Independence of the Voluntary Sector 2013, 25):

> 26% of small and medium size enterprises badge themselves as Social Enterprises. The voluntary sector brand is being abused: "Social Enterprise" is a totally unregulated or defined concept and, for some, just a convenient brand.

Concern was also expressed about "compromised independence, fears of 'mission drift', loss of responsiveness and innovation, and the growth of competition and polarisation within the sector" (Dickinson et al. 2012). Larger and more experienced TSOs and for-profit organisations were "squeezing out" smaller, local TSOs from the market and "cherry picking" services, leaving TSOs to pick up more difficult cases (Harlock 2012, 13).

SITF and Big Society Capital

From 2000 onwards, Cohen had claimed that venture capital can "harness the most powerful forces of capitalism: entrepreneurship, innovation and capital to tackle social issues more effectively" and "connect [social sector organisations] to the capital markets" (Chiapello and Godefroy 2017, 178). From Cohen's series of SITF Reports (SITF 2010; 2005; 2003; 2000) policies of social investment began to emerge, under which outputs and outcomes provide a basis for returns to private investors.

Cohen's April 2010 Final Report "Social Investment: Ten Years On" projected £14.2bn from private sources for social investment (SITF 2010, 16). In the meantime, the Third Sector Task Force Final Report in 2009, led by ACEVO (Voluntary Sector Chief Executives) and NCVO were already pinning their funding aspirations on a proposed Social Investment Bank and their becoming subcontractors to private sector prime contractors. "(T)he scale of the new contracts and the 'reward' mechanism for providers will create a greater opportunity than ever before for the third sector to support prime contractors in the delivery of public services" (ACEVO 2009, 6).

As a precursor to a Social Investment Bank, Cohen set up a Commission on Unclaimed Assets (CUA) which recommended the transfer of unclaimed bank accounts, mainly from dead people, to a new entity, the Reclaim Fund. Following lobbying to implement CUA recommendations, in 2008 the government introduced the Dormant Bank Accounts Act 2008. In its December 2009 Pre-Budget Report, the Treasury spelled its intention clearly (HM Treasury 2009, 88, 89):

> To fund its initial capitalisation, the Government announces its intention to commit up to £75mn of the funds expected to be released through the Dormant Accounts Scheme in England… for the establishment of a Social Investment Wholesale Bank, subject to the final volume of funds available for distribution in England.

Big Society Capital (BSC) was set up in April 2012 as the government's dispensary for social investment funding. Under the Dormant Bank Accounts Act in November 2008, the Cabinet Office tasked BSC to manage £600mn from dormant bank accounts and "Merlin Banks" as a social investment wholesaler. BSC acknowledged support it received from national TSOs (Big Society Capital 2013, 11). In January 2021 it was announced that a further £800mn of dormant assets, mainly from dormant pensions, insurances and securities accounts, would be made available to the third sector, though further details have not been provided (Weakley 2021).

Alongside BSC, after delivering the second Futurebuilders Fund from 2008, the intermediary Social Investment Business became the repository for a range of funds, including the Communitybuilders Fund and Department of Health SEIF in 2009, the Cabinet Office Social Action Fund in 2011 and Investment and Contract Readiness Programme in 2012. Following the Coalition Agreement in May 2010, the government rapidly set out its broad direction of travel on public service reform:

- "Modernising Commissioning: Increasing the Role of Charities, Social Enterprises, Mutuals and Cooperatives in Public Service Delivery" (Cabinet Office 2010)
- "Growing the Social Investment Market: A Vision and Strategy" (Cabinet Office and HM Government 2011)
- "Open Public Services" White Paper July 2011, (HM Government 2011) with its presumption in favour of open commissioning.

TSOs continued their encouragement of these government policies. These formed a Social Economy Alliance in June 2013 to influence elections, leading to a 2015 UK General Election Manifesto. Led by Social Enterprise UK, the Alliance includes a wide range of third sector representative organisations in England and demonstrates their continuing support for outsourcing public service delivery. The Alliance May 2017 "Manifesto for an Inclusive Economy" included (Social Economy Alliance 2017, 4):

> We can reinvent capitalism for the 21st century, reframe the debate about the role of business in society and show that entrepreneurship can be a force for

good by spreading wealth and opportunity, solving the major social challenges of our times and creating a more shared society.

But recent comments continue to show BSC's essentially limited success. The third sector took up around £730m of social investment in the year ending 2017, compared with £22bn in grants and donations in the same period. This represents a take-up by less than 1% of TSOs annually (Litchfield 2019).

Procurement difficulties for third sector organisations

There are considerable difficulties for social enterprise in many procurement processes. The 2019 Social Enterprise in Scotland 2019 Census shows that only 36% of social enterprises with a turnover of less than £100,000 are trading with the public sector, only 17% have won a contract, since 42% have an income of less than £50,000 and 55% have an income of less than £100,000 (Coburn and CEIS 2019, 31, 44). The 2019 UK Census shows that one third have a turnover of less than £50,000 and 61% less than 3 years old less than £50,000 (Mansfield and Gregory 2019, 15, 17). Previous social enterprise censi show that almost two thirds of social enterprises have annual turnovers of less than £100,000, so that they are handicapped in most procurement competitions (BMG Research 2017; Coburn 2015; 2017; Villeneuve-Smith and Temple 2015).

The 2010 Coalition Government increased the pace of the "marketisation" of hitherto public services (Macmillan 2011). Following the Health and Social Care Act 2012, the National Health Service was further opened to bidding by corporations as well as TSOs (Aiken and Harris 2017, 334). Many smaller TSOs now appear to be withdrawing from a local, community or minority focus and surviving – if at all – by cobbling together projects for which governmental or foundation funding is more readily available. The period since 2010 under the Coalition Government has seen a contraction with an anticipated loss of £3.3b income over the period 2011–2016. There were 70,000 job losses in London's voluntary sector in 2011" (Murray 2013, 4). Survival may well be at the cost of losing local and specialist knowledge, credibility and support". Following Rhodes' (1994) concerns about the "hollowing out" of the British state through these policy processes, Aiken and Harris conclude (Aiken and Harris 2017, 336):

> In the light of the evidence presented here about how recent trends in public policy have been impacting on small and medium third sector organisations (SMTSOs), we would suggest that there are now equivalent deep changes under way in the third sector; a process of erosion of the core features of SMTSOs, which have up to now tried to work for specialist and local interests.

Article 77 of 2014/24/EU (the EU Procurement Directive) enabled national governments in a range of circumstances to give preference to social enterprises and mutuals within a restricted competition for provision of social, health, education and other services, with interpretations left to national governments. "It is obvious that these entities cannot face competitive challenges within the contemporary economy. Therefore, the support of governments is necessary" (Pirvu and Clipici 2015, 19). "These tensions ....raise pressing questions about the ability of VSOs in the area to contribute to the longer-term maintenance of effective services that create meaningful outcomes for clients and citizens more broadly" (Rees and Rose 2015, 89). However, following Britain's exit from the EU, the government has recently initiated a consultation on its "Transforming Procurement" proposals, which though they include social value, will discontinue this "light touch regime" under Article 77 (Cabinet Office 2020, 32). Though more details of a proposed "competitive flexible procedure" will only emerge after consultation, as projected throughout this book, the new procurement regime is part of a continuing trend where social enterprises, co-operatives and mutuals will face increasing competition from the private sector.

Social investment goes global

At the G8 Social Impact Investment Forum in June 2013, Prime Minister Cameron announced the setting up of a Social Impact Investment Taskforce under Ronald Cohen to act as a catalyst to the development of a social impact investment market. The UK government committed £60mn to a new social investment Access Foundation (Maude 2015, 2). The Taskforce held meetings in the White House in Washington, London, Berlin, Paris, Rome and Toronto, with the UK Cabinet Office providing the secretariat. In August 2015 the Taskforce was superseded by the Global Social Impact Investment Steering Group (GSG) with a membership including thirteen countries. The bulletin from its September 2014 meeting stressed that "it was important for the GSG to dedicate time and money to communications, with a communications budget set at $1mn in its first year, about 20% of which will be spent on analysis of the narratives around impact investment in the UK and USA" (Global Social Impact Investment Steering Group 2015, 2).

All this is now amplified internationally by Ronald Cohen as a global version of his SITF, with many of its activities funded by UK and US governments as part of their central mission during austerity. The Leaders' Declaration from its September 2020 online meeting emphasised "incentives to accelerate impact investment, which seeks social as well as financial returns in order to create sustainable jobs, advance education, improve healthcare, and fund the expansion of non-profit organizations that support the most vulnerable" (Global Steering Group for Impact Investment 2020). This Declaration has now been signed by over 1,000 international central and local public officers, academics and practitioners in what the author believes will be a dominant influence.

The author believes that the British Council's 2014 admission was prophetic. "There may well not be a recognisable 'social enterprise sector' by 2020. Certainly any attempts to confine social enterprise to specific legal structures or models of governance will have ceased" (Catherall and Richardson 2014, 7).

Conclusion: New Labour's critical period

Events from 1998 to 2002 represent a critical period in social enterprise development, which was dominated by New Labour policies to transform the role of collectivist, mutual and locally democratically accountable third sector structures to become more individually accountable within a marketised environment. Though some contributions (Haugh and Kitson 2007) have described this as a smooth transition, interviews in this chapter show that this caused a major political rupture between Labour and the Co-operative Movement.

But underlying this rupture the author has discerned a series of demi-regularities which may be retroduced in evidence of underlying causal mechanisms, showing policies which sought more flexible delivery of lower cost public services and a diminution of the public sector. After 1998, SEL widened the meaning and interpretation of social enterprise. The SEC (2002) widened definitions further, followed by the DTI Social Enterprise Strategy document in July 2002 (Department of Trade and Industry 2002) and September 2002 HM Treasury Cross Cutting Review (HM Treasury 2002), the Cabinet Office "Private Action, Public Benefit" (Cabinet Office 2002) and proposals for a CIC (Department of Trade and Industry 2003). Peter Lloyds's report for the SEC then projected a funding and contracting regime which has endured through New Labour Conservative governments (Lloyd 2003a; 2003b). Apart from the introduction of a CIC structure (Department of Trade and Industry 2004), which loosened requirements for collective oversight and governance, four years of New Labour policy from 1998 to 2002 set the stage for social enterprise for the next twenty years.

At that time from Scotland, a prescient John Pearce summed up these developments, especially the repositioning of the third sector for delivery of public services (2003, 58):

Will it build its vision for radical change and promote, argue, lobby and work for a social and economic system founded on third-system values, or will it settle for being no more than a reformist mechanism, helping to make the first and second systems work better by being "an additional tool in the box" and "an adjunct to the mainstream economy"?

Notes

1 Differences between cooperatives and individually accountable social enterprise structures are explained further in Appendix 2.
2 "Creating a Social Economy" sought commitments from the Labour Party on "some specific policy issues": 1) Recognition. Using a range of forms of legal status to establish their enterprises, co-operatives can be hard to identify. This militates against any positive action which might be taken to support them. The passing of a Co-operatives Act which is "friendly" towards the new co-operatives – as is being proposed by the UK Co-operative Council – would help. 2) Investment. If the sector is going to grow at any speed, there needs to be investment capital available tailored to its needs. ICOF should be refinanced to further develop its twenty-one years' experience of supporting co-operative enterprises; and consideration should be given to a UK equivalent of the Italian Marcora law which has helped numerous failing private enterprises to be transformed into successful worker co-operatives.
3 ICOM's 14th Annual Report also demonstrated its links with the Cooperative Party: "ICOM has developed very close links with the Co-operative Party throughout the year and continues to focus much energy into the United Kingdom Co-operative Council which has emerged as the main overarching body to represent the interests of all co-operative sectors."
4 In support of its relationship with New Labour, the Cooperative Opportunity for All campaign continued:

   in amending Clause 4 of the (Labour) party's constitution, a new reference to cooperatives was introduced;

   - a commitment has been given to introducing the UK Cooperative Council's proposals for a new Cooperatives Act to improve and update the legislative framework;
   - according to the Road to the Manifesto, "We are keen to encourage a variety of forms of partnership and enterprise, including cooperatives."

5 As shown later, Andrea Westall was involved in key policy discussions for development of social enterprise policy and refers to the conflation of social enterprise and the social economy. See Westall (2001a).
6 The PAT3 Report also found an "echo" of EMES and WISEs in Chapter 4 on providing work experience and employment opportunities. See Policy Action Team 3 and Stephen Timms (1999).
7 Despite recent antecedents, Westall makes no mention of co-operatives and instead focuses on US examples which include air traffic control and the National Centre for Social Enterprise. See Eikenberry and Kluver (2004).

8 The consultancy research brief included: 2) to investigate the need and the potential for providing an integrated and unified London-wide service of development and support for cooperative and democratically managed businesses. This work is being earned out in part by the two organisations described above and the locally managed CDAs / CSOs; 3) to investigate the need for, and the resources required to maintain, a federation of worker coops; 4)to inform London Boroughs Grants Committee on the future funding needs of this sector.Particular issues which need to be examined are: the facilitation of information and communication between Cooperative Support Organisations, cooperatives and social economy organisations.

9 The London ICOM Fifteenth Annual Report said: "There had been a period of consultation with remaining cooperative support organisations throughout London over the previous two years which had culminated in a report in 1996. In February 1997, a day conference attempted to pull all the loose strands together and take a number of initiatives which would lay the groundwork for a new operational framework. The resulting proposal for tender to external consultants involved a close examination of London ICOM, London Cooperative Training and the London CDA's/CSO's."

10 The CAG Report recommended a Steering Group to oversee the development of the new body be made up of people broadly in agreement with the proposed approach; provide continuity with the existing working party, retaining participation from LC1 and LICOM; and include additional participation from worker cooperatives and other community enterprises.

11 Though the Director has been anonymised in this text, this was a significant resignation, driven by the need to ensure, in his words, that "LICOM Council's energies would better be used influencing the strategy process rather than dragging tired old London ICOM on for the last few miles".

12 The Objects of the Company included:

   i)   To promote the principles and values of the social enterprise economy in Greater London and its environs
   ii) To promote cooperative solutions for economic and community development
   iii) To promote social enterprises, in particular cooperatives and common ownerships, social firms and others organisations and businesses which put into practice the principles of participative democracy, equal opportunities and social justice.

   SEL's Articles of Association prefaced a wide ranging membership:

   Articles of Association – A) Membership

   1 The Management Committee may at its discretion admit to Membership organisations which are based or have an active presence in Greater London, which support the objects of the Company and which qualify for admission to one of the following categories of Membership:

      i)   Cooperative Support Organisations

ii) Social and Ethical Enterprises, in particular cooperatives and common ownerships, social firms and other organisations which put into practice the principles of participative democracy, equal opportunities and social justice

iii) Partnership and Support Agencies, being organisations which wish to support the work of the Company but which do not qualify for either of the above categories of Membership.

13 SEL's structure:

SEL is a non-profit making voluntary organisation, established as a company limited by guarantee. It has a management Board based on three categories of membership: Local agencies promoting social enterprise development; social enterprises; partnership organisations who share SEL's objectives.

Each category has four seats on the board, plus an additional three places for cooptees who can support SEL's work with special areas of expertise.

The Board is currently made up from an initial steering group that has been involved in setting up Social Enterprise London. An AGM is planned for early October, which will elect a full Board that will support SEL's development and help shape the promotion of Social Enterprise in London for the 21st century.

14 Social enterprises use many different kinds of legal structures but share a set of common characteristics:

- Democratic management structures on a membership basis – participation by the workforce and in some cases other groups (e.g. users or clients, and local community groups, etc.)
- Explicit social and ethical aims and values including a commitment to empowerment
- Enterprises in the sense they have to be viable trading concerns. They may be profit making or non-profit making. If profits are distributed it should be done on an equitable basis in relation to work done or for community benefit rather than simply as a return on share capital.

15 Ministerial contributions at the seminar contributions included: the role of social enterprise in public sector reform and delivering public services; the need to avoid grant dependency; and complementarity with private sector corporate social responsibility. The ensuing discussion included the following ideas:

- The need to find ways to make social enterprise more attractive to funding from the private sector
- The public services agenda and the vital importance of recognising the sector's potential
- Links with the private sector being just as important as links across Whitehall
- The unsatisfactory state of models and legal structures, with IPS regulations impeding growth
- The need to actively pursue the procurement issue to enable social enterprises to benefit from central and local government contracts.

16 The purpose of the Review was (Cabinet Office 2001a, 4) "to review the legal and regulatory framework for the sector in order to assess how it could better

enable existing organisations to thrive and grow, encourage the development of new types of organisation, and ensure public confidence".

17 The Co-operative Union briefing stated: "Returns varying according to profits are incompatible with small social and cooperative enterprises, being hostile to anything other than profit maximisation. Similarly, external voting equity and control is more concerned about getting money back than social objectives".

18 Gareth Thomas MP's Private Member's Bill sought "to require at least 50% of the members to take part in a vote to demutualise the Society (i.e. to convert it to a share company), which already requires a 75% majority of those voting, in order for the vote to be effective". The Co-operative Union also proposed an alternative "Community Mutual" proposal, building on work done by the Cooperative Party and Cobbetts solicitors.

19

> First of all, the cross-cutting review that I am responsible for taking forward at this time ... in terms of the involvement of the voluntary sector in the delivery of public services ... The aim is to understand more fully, how the government can work with the voluntary sector, to deliver high quality services ...

> Secondly, the Performance and Innovation Unit Review which Geoff Mulgan and my colleague Baroness Morgan are taking forward ... to look at the challenges for charities and the wider voluntary sector, from a particular angle that looks at the modern role of charities; the links between the public and the voluntary sectors; and developing proposals for modernising the legal and regulatory framework for charities and the voluntary sector.

20 This earliest note of a meeting in House of Lords, dated 26 April 2001, headed "Towards a Charter for Social Enterprise and the formation of Social Enterprise UK", includes recollection of "first meeting of January 11 2001" and foreshadowed the emergence of a Coalition for Social Enterprise, which became the Social Enterprise Coalition. The note on resistance from the Cooperative Movement is significant.

21 The Objects of the Company are:

- To promote the principles and values of the social enterprise economy in the UK through a national voice for social enterprise to establish a sufficiently clear public and policy understanding of the social enterprise sector amongst practitioners, policy makers at all levels, and media and opinion-formers.
- To promote social enterprise solutions.
- To promote social enterprises.
- To promote the creation of a strong framework, and access to resources, in the regions and nations of the UK, in order to support the development of social enterprises.

22 The Implementation SubGroup continued in the same vein, including:

> Send out notice w/b 17th June – by email and letter, explaining that we intend to have a founding AGM, to get things moving, but that next April we will have formalised the membership and will have a full AGM. The people on the list are those who have signed the charter.

From SEC Notes of Meetings held in May: Preparations for the AGM, there was agreement about membership categories and procedures:

> Currently there were two directors – John Goodman and Helen Barber. It was agreed that, until the AGM and the election of a new board, the implementation committee would become the directors of SEC.

23 Birchall also describes New Labour's 2003 Health and Social Care Act, which "offered existing hospital trusts in England the chance to gain more autonomy by applying for 'foundation' status'. The legislation describes NHS Foundation Trusts as being "modelled on cooperative societies and mutual organisations" (Birchall 2008, 8).

6

Explanations

Introduction

As shown throughout this book, the emergence of social enterprise as a service delivery platform in a public services marketplace has been endorsed and encouraged by many UK academic contributions. Many of these seem to have approached the third sector through their academic endeavours rather than through any practice and implementation experience. Using sources in North America, mainland Europe and elsewhere, this chapter seeks provide explanations for continuing UK misunderstandings and misconceptions.

North American influence

North American cross-sectoral approach

Many UK contributions have borrowed extensively from a North American business school academy, where there is little mention of sector boundaries, which is one of the most prominent reasons why many UK social enterprise interpretations overlooked any connection with governance and local democratic accountability.

Most North American interpretations are "sector blind". Social entrepreneurship "captures a unique approach to economic and social problems, an approach that cuts across sectors and disciplines... innovations that use elements from both sector to create social value" (Dees and Anderson 2006, 48). Social entrepreneurship can include social purpose business ventures, such as for-profit community development banks, and hybrid organisations mixing not-for-profit and for-profit elements (Dees 1998b, 2) Social entrepreneurship can occur within the public, private or non-profit sectors – a hybrid model involving both for-profit and non-profit activities as well as cross-sectoral collaboration" (Johnson 2000, 7). Dees and Anderson's school of "enterprising social innovation" suggests that if philanthropy mixed with economic motivations are not needed for social impact "the organization could be run purely as a business, which poses few interesting intellectual issues beyond the discovery of the opportunity" (Dees and Anderson 2006, 51). The objective of creating social value does not require to be captured within organisational boundaries. The social entrepreneurial venture can thus be conceptualised as a vehicle for creating social value, either directly or through facilitating the creation of social value with and by others (Austin, Stevenson and Wei-Skillern 2006, 16, 18).

Suchman warns of dangers in this cross-sectoral approach. Though society imposes heavier obligations (such as "fiduciary duty" and "strict liability") on those entities that hold themselves out as providing certain particularly important or problematic goods and services, by "adjusting organisational goals, managers often can select among alternative moral criteria, such as efficiency, accountability, confidentiality, reliability, responsiveness, and so on (Carroll, 1979)" (Suchman 1995, 590). "Scholars have traditionally tried to define the field in terms of the entrepreneur or what the entrepreneur does but because there are fundamentally different interpretations of these two concepts, consensus on a definition of the field is perhaps not possible" (Venkataraman 1997, 120). Institutional theories (DiMaggio and Powell 1983) have stressed that many dynamics in the organisational environment stem not from technological or material imperatives, but rather from cultural norms, symbols, beliefs and rituals. The stronger the institutional environment, the greater the need for cognitive legitimacy of all kinds and for moral legitimacy based on procedures and structures (Suchman 1995, 571).

Mort et al. look for a middle ground between the "currently fragmented status of the literature and a measure that will effectively capture the entrepreneurial activity in not for profits" (2003, 77). Light argued for a "bigger tent" to include the private sector. Advocates of social entrepreneurship have excluded large number of organisations that deserve the financial support, networking and training now reserved for "the current definition of social entrepreneurship and prevailing model of the self sacrificing entrepreneur" (Light 2006, 48). Others wrote that parameters for social enterprise were already too fixed, settled and "inappropriate at this stage of development because organisations are complex, variable-rich phenomena that can be studies from multiple perspectives" (Daft and Lewin 1990, 2).

Others view social entrepreneurship as "a process consisting of the innovative use and combination of resources to explore and exploit opportunities, that aims at catalysing social change by catering to basic human needs in a sustainable manner" and argue for "economic value creation", including for-profit structures, to ensure "sustainability and financial self sufficiency" (Mair and Marti 2006, 37, 38). Martin and Osberg later continued an emphasis on institutional behaviour beyond the firm, describing a "chain reaction, encouraging other entrepreneurs to iterate upon and ultimately propagate the innovation to the point of 'creative destruction'" (2007). Petrella and Richez-Battesti summarise Martin and Osberg's approach. The difference between entrepreneurship and social entrepreneurship lies "in the value proposition itself" (Petrella and Richez-Battesti 2014, 146).

While all these contributions on North America are significant in their search to define social entrepreneurship, UK contributions which borrow from them have created an interpretation of social enterprise policy where intrinsic structure and governance are less specific. As shown at the end of Chapter 5, this has enabled a wide range of structures and organisations to label themselves "social enterprises".

Influence of US foundations

UK interpretations of social enterprise continue to be heavily influenced by North American foundations like Ashoka, Skoll and Schwab, which are active in the UK and have oversold a model of individual "hero" or "change maker" social entrepreneurship, encouraging procurement and contracting and the incursion of private finance from foundations and social investors. This represents the operationalisation of North American non-profit models in a UK marketplace.

Apart from a cross-sectoral approach, North American nonprofits have their own history, which is often ignored in UK contributions. During the 1960s John D Rockefeller III admitted that big philanthropy needed to change way it works. Following previous abuses about tax-exempt foundations' using tax relief for political purposes, he set up his Commission on Foundations and Private Philanthropy, which became the Filer Commission and which reported in 1977 (Filer Commission on Private Philanthropy and Public Needs 1975).

The Commission's most enduring contribution was its suggestion that all tax-exempt entities, including donors and donees, formed a distinctive "third", "non profit", or "independent" sector whose welfare was essential to the future of democracy. The Commission sought to establish a permanent quasi-governmental agency – modelled on the British Charity Commission – within the Treasury Department (Dobkin Hall 2001, 78), which Rochester describes (Rochester 2013, 43):

> [W]hile in the UK existing organisations such as NCV (National Council for Volunteers) and CAF (Charities Aid Foundation) had to be manoeuvred into

new coalitions, in the USA a new advocacy coalition at national level had to be created in the form of the networks that formed independent Sector in Washington (it took almost four years to do this). (6 and Leat 1997)

The Commission sought a permanent "bureau of philanthropy" in the Treasury Department (Dobkin Hall 2006, 2:55). But President Carter's Finance Secretary, Michael Blumenthal, questioned whether such a body could "represent the public interest and defend a private one" (2001, 247).

This controversial background of funding from foundations through tax exemption represents a policy direction very different from the UK. Dobkin Hall gives the example of the Ford family's ability able to pass on control of the Ford Motor Company to the next generation without paying taxes. He asks whether "the increasingly tax sensitive public would regard as genuinely charitable the overt use of tax-exempt foundations to help the wealthy avoid taxes and concentrate wealth to promote liberal policy agendas with which they were not in sympathy" (2001, 64). Many organisations enjoying tax exemption seek to benefit the needy. But others point to ways in which philanthropy, despite the 1969 Tax Reform Act, continues to serve the purposes of the wealthy far more than it does those of the population as a whole (82).

Initially, following the Filer Commission, increasing numbers of nonprofits benefitted from more government funding. From 12,500 foundations in 1940 and 50,000 in 1950, by 1967 there were 309,000, by 1977 790,000, and by 1989, just under one million – an eightyfold increase in forty years (Dobkin Hall 2001, 62). By the late 1970s, government funding accounted for more than 30% of the overall operating revenues of non-profit charitable service agencies. In social services it reached almost 50% (Salamon and Anheier 1997b, 305). Nonprofits were delivering a larger share of government-financed human services than all levels of government, and government support had outdistanced the support for these institutions from private charitable donations by a factor of almost two to one (Salamon and Anheier 1997a, 289). Partnership between government at all levels and non-profit organisations extended the size and scope of non-profit action (Dancuse, Bouchard and Morin 2013, 103).

But this pattern of increased US government spending did not last. The Reagan Administration retreated and proposed to help the non-profit sector chiefly by "getting government out of its way" (Salamon and Anheier 1997b, 305). Outside the health field, "federal support to non profit organisations declined by one fourth in the early part of the decade, and did not return to its 1980 level until the early 1990s" (305). In his 1989 Inaugural Address, George H. W. Bush spoke of "a thousand points of light, the community organisations that are spread like stars throughout the Nation, doing good"

(Bush 1989). Both Reagan and Bush pretexts of "returning government to the people" concealed industrial deregulation, business tax breaks and reductions in services and social programmes for the very poor or persons of more modest means. To replace existing social welfare provision, each "point of light" represented "a voluntary, community-based initiative serving the dependent and disabled" (Dobkin Hall 2006, 56).

"[F]ederal spending cuts would cripple non profits, rather than empower them" (Dobkin Hall 2006, 2:55). After federal expansion of health and social welfare spending from 1965 to 1972, the funding lost between 1980 to 1994 was equivalent to total foundation grants between 1970 and 1990 (Salamon 1999, 9). Funding reductions in the Carter and Reagan years increased the power of foundations, so that nonprofits found themselves in competition with private sector businesses (Dancuse, Bouchard and Morin 2013, 104). All this represented the "pervasive marketisation" of the American social welfare system, as "non profit organisations have been sucked increasingly into market type relations and for-profit firms have steadily expanded their market niche" (Salamon 1993, 36).[1] The US government shifted its emphasis from "using grants to contracts and vouchers, with increased emphasis on competition and performance measurement for the delivery of social services" (Eikenberry and Kluver 2004, 134). There was also a paradigm shift in philanthropy, with donors "scrutinising charitable causes like potential business investment" (Eikenberry and Kluver 2004, 344). This also raises the issue of whether marketisation of the nonprofit sector is undermining critical roles that it plays in building civil society (Eikenberry 2009, 10).

US nonprofits and social enterprise

Through their increasing financial difficulties, many US nonprofits were driven to activity which was soon labelled as "social entrepreneurship". Despite advantages which allow social enterprises to adapt internal organisation to problems described above, this also makes social enterprise a fragile organisational model, extremely sensitive to changes in market conditions and public policies (Bacchiega and Borzaga 2001, 291).

In an earlier study of Canadian charities and commercial activity, Zimmerman and Dart (1998) commented that the language of the marketplace has put management at the centre of these organisations, corporate business at the centre of society and defined government and non-profit organisations as non-productive or burdensome – "a nearly pervasive ideology that views all aspects of human society as a kind of market". Dart (2004) echoes this view. Social enterprise and social entrepreneurial organisations are different from traditional non-profit organisations.

Johnson (2000) notes that – despite the range of specific forms – they differ from traditional nonprofits in that they blur boundaries between non-profit and for-profit and that they enact hybrid non-profit and for-profit activities (cited in Dart 2004, 415).

Young and Brewer describe structural differences between nonprofits and social enterprise. Nonprofits have difficulty raising capital, are restricted in charging, are not profit seeking and only operate in certain sectors. In some areas social enterprise has advantages, through internal efficiencies, using free resources and an ability to motivate employees and offer wider incentives. It may also undertake profitable activities and can address the free rider problem. Though these diverse forms of enterprises represent a "social enterprise zoo", they have difficulties in accommodating European structures such as co-operatives and mutuals (Young and Brewer 2016, 6–9). This again shows the difficulties of extending North American analyses into mainland Europe and the UK.

Dart had earlier expressed a similar view – that social enterprise and social entrepreneurial organisations are different from traditional non-profit organisations, since they blur boundaries between non-profit and for-profit and they enact hybrid non-profit and for-profit activities (2004, 415). Dobkin Hall is more insightful in recalling Dees' suggesting that social enterprises were within "a spectrum of activities that spanned a range of undertakings from the purely philanthropic to the purely commercial and involved both for-profit businesses and non profit organisations as well as various hybrid entities" (Dobkin Hall 2013, 24). Dobkin Hall also highlights an expanding diversity of nonprofits which forms the platform for social enterprises. "Non profits were once constrained by legal definitions of charity that required them to serve a fairly narrow range of charitable, educational, or religious purposes; today all that the law requires of non profits is that they not distribute their surpluses (if any) in the form of dividends and that their beneficiaries be a general class of persons rather than specific individuals." Since nonprofits are not given automatic tax exemption in most states, social enterprises are vulnerable through hostility to non-profit commerciality (Dobkin Hall 2013, 60; 2006, 57).

Kerlin (2006) also describes the emergence of North American social enterprise. Responding to a downturn in the economy in the late 1970s, the 1980s brought welfare retrenchment and large cutbacks in federal funding resulting in the loss of some $38bn for nonprofits outside the health care field (Salamon and Anheier 1997b). Nonprofits began to seize on social enterprise as a way to fill the gap left by government cutbacks dramatically expanding the use of non-profit commercial activity (Crimmins and Keil 1983; Eikenberry and Kluver 2004; Young 2003; cited in Kerlin 2006, 251). With decline in funding from governments, these developed business activities, so that in certain cases they became "social enterprises (Borzaga and Defourny 2001, Nyssens 2006)" (Fecher and Lévesque 2008, 694).

Thus, in the United States, nonprofits moved into social enterprise activities to finance provision of services. Reliance on these models has driven UK social enterprise policy in the direction of the market and further away from concepts of a social economy and social solidarity.

Filer and Wolfenden

The UK's Wolfenden Commission in 1978 coincided with the Filer Commission report on Private Philanthropy and Public Needs in 1977. Both sought to define nonprofits and the third sector. Rochester comments (Rochester 2013, 45):

> To a great extent, the comparative indifference or hostility of the state and the weakness of sector-wide organisation in the USA have been counterbalanced there by the development of a strong and comparatively well-resourced non-profit academic community and lobby, which has also made a contribution to the vigour of the voluntary sector concept in Britain.

The main difference from the UK is that non-distribution or "non inurement" continues to form a basis for US tax exemption and continues to dominate policy on nonprofits. Thus in the United States, these developments have been "synonymous with non profit organisations, focuses solely on economic activities and assumes the third sector 'exists with some meaningful degree of independence from the state and the corporate sector'" (Alexander 2010, 213). In Europe, the distinction is not between profit and non-profit groups, but between "maximising returns for individual investors and collective or mutual benefit" (214).

Rose-Akerman comments on this favourable treatment of nonprofits. She argues that there is no market in ownership shares to discipline run away managers. The success of the non-profit sector is viewed as an artefact of favourable treatment by government. Exempt from the corporate income tax and the property tax, nonprofits can thrive even when they fail to attract many private donations (Rose-Ackerman 1996, 717). She concludes that there is little doubt that "non profits will continue their dominance in religion and the government's role will remain small in light of the constitutional guarantees of religious freedom and free speech" (725). All this represents a different environment and context compared with emerging third sector discourses in the UK.

It is against this non-profit background that Dees wrote his "Meaning of Social Entrepreneurship" (1998b), with its many interpretations that followed. As an example, Jeff Boschee set up the US Institute for Social

Entrepreneurs in 1999, having previously been President and Chief Executive of the US National Center for Social Entrepreneurs. His contribution is significant, since he was a consultant with the Social Enterprise Unit in the DTI from 2001 till 2004 (Boschee and McClurg 2003). This shows one of the avenues through which North American interpretations have made headway in the UK.

EMES and WISEs

Apart from North American influences, in other UK contributions there has been excessive reliance on the interpretation of social enterprise by the EMES. The EMES WISE model descends from an extended lineage of third sector structures which have traditionally delivered public services in many European countries. Especially in France the WISE model under the RMI programme was later further enhanced with European funding. EMES has become a dominant discourse for these market models, which in the UK has meant the marginalisation of other mainland European contributions on the wider social economy. The EMES WISE model is only applicable to a smaller number of UK social enterprises which project their future within a procurement market for public service delivery.

UK reliance on these North American and EMES marketised approaches has excluded other European and Canadian literatures on a social economy, so that the effect of neglecting other discourses and narratives had meant that an opportunity for development of a social economy for the UK has been forgone, with a restricted path for marketised social enterprises charted for the future. The only part of the UK which still retains the possibility of moving into a more EU mainland or Quebec regime is Scotland, where the Scottish Government still funds considerable third sector infrastructure.

RMI

The EMES WISEs approach began from a proliferation of a temporary employment subsidies. WISEs as "labour market programs provided new support for hiring or retraining unemployed people in not-for-profit organisations, while the development of quasi markets fostered contractual relations with public authorities in a more competitive environment" (Defourny and Nyssens 2010c, 39). The main difficulty for contributions which seek to interpret this model for the UK is that there is no similar UK funding programme – though EU funding has been used to support UK WISEs. WISEs and wage subsidy programmes are expensive.

The main component of this subsidy was the RMI, based on a 1987 report on homeless projects. The French National Assembly voted for its introduction in 1988. "The RMI is the main means-tested benefit and is claimed by 43% of the working age population receiving benefits in mainland France and up to 64% in overseas departments" (Legros 2009, 13). RMI recipients received significant employment contract subsidies (Legros 2009, 17):

> Job seeker's contract – minimum employment income. This contract is offered to recipients of means-tested benefits (RMI-API-ASS). It is for a minimum period of 20 hours work, for a maximum of 18 months, paid at the minimum hourly wage. ...The employer receives the amount of the RMI and is exempted from paying any social security contributions.

The RMI recipient undertakes to participate in certain acts while the community generates resources to enable completion of his or her project in addition to paying the financial benefit. Support includes services to develop social independence, public employment services, improving professional skills, internships and subsidised employment (Legros 2009, 18).[2] This represented an "insertion contract" with the state to integrate clients into the labour force ('insertion'), where the state provided the funds and non-profit organisations and local government agencies implemented the contract (Archambault 1997, 125). Since work integration was key to the RMI Programme, during the 1990s, various associations made reintegration of the excluded their objective. "They intervene in very different spheres, receive public funds, and often work in partnership with the state, social workers, or administrative personnel belonging to local communities in particular, with which they are associated in setting up fixed-term local projects" (Boltanski and Chiapello 2005, 350).

RMI and WISEs

RMI resulted in a large expansion of temporary work in France. "In the second half of the 1980s, the total of temps, trainees and fixed-term contracts increased from approximately 500,000 in 1978 to around 1,200,000 in 1989. In March 1995, they stood at more than 1,600,000, or a little under 9% of wage earners. In 1997, their number increased still further" (Boltanski and Chiapello 2005, 225). RMI developments have enabled recent EMES literatures to use a narrower conceptual overview of social enterprise. "Most of the (WISE) schemes established from the 1990s onwards offer temporary compensations for "temporary unemployability" of the employees and intend to support the transition from unemployment to employment in the "regular labour market" (Defourny and Nyssens 2008, Van Opstal, Deraedt and Gijselinckx 2009, Deraedt and Van Opstal 2009, Jacobs et al. 2012, Jacobs and Gijselinckx 2013)" (De Cuyper, Jacobs and Gijselinckx 2015, 270).

EMES published a series of research papers (Defourny and Nyssens 2006; Defourny 2001; Defourny, Pestoff and EMES 2008; Defourny, Develtere and Fonteneau 1999; Defourny and Nyssens 2006; Defourny and Shin-Yang Kim 2011), which describe third sector and social enterprise structures in a contemporary marketplace. These offer a different vision of society from Lipietz, French Regulationists and CIRIEC, as described in detail in Chapter 3. Fecher and Lévesque (2015) compare the social economy of CIRIEC (Monzón and Chaves 2008) with social enterprise as proposed by EMES (Laville et al. 1999). For CIRIEC, the social economy includes non-commercial sectors whereas for EMES the social enterprise excludes the non-commercial. The EMES version "could not really distinguish itself from that which predominates in the USA ... because of the lack of the democratic dimension, a conditio sine qua non for the social economy" (Fecher and Lévesque 2015, 184). Following Claude Vienney (2000) the definition of academic social economy was further established, after Leon Walras, combining economics, law and sociology, with "references to social justice or to the irrelevance of explanations based solely on the market (Vienney [2000] p38)" (Demoustier et al. 2006, 14).

Fecher and Lévesque compare social enterprise with the social economy. "The conceptualizations of academics limit themselves here to the comparison of the social economy advanced by CIRIEC (Chaves and Monzón Campos) with the social enterprise proposed by the research network EMES (Borzaga, Defourny and Nyssens)".

The concept was extended. Contemporary social enterprises expanded the scope of beneficiaries, previously reserved for their own members, in order to attend to different excluded groups or even an entire community" (Gonçalves, Carrara and Schmittel 2015, 1595). Though Defourny and Nyssens (2010c) and Kerlin (2010) and others describe the context of public funding reductions, their focus on earlier structures is minimal. "The study of these enterprises is the object of a European programme, at the heart of the network of EMES researchers" (Borzaga, Defourny and Adam 2001)" (Demoustier and Rousselière 2004, 19).

Defourny and Nyssens describe four different types of WISEs. The first group offers occupational integration supported by permanent "subsidies" – those for the handicapped. A second group provides permanent, self-subsidised employment to people disadvantaged in the labour market, including UK community businesses and social firms. A third type mostly aims to (re)socialise people through productive activities, including sheltered employment. The fourth group offers transitional employment or traineeships, most of which operate fixed-term contracts and include UK Intermediate Labour Market organisations (Defourny and Nyssens 2006, 15, 16).

Defourny (2001) and other EMES authors suggest that social enterprises, unlike traditional NGOs and nonprofits, engage in continuous production of goods and/or services and take economic risks, with bankruptcy as a possible outcome. A minimum amount of paid work, ie. a workforce not only composed of volunteers, is also suggested as an element differentiating social enterprise (Huybrechts and Nicholls 2012, 36). Earlier EMES descriptions of co-operatives in Italy, Belgium, France and Portugal are described above (Petrella and Richez-Battesti 2014, 149). But in an important distinction for the EMES approach, Defourny and Nyssens later explain this provision of goods and services (Defourny and Nyssens 2010c, 45):

> Accordingly, social enterprises, unlike some non-profit organisations, are normally neither engaged in advocacy, at least not as a major goal, nor in the redistribution of financial flows (as, for example, grant-giving foundations) as their major activity; instead, they are directly involved in the production of goods or the provision of services on a continuous basis.

There are challenges to this WISE activity. Policymakers have focused on the challenges of reproducing regimes of precarious work and mobilizing the poor for low-wage employment" (Peck and Tickell 2002, 390). The "economic realism" to achieve the social goal does not allow the workers to be deeply involved in management (Davister, Defourny and Grégoire 2004, 24). There are fears of "excessive confidence in market oriented social enterprises" by private organisations (foundations and corporations within corporate social responsibility strategies) or public policies to combat social problems with reducing budgets (Defourny and Nyssens 2010a, 49).

WISEs lack "the democratic dimension, a conditio sine qua non for the social economy". WISE directors seek to mitigate negative effects of diversity of stake holders by forming subgroups and by "arming themselves with appropriate institutional arrangements for a balanced representation" (Fecher and Lévesque 2015, 184, 189). These are "pseudo-market schemes as in the UK's 'New Deal' third-sector initiatives – preparing social economy initiatives to reintegrate with the market" (Moulaert and Ailenei 2005, 2049). This is registered most strongly in the neoliberal transition from welfare to workfare regimes in many national states in Europe, led by the UK (strongly influenced by the USA) (Hudson 2002, 330). "(T)hey are people whose self-responsibility and self-fulfilling aspirations have been deformed by the dependency culture, whose efforts at self-advancement have been frustrated for so long that they suffer from 'learned helplessness', whose self esteem has been destroyed" (Rose 1996, 59). This approach is endorsed by Giddens: "With expanding individualism should come an extension of obligations. Unemployment benefits, for example, should carry the obligation to look actively for work" (1998, 65).

Even in France, the birthplace of most WISEs, there is increasing scepticism about the model through increasing modulation of performance contracts. "To 'stick' to the predetermined return-to-work target, WISEs now face a trade off: pre-screen the employees being integrated or strengthen the mentoring" (Gianfaldoni and Morand 2015, 212). "Incentive contracts or performance-pay subsidies may induce some WISEs to provide little assistance to those with either insurmountable or high barriers to obtaining work, or who have little likelihood of achieving payable outcomes" (2015, 216).

This means that "changes in strategy by firms have been paid for largely by the community" and "firms maximize their profits by offloading on to the state – and to its detriment – costs bound up with maintaining the labour force". Habermas foresaw that this induces a legitimation crisis of the state, "because of a systematic overloading of the public budget" (Boltanski and Chiapello 2005, 376). Because regular work might be unrealistic, "any 'project' will be regarded as a (worthy) endeavour if it aims to help arrest 'marginalisation' ... is deemed to be a precondition for reconstructing links" (Boltanski and Chiapello 2005, 393). The EMES approach seeks to "reintegrate the individual as a stepping stone to full participation in society" and through "social management" of unemployment, to offer more fixed-term jobs. But this assumes that most without work are excluded from the labour market only because they need work preparation and that "economic recovery could eliminate unemployment through a resumption of corporate hiring" (Laville 1996, 46). Aglietta describes WISE approaches as "part of an extension of Fordism, based on the premise that the enterprise was still a vehicle of social integration ... It is hardly surprising, then, that such aid has had little effect ... The employment and poverty traps that this array of assistance schemes creates are being denounced from all sides" (Aglietta 1979, 444).

Though there are UK ILM programmes which offer work integration, they are rarely mentioned. "Although they often operated within the 'social economy' what has distinguished British and other ILMs from market focused social economy firms was that their primary purpose was improving employability and moving people into regular jobs as soon as possible" (Finn and Simmons 2003, 65). Most UK commentators have discounted the development of ILM operations, especially those promoted by the WISE

Group in Glasgow. Despite "substantial commitments of public funding and readily digestible measures of achievement – such as the training schemes designed to respond to unemployment in the 1980s, or the growth of contracts with social care providers in the 1990s" these were seen as "owned" by the Employment Department and Social Services (Kendall 2000, 546).

This need for additional funds was prompted by funding difficulties for those Christian Democrat governments to support active labour market policies (ALMP) beyond traditional passive employment related policies. Apart from France, few of these governments operated RMI programmes. One reason for neglect of earlier RMI funding of WISE delivery structures before New Labour may be that most UK contributions have relied on internet sources, so perhaps did not recognise the significance of RMI support.

Third sector and welfare reform

The direction of UK social enterprise and third sector policy has also been driven by third sector infrastructure organisations as policy entrepreneurs. The significance of representation for voluntary and community organisations at national level is not always recognised.

After the Wolfenden Report in 1978, it was the voluntary and community sector itself which laid foundations for later social enterprise policies under New Labour. In the UK and in Europe major policy drivers and deliverers of ALMP, especially in ILMs wage subsidy schemes (the UK version of WISEs), were TSOs rather than traditional left and social democrat forces as described by Esping-Andersen (1990). A pertinent comment about New Labour's belated recognition of the need to support communities in their own right is made by a former senior civil servant (Former Senior Civil Servant IV 2015):

> We had just had how many years of Thatcherism and Majorism where a lot of these organisations had been campaigning against things they didn't like. Now they needed to be, that energy needed to be harnessed not to complain about government but actually with money from government, because there was a lot of that, to take and go out there and make stuff happen and that's why it was so fast.

Though a post-Fordist period produced different welfare systems in the UK, the USA and continental Europe, most UK contributions have not recognised that work integration and other ALMP policies cannot be "bolted on" to existing programmes since, as in the RMI programme above, these involve cash transfer and wage payments to compensate for hardship or exclusion. While trade unions and social democracy fostered previous "passive" welfare policies such as unemployment benefits and pensions, European funding after deindustrialisation and austerity afforded more opportunity for voluntary and community organisations and social enterprises as service deliverers to become policy influencers. The ESF is especially relevant to the EMES WISE model, since its intervention rate effectively doubles the amounts available for wage subsidies and cash transfer payments. On account of their cost, without an RMI type programme, ALMP wage subsidy programmes are not usually prioritised. As an example of the significance of RMI support, the author retains a 1988 letter from Jacques Delors, in which President of the European Commission endorses the use of European funds for paying unemployment benefits.

Post-Fordist deindustrialisation, large-scale unemployment and complex social problems, with many not directly related to employment, necessitated different responses beyond passive benefits related to employment. Prior to ALMP development, Salamon et al. wrote "in the corporatist model, by contrast, extensive cooperation between government and the non-profit sector is anticipated, so that governmental sources are likely to be far more important" (Salamon and Anheier 1997b, 20). Through domination of corporatist welfare systems and influence from Christian Democracy through the Church and political parties in Germany, Italy and the Netherlands (Esping-Andersen 1990), provided that adequate funding is available, the evolution of social enterprise as a delivery vehicle in continental Europe has been more consensual than in the US or UK.

ALMP

"In many ways, Active Labour Market Policies (ALMP) are the most European of policy tools" (European Trade Union Congress 2019, para. 390), of which this is a comprehensive list (Martin and Grubb 2001, 4):

- Public employment services and administration includes the activities of job placement, counselling and vocational guidance, administering unemployment benefits and referring jobseekers to available slots on labour market programmes.
- Labour market training – vocational and remedial training for unemployed adults and for employed adults for labour market reasons.
- Youth measures – special programmes for youth in transition from school to work.
- Subsidised employment covers targeted measures to provide employment for the unemployed and other priority groups (excluding youth and the disabled).
- Special programmes for the disabled.

This need for additional programmes of active support is explained by "insider-outsider" labour markets – low unemployment alongside huge numbers of newly excluded or marginalised workers (Esping-Andersen 1996b, 76, 77). Defourny and Nyssens explain these policies in countries with a Bismarckian tradition, which, according to the Esping-Andersen typology, belong to a "corporatist" group, namely Belgium, France, Germany and Ireland. They describe how non-profit organisations, financed and regulated by public bodies, play an important role in the provision of social services (Defourny and Nyssens 2010c, 34).

Esping-Andersen describes post-industrial societal changes, including "much greater occupational and life cycle differentiation" and "more heterogeneous needs and expectations" with "two earner, double career units" alongside "a rise in divorced, single person, single parent households" (1996a, 9). "Welfare regimes must be identified much more systematically in terms of the inter-causal triad of state, market, and family" (1999, 35). Europe was leaving behind a social order that was much understood to enter another, the contours of which could be only dimly recognised (1990).

The role and influence of the third sector

Though the Introduction of this book describes the influence of TSOs as policy entrepreneurs, neither Esping-Andersen nor Hall and Soskice (Hall and Soskice 2001a) recognise their major roles in influencing welfare or labour market changes (Esping-Andersen 1996a; 1990; Hall and Soskice 2001b; Crouch 2005; Amable 2000; 2011). Though Esping-Anderson examines the influence of "working class mobilisation" and left influences and accords a role to the politics of Christian Democracy, he does not mention pressure from TSOs (1990). His classification of welfare states does not take into account their role, even though it has been documented that voluntary organisations play an important part in overall welfare service provision of most of the countries included in the typology (Kuhnle and Selle 1992, 15). Hall and Soskice's analysis is dominated by a description of Keynesian economics' being replaced by "a starkly utopian intellectual movement, aggressively politicised by Reagan and Thatcher in the 1980s before acquiring a more technocratic form in the self-styled "Washington consensus" of the 1990s" (Peck and Tickell 2002, 380). Much of this omission is because these analyses focused on transfer payments rather than services, which are easily deciphered.

Others confirm this absence from literatures and discourses of the third sector involvement. "In the welfare regime literature, the third sector is conspicuous by its absence" (Lewis 2004, 170). "The role of the third sector in service delivery is also absent in much of the comparative quantitative research to date" (Pestoff 2009, 78). "Not only has the influence of the third sector been left out of mainstream regime typologies but these approaches ignore the local level, where many government – third-sector partnerships appear to have been realised regardless of the type of regime" (Pestoff, Osborne and Brandsen 2006, 594). Pierson's interpretation is that the weakening of organised labour need not translate automatically into a commensurate weakening of the welfare state. He describes "maturing social programs" which develop new bases of organised support, autonomous from the labour movement, with moderate cutbacks carefully designed by a "de facto bipartisan coalition" and orchestrated to prevent a political outcry (Pierson 1996, 151, 161).

Iversen and Cusack point out that to account for increased welfare spending, and to understand the driving force behind expansion, "it is necessary to look beyond standard class-power explanations" (Iversen and Cusack 2000, 324). "In combination with the large losses in the traditional sectors, this has led to a tremendous reduction in employment possibilities for those formerly active" (Iversen and Cusack 2000, 315). Christian Democrat governments were less willing to compensate for losses of traditional jobs through expanding public service provision (Iversen and Cusack 2000, 338). So an expansion of third sector work integration structures formed part of their response.

The influence of the third sector is borne out elsewhere. As WISEs and TSOs became dependent on national and EU funding, Vaillancourt et al. confirm that relying solely on the state, it is difficult to obtain an adequate social and public policy. Some had "acquired the habit, in left-wing intellectual circles, of valuing intervention by the state in defining its role as if the state were the sole architect of social and public policy" (2013, 131). There has, however, been some belated recognition of the role of the third sector in UK contributions. Pressure from TSOs fed into a declared proactive stance in favour of recognising the benefits and potential contribution of a vibrant, active and engaged third sector (Haugh and Kitson 2007, 982). Third sector and social economy programmes aim to compensate for the simultaneous fragmentation of the traditional structures of market and state (Mayer 2003, 124).

However, Esping-Andersen later recognised a role for the third sector (Pestoff 2009, 222):

> In addition to the state, family and labour market, Esping-Andersen recognizes, in some footnotes in later works, the importance of another institution for producing welfare, that is, the third sector. He acknowledges that his triad should perhaps be extended by adding the third sector, since it plays "a meaningful, even significant, role in the administration and delivery of services.

Above all, most of these contributions take insufficient account of the emergence of ALMP and how these policies might be funded (OECD 2014, 183). As part of this process, there was an "embryonic pattern of interest intermediation emerging ... in which a series of peak organisations has been selected by the European Commission and placed in a 'structured context' that allows the Commission significantly to influence" issues and outcomes (Atkinson and Da Voudi 2000, 433). The European Commission rewarded states where organisations supported its policies, so that not only were third sector infrastructure organisations directly benefiting from EU funding, but support was available to enhance their lobbying in Brussels for this to be extended. "It funds EU-level groups and groups that promote a European identity through pro-EU activities, EU integration promotion, democracy and civic engagement promotion, and intercultural exchange and youth education and engagement" (Mahoney and Beckstrand 2011, 1358). As shown later, these developments are recognised as an important factor in third sector policy entrepreneurship in mainland Europe – to which the UK was only admitted as a late partner.

Having neglected and in contrast to these developments, in the UK Leadbeater and others argued for a different "new welfare settlement" based on third and private sectors as an agent of welfare reform (Leadbeater 1997, 18). They developed "welfare pluralism" as a concept only later pursued in several EU funded projects (Edmiston 2016a; 2016b; Edmiston and Nicholls 2017).

Christian Democracy and welfare

Mainland European third sector reactions to deindustrialisation and welfare reform have largely been influenced by the search of Christian Democrat welfare states for funding for ALMP. Instead of seeking additional funding, the UK saw a major political shift under New Labour which projected the third sector as a lower cost delivery contractor, competing against the private sector for public service delivery.

Laville et al. provide a good overall description of the role of mutuals in mainland Europe (2005, 3):

> [M]utual societies became social protection organizations complementary to compulsory schemes. They became subject to State-prescribed standards to supplement social transfers, even if it meant altering the principle of voluntary membership to be able to provide contingent and complementary support. In Denmark, Spain, France and Italy, mutual societies pooled their health insurance activities with those of administering health care and social welfare institutions.

Christian Democrat parties and politics were constantly under pressure from social democrat parties, trade unions and a post-Fordist threat from Communism. After the Paris Commune in 1871, Bismarck, who had been Ambassador to Paris, wrote that "to counteract such developments the state had to actively engage in issues stressed by social democrats and to implement what was legitimate in these demands" (Korpi 2008, 11). When they entered a post-Fordist period, Christian Democrat parties searched for funding for their interpretation of ALMP.

Early welfare state reforms were rarely, if ever, initiated by socialists. The "most influential answer came from those who show that Christian Democracy (or Catholicism) constitutes a functional equivalent or alternative to social democracy" (Van Kersbergen 2003, 24; see also Wilensky 1981; Korpi 2008, 5). The need for additional funding to support ALMP policies cannot be understood without understanding the influence of Christian Democrat policies. Eligibility for benefits is based on a combination of contributions and on belonging to a specified occupational category" (Korpi and Palme 1998, 668). A Protestant and Catholic coalition in the Netherlands and Christian Democratic parties in Germany produced similar welfare patterns. Christian Democratic parties seek to ameliorate suffering resulting from inequities of the marketplace and to help the privileged maintain their position in the face of adversity or old age, rather than to replace or shape the market itself (Huber, Ragin and Stephens 1993, 717).

In many contributions, especially those from the UK, there has been "little or no account of political intermediation" or of the political domination of Christian Democracy (Van Kersbergen 2003, 11). Lynch comments that in Italy a Christian Democrat Welfare State has meant few publicly provided services, particularly for families; a male-breadwinner bias in both tax and transfer systems; and a tendency to devolve authority over delivery and implementation of social policy to non-state actors (2009, 93). She concludes that the passive familialism of a welfare state that leaves social service provision to non-state actors derives from the liberal state's choice not to challenge the Church's control over this domain (115). While Christian Democrat welfare systems sufficed for passive labour market benefits, they were inadequate for funding delivery of ALMP. There were also problems with the "explosion" in cost of pensions (Esping-Andersen 1996a, 73) and some tax systems still had punitive tax treatment of working wives. Christian Democrat power has been a major obstacle to the economic emancipation of women and does not acknowledge the primacy of politics (Van

Kersbergen 2003, 175, 186). "Post war Christian Democracy in power has indeed fostered a distinctive political economy, social capitalism" (Van Kersbergen 2003, 237).

As shown by Van Kersbergen, Esping-Andersen and others (Van Kersbergen 2003; Esping-Andersen 1990), welfare systems in France, Belgium and Spain are similar. Huber et al. explain the search for their additional funding: "Accordingly, public sector expansion is less central and expansion of transfer payments more central to this political project than the social democratic project. Finally, this implies a lesser willingness to expand taxation" (Huber, Ragin and Stephens 1993, 718). ALMP are thus carried out by arms' length organisations, rather than directly by the state. Welfare systems based on Christian Democracy are "not associated with quality of social rights outside labour market or redistributive effects of taxes and transfers" (Huber, Ragin and Stephens 1993, 718). This more limited conception of the appropriate role of the welfare state vis-a-vis the market held by Christian Democratic parties emphasises transfer payments (Huber, Ragin and Stephens 1993, 740).

European funding for ALMP

As Christian Democrat welfare systems encountered funding problems in moving beyond insurance-based systems and into ALMP, WISEs have become the dominant delivery agents these policies. Whether they are mainly funded through the market (including public sector contracts), through public subsidies or through donations or volunteering (Davister, Defourny and Grégoire 2004, 15), public subsidies and funding are important. "This latter situation (primacy of work integration) is particularly true for a majority of WISEs in countries such as Denmark, Germany or France, where most public subsidies they receive seem clearly linked to ALMP and/or to specific profiles of disadvantaged unemployed persons" (Campi, Defourny and Grégoire 2006, 35). In addition to EU funds, other sources of funding include subsidies, donations and volunteering, revenue from trading, grants, exemption from social security contributions through volunteering, and funding agreements and contracts with various government departments and structures (Spear and Bidet 2003, 19).

For individual countries, Anheier et al. describe their dependency in Germany on public sector funding. They explain that "non profit welfare agencies have become central actors in the provision of social and health care services … the welfare agencies became ever more dependent on government support" (Anheier, Toepler and Sokolowski 1997, 191) Bode describes the strong role of French and German third sector structures before they were described as WISEs: "Regarding the whole field, it has to be stated that, above all, it is very much dependent on public policies. These policies are increasingly oriented towards creating employability and towards strategies of rapid placement" (Bode 2006, 14). Vidal provides a similar description of the background of Spanish WISEs. The success of co-operatives and worker-owned companies that appeared in response to the industrial crises of the late 1970s to mid-1980s provided a chastising lesson for those determining employment policy (2005, 809). Kerlin also describes "the institutional environment for strategic support of social enterprise" as "much more tied to government and European Union support … Public authorities' legal recognition of social enterprise integration through work does allow, in most cases, a more stable access to public subsidies, but in a targeted and limited way" (Kerlin 2006, 256).

In contrast, only a small number of UK contributions show the importance of public and external funding. "One major source of financial support for Intermediate Labour Markets (ILMs) was provided by EU funding. These were delivered by 'integration' and 'insertion enterprises' or co-operatives and "community businesses." In contrast to market-based mainland European programmes, UK ILMs paid wages for "real work" (Finn and Simmons 2003, 18, 19). "The turnover of UK ILMs more than doubled (118%) since 2000/2001, with the non-New Deal ILMs increasing by 248%. The European Commission developed a systematic approach to these and has supplemented direct financial support with reviews of impacts and best practice (Finn and Simmons 2003, 29, 65).

Though this does not usually feature in contributions on the development of social enterprise and the third sector, there is a wide range of literature describing the use of EU funding for ALMP (Depedri 2014; Graziano, Jacquot and Palier 2011, 19; Jacquot, Ledoux and Palier 2011, 42; Johnson 2007, 6; Kleinman and Piachaud 1993, 9; Obinger, Leibfried and Castles 2005, 558, 568; Stiller and van Gerven 2012, 129; Van Gerven, Vanhercke and Gürocak 2014, 523; Verschraegen, Vanhercke and Verpoorten 2011, 56; Viso 2010, 369).

The search for funding for ALMP "shifted the debate from merely focusing on the issues of income inequality and material exclusion, to incorporating the social and cultural dimensions of the exclusionary processes" (Atkinson and Da Voudi 2000, 438). The EMES WISE model emerged because there was little pressure to widen funding for the social economy beyond work insertion, "because it would require a major politico-ideological shift on the part of Member States with regard not only to their systems of citizenship but also their welfare regimes and an expansion of the Commission's role" (442).

For the author, a more detailed examination of mainland European Christian Democrat politics shows that while corporatist welfare systems were adequate during periods of substantial growth until the 1970s, after the RMI Programme in France, for ALMP EU funding was later necessary to broaden the range of delivery agents. Despite many contributions from the EMES on work integration, labour market and care related services, most UK contributions usually do not recognise their need for substantial funding programmes or the role of the RMI Programme in fashioning WISEs.

European social economy and UK neoliberal market

Influenced by EMES and WISE models, UK TSOs moved to a marketised approach, with an expanding role of public service delivery by contract. Boltanski and Chiapello support the author's appraisal of the UK position (Boltanski and Chiapello 2005, 178):

> The history of Great Britain is a very different one, having been marked by the Thatcher revolution. Indications are that different organisational models and spirits of capitalism will ultimately prevail in each of these two countries: that they will be more market-oriented in Great Britain (in the sense that our justificatory regime analysis lends to this term); and more "connectionist" in France.

Following Jessop's analysis, the Schumpeterian Workfare Postnational State emerging in the UK had three key features: (a) the "hollowing out" of the form and functioning of the national state; (b) a "resurgence of local and regional governance" embracing a medley of stakeholders; and (c) a subordination of Keynesian social and regional redistributive policies in favour of supply-side initiatives to promote international structural competitiveness (MacLeod and Jones 1999, 578). These ideas provided a "seedbed of a Thatcherite societal paradigm of a 'popular capitalism' and the 'enterprise culture'" (MacLeod and Jones 1999, 585). "The reorganisation of the state under the past Thatcher governments has been marked by permanent improvisation, trial and error and institutional Darwinism (Jessop et al. 1988)" (O'Toole 1996, 34).

Despite this, the author contends that developments in mainland Europe, especially in France, were relevant for the UK. In 1981, Aglietta, Boyer, Coriat and Lipietz as Regulationists became advisors in Mitterrand's "Union de la Gauche" government in France. Mitterrand "pursued old-style Keynesianism in one country (a return to an already exhausted mode of regulation), together with a more productivist restructuring programme to make French industry more competitive, based on technological modernisation" (Jessop 1997, 509). While this was happening, the UK Labour Party headed in the direction of "market socialism" (Le Grand and Estrin 1989) and began to lose sight of common origins with co-operatives and associations, so that it now refers to the third sector rather than the social economy (Dancuse, Bouchard and Morin 2013, 100).

There are major differences between the French and UK approaches. A distinct macroeconomic model of development in France, the specification of its characteristics and its explanation constitute the fundamental claims made in theories of regulation (Dunford 1990, 315). "In France, the contemporary (as of the 1980s) re-emergence of the social economy as "'social and solidarity economy' is narrowly linked to the reaction against neoliberal principles and individualist ideology" (Moulaert and Ailenei 2005, 2041). But for the UK, the meaning of a social economy is still evolving and is susceptible to many often-contradictory interpretations (Pearce and European Network for Economic Self-Help and Local Development 1999, 2; Amin, Cameron and Hudson 2003, cited in Moulaert and Ailenei 2005, 2043).

UK exclusion from EU Social Chapter

Following the introduction of RMI in France, this sector organisations in mainland Europe benefitted from increased funding during the emergence of the EU Social Chapter under Jacques Delors as President of the European Commission from 1985 until 1994. The UK disputed EU competence in many of these areas, especially during Thatcher governments (Margaret Thatcher Foundation 2014). Despite this, across mainland Europe a grand coalition of EU member state governments, political parties, trade unions and EU TSOs agreed on an EU wide consensual approach, which resulted in an increasing contribution to member states' domestic welfare expenditure from the EU Commission.

A possible rapprochement between UK and European approaches was more difficult through UK exclusion under Thatcher and Major Governments from Delors' initial projects as President of the European Commission from 1985 to 1995 to progress an EU Social Chapter – during which period the author was a Member of the European Parliament. This exclusion may have contributed to some UK contributions' underestimation of the significance of EU member states using EU funds to augment delivery of public services, especially for programmes involving wage subsidies or cash transfers.

UK government resistance crystallised after Jacques Delors' address on the Social Chapter to the Trades Union Congress in Bournemouth on 08 September, which was abruptly followed on 20 September 1988 by Margaret Thatcher's Bruges speech: "We have not embarked on the business of throwing back the frontiers of the state at home, only to see a European super-state getting ready to exercise a new dominance from Brussels" (Margaret Thatcher Foundation 2014). Negotiations for the European Social Chapter included Recommendation 92/441/EEC on common criteria concerning sufficient resources and social assistance in social protection systems. (European Council of Ministers 1992). Laville et al. provided a good overall description (2005, 7):

> Extending these investigations, the European Commission conducted a programme to enhance the value of local initiatives intended to stimulate exploration and action in this area, in particular by reconfiguring structural funds, and via a pilot programme of the Directorate-General for Employment on the "third system" to get a better assessment of the system's impact on job creation.

The Commission's recommendation recognised "that economic growth alone is not sufficient to guarantee social integration and specific policies geared to that purpose are needed" (Ferrera, Matsaganis and Sacchi 2002, 228). On involvement of the third sector Ferrera et al. conclude: "The involvement of such organisations (and, arguably, of representatives of the poor and the socially excluded) could be made more substantial if semi-formal procedures of consultation were set up at national as well as European level" (Ferrera, Matsaganis and Sacchi 2002, 237). Through opposition from the UK Conservative government, this recommendation was never included within the 1992 Maastricht Treaty (Ferrera, Matsaganis and Sacchi 2002, 228):

> It highlighted "the multi-dimensional nature of social exclusion" and how "people with insufficient, irregular and uncertain resources are unable to play an adequate part in the economic and social life of the society in which they live and to become successfully integrated economically and socially".

The Delors' Commission established the Social Economy Unit in 1989. In its 2001 White Paper on European Governance, civil society was "identified as the key mechanism for bringing together the EU and its citizens" (Alexander 2010, 218). Discussions about the Social Chapter were led by those Northern European member states with Christian Democrat welfare systems. "This welfare regime was closely associated with the European social model promoted by Delors, which in turn was strongly linked to the notion of a social market economy" (Atkinson and Da Voudi 2000, 429). The main policy emphasis was based on the RMI minimum income guarantee for "re-inserting the young and long-term unemployed into the labour market" (434). All this encouraged development of an EMES WISE model.

　　Though an incoming UK Labour Government later ratified the Agreement on Social Policy to be included in the Treaty of Amsterdam in July 1997, this policy was downgraded to a request for the Commission to "encourage cooperation between the Member States and facilitate the coordination of their action as regards social policy (Article 140)". The Commission sought to augment the role of the third sector in these processes: "the holding of the first European Social Policy Forum in March 1996, which brought together over 1000 participants mainly from NGOs, on the eve of the beginning of the Intergovernmental Conference … a strong civil dialogue … alongside the policy dialogue with the national authorities and the social dialogue with the social partners" (European Commission 1997, 7).

Since little of this had been written into the Treaties of Maastricht in 1992 or Luxembourg in 1997, with dialogue left to member states, this was a process in which the UK was a late arrival. In 1999, the Commission published "A Concerted Strategy for Modernising Social Protection" (European Commission 1999, 12). After the Lisbon Summit in March 2000 and Nice Summit in December 2000, each member state was required to publish national plans for employment annually and for social protection biannually (European Commission 2000). Under an Article of the Treaty on the Functioning of the EU – the Treaty of Lisbon, December 2007 – work for Social Inclusion and Social Protection was again downgraded to the Social Protection Committee as an Advisory Body to Employment and Social Affairs Ministers in the Employment and Social Affairs Council.

However, despite its considerable dilution after Delors' initial endeavours for the Social Chapter, member states' earlier influence on use of EU Structural Funds for ALMP has endured in regulations for current 2014–2020 EU Programmes. ESF Regulation No. 1304/2013 is an example of current regulations which specifically refer to ALMP "Promoting social entrepreneurship and vocational integration in social enterprises and the social and solidarity economy in order to facilitate access to employment" (European Commission 2013, para. v).

Not only was New Labour too late joining in the pressure from other EU member states for increased EU funding for these ALMP but many UK contributions have not recognised the significance of these discussions.

Conclusion

Through failing to recognise a different context for North American nonprofits and perhaps through misreading an increased third sector role in public service delivery in mainland Europe, the UK has developed a social enterprise and third sector policy which is marketised and leading to the disintegration of many TSOs.

The funding difficulties described above for ALMP and the role of the TSOs as policy entrepreneurs do not feature in most UK contributions. In a completely different context in the UK, Leadbeater and others argued for a "new welfare settlement," based on the third sector as an agent of welfare reform (Leadbeater 1997). He argued that the social entrepreneur would become an effective and cheap alternative to the welfare state (Hulgård 2010, 296).

The most significant omission in many UK contributions which have relied heavily on the EMES WISEs model has been neglect of programmes like RMI in France and Christian Democrat welfare policies funding difficulties for ALMP. A combination of RMI programmes and EU funding has helped to shape various models of WISEs in mainland Europe, which are not easy to replicate in the UK without appropriate funding.

Some of this difficulty in understanding the funding problems of wage subsidy models, which are expensive, may be due to UK exclusion from initial EU Social Chapter discussions during the EU Presidency of Jacques Delors.

Notes

1 For further details about the marketisation of US nonprofits, see Eikenberry and Kluver (2004); J. A. Kerlin, 'Social Enterprise in the United States and Europe: Understanding and Learning from the Differences", *Voluntas: International Journal of Voluntary and Non-profit Organizations* (2006) 17 (3): 246; L. M. Salamon, 'The Marketization of Welfare: Changing Nonprofit and For-Profit Roles in the American Welfare State', *Social Service Review* 67 (1) (1993): 16–39; L. M. Salamon and H. K. Anheier, 'Defining the Nonprofit Sector: A Cross-National Analysis', *The State of Global Civil Society and Volunteering: Latest Findings from the Implementation of the UN NonProfit Handbook* (Baltimore, MD: Johns Hopkins University Press, 1997).

2 For further details of the RMI programme, see M. Legros, 'France: Minimum Income Schemes: From Crisis to Another: The French Experience of Means-Tested Benefits', *Report to European Commission* (2009), 1–27, https://ec. europa.eu/social/BlobServlet?docId=15304&langId=en.

7

Conclusions

This book has sought to show that though third sector and social enterprise historical antecedents are causal, they have been lost. Labour and Co-operative Movement political support has been replaced by a depoliticised sector which functions increasingly as a player in a competitive market for the delivery of public services. This has limited the development potential for a wider social economy, leaving models based on a marketised approach that are failing in the UK. Social enterprise structures are unable to maintain their values in a changed funding environment and academic contributions have failed to analyse the social economy as a means to advance better forms of local economic democracy. Social enterprise and the wider third sector have been institutionalised as a neoliberal agent for public service delivery, increasingly based on external private investment, with a shift from politics to practical solutions. They are now part of the welfare state and no longer necessarily considered as critical to democracy or economic development. UK and Scotland censi of social enterprise show that the sector is now fragmented, small, undercapitalised and unable to meet its social welfare expectations, with public and social values replaced by value for money, impact and output measurement and cost of delivery.

Neglect of sources

In contrast to most current academic contributions, the author, using a Critical Realist approach, has traced the antecedents of social enterprise and TSOs from an earlier period. Following earlier patterns of demi-regularities, which actualised through retroduction to produce causal mechanisms, most of these indigenous structures are ill-suited for the public service delivery role in which they are now cast.

Though significant influence is attributed to UK contributions from Leadbeater (Leadbeater 1997) and first North American definitions of social enterprise from Dees and others (Dees 1998a; 1998b), in most UK contributions there is almost no recollection of the role from 1978 onwards of Beechwood College, Leeds, which earlier described social enterprises in detail (Spreckley 1981). Neither is there reference to the many contributions on UK co-operatives from the Open University during the 1980s, despite their description of structures and registrations similar to today's social enterprises. Data collection and interviews for this book, with supporting evidence from ICOM and others, show that many local structures during earlier periods would today merit the description "social enterprise". Considerable data also shows that for thirty years after the Labour Government's first UP in 1968, the encouragement of local community structures in their own right was not a policy priority (Fordham and Victor Hausner and Associates 1991).

Data collection and interviews during the key 1998 to 2002 period demonstrate a sequence of events different to that in other UK contributions, representing a fundamental strategic change of direction. This shows a major paradigm shift, as interpreted by Kuhn and Hall (Kuhn 1962; Hall 1993) so that social enterprise was reinstitutionalised in a new normative role of public service delivery. Description and analysis of this paradigm shift are largely absent from most academic literature and discourse.

Community responses

1960s to 1980s developments have been described, since they are omitted from most UK academic contributions. Moulaert et al. describe three "waves of social innovation" in the second half of the twentieth century (2017, 18):

> [T]he "radical emancipation wave" of the 1960–70s, the neighbourhood and community (re)development period (1980s–2000) and the "social and solidarity economy", with received a new impetus with the financial crisis of 2008. ... The neighbourhood and community (re)development movement targeted urban neighbourhoods in decline due to industrial restructuring and threats by large development projects and worsening ecological conditions. ... It is in this last period that the emancipatory element was weakened in some SI research and the social economy became instrumentalised in the process of rationalising the welfare state, including privatising parts of the welfare state services.

Though Moulaert's first two waves are rarely described in most UK contributions, from the 1960s to the 1990s the UK showed many examples of Moulaert's first wave social innovation responses to deindustrialisation and job losses (Fordham and Victor Hausner and Associates 1991; Gostyn et al. 1981; Keltie and Meteyard 1991; Knight 1993; Woodin, Crook and Carpentier 2010). These responses to deindustrialisation (Hudson 2010) were later supported by local government frameworks for alternative local social economies and enterprise support agencies (Patel, Carter and Parkinson 1999a; 1999b; Wood, Reason and Egan 1999; Martinelli et al. 2003; Cornforth et al. 1988).

The author's contention about the omission of earlier developments is reinforced by Moulaert at al in their summary of recent policy (Moulaert et al. 2017, 19):

> [I]t tends to overlook the importance of grassroots initiatives movements and other players in the solidarity economy, the transition movement, the Co-operative Movements, post-foundationalism, the agro-ecological movement, neighbourhood and community organisations, seeking to team up their initiatives and scale out their democratic governance systems.

Many academic contributions still argue that the 1998 Memorandum and Articles of SEL (Social Enterprise London Ltd 1998) represented both a co-operative and Blairite Third Way (Haugh and Kitson 2007, 982). But the basis of Mulgan and Landry's advocacy of structural changes (Mulgan and Landry 1995) and Leadbeater's contribution was welfare reform and lower cost delivery, so that many of his conclusions pointed to the private sector (Leadbeater 1997, 78). By the time that Peck and Tickell wrote about the "mobilisation of the little platoons … in the service of neoliberal goals" (2002, 390), Conservative and New Labour administrations had "not only encouraged the expansion of the non-statutory sector, but attempted to shift the burden of welfare provision away from both the state and non-statutory agencies onto the shoulders of private citizens themselves" (May, Cloke and Johnsen 2005, 708). The operation of underlying causal mechanisms meant that any opportunity for promotion of community structures within an alternative social economy had already been overtaken by New Labour's transposition of the third sector. Many of these structures were now constrained in a contractual relationship with the state (Osborne and McLaughlin 2004, 580).

There is an unbroken chain of academic and other contributions for the promotion of a marketised UK social enterprise policy, stretching from Le Grand and quasi-markets in the 1980s (Le Grand 2013), through Mulgan et al. in the 1990s (Leadbeater 1997; Mulgan and Landry 1995; Leadbeater and Christie 1999) to Murray et al. (2010), which represent a New Labour contribution to welfare reform in the UK and then to later EU social innovation discourses. These contributions – many by the same authors – though they are sometimes described as a change from co-operative and mutual structures in initial New Labour years – are now reinvented as an "entrepreneurial/instrumental" interpretation of social innovation. All this took place in a context of marketisation – "pseudo-market schemes as in the UK's 'New

Deal' third-sector initiatives –preparing social economy initiatives to reintegrate with the market" (Moulaert and Ailenei 2005, 2049). "[T]he entrepreneurial discourse appears to dominate relevant EC policy documents and programmes" (Moulaert et al. 2017, 33). EU policy documents also reflect this. "[A]nother such barrier lies in a general culture that views the solution to social demands as a prerogative of public institutions, thereby giving only a passive role to citizens, stakeholders and users" (Hubert and Bureau of European Policy Advisers 2015, 115). Based on earlier NCVO managerialism and Demos policy initiatives, having secured the transformation of social enterprise within the UK, through similar causal mechanisms these same organisations later sought to dominate an EU policy perspective, based on earlier frameworks in the UK to promote a less accountable social enterprise in lower cost public services.

UK marketisation vs European and Quebec social economy

The author also argues that, apart from overlooking the significance of UK 1970s and 1980s indigenous structures, other contributions which support his main contention on the legitimate origins of earlier social enterprises and their original role and purpose have also been overlooked. Many current contributions neglect the "Regulationist approach" to deindustrialisation and Post-Fordism, led by Michel Aglietta and Alain Lipietz. During the 1980s Lipietz was developing the concept of a "third sector" (Lipietz 1989). Most UK contributions also overlook the wide range of contributions on a social and solidarity economy, especially from France and Quebec, which might have relevance for the UK (Eynaud et al. 2015; Biewener 2006; Bouchard 2012; Laville, Young and Eynaud 2015; Laville 1996; 2010b; 2010c; Laville et al. 2000; Lévesque 2013; Mendell, Lévesque and Rouzier 2000). Despite Lipietz's report to French Minister of Employment Martine Aubry in 2000, very few UK contributors recognise his projection of a role for social economy organisations which are distinctive from the state and private sector (Amin 2009, 31).

This means that most UK contributions are dominated by a North American marketised influence and the EMES focus on a WISE marketised variant of social enterprise, where economic and entrepreneurial dimensions are dominant (Amin 2009; De Cuyper, Jacobs and Gijselinckx 2015; Fecher and Lévesque 2015; Gianfaldoni and Morand 2015; Gijselinckx and Develtere 2008). EMES research focuses on "work integration of low qualified job seekers (Nyssens 2006)" or "aid for certain categories of disadvantaged persons (abused children, refugees, immigrants etc.)" (Defourny and Nyssens 2013, 43). Augmented by social investment and impact measurement, the author recognises that the task of returning social enterprise and third sector structures to the forms of their antecedents is now impossible.

Miscasting a role for social enterprise

Since UK social enterprise and the wider third sector are now transposed to providing piecemeal practical solutions in a market setting, many academic contributions fail to recognise any abandonment of a role for the social economy in local economic democracy. This constitutes a paradigm shift (Hall 1993; Kuhn 1962) to allow social enterprise to be reinstitutionalised in market competition against the private sector rather than as an alternative social economy as in mainland Europe. Despite surveys showing 1970s and 1980s indigenous community structures, many current contributions "overlook the importance of grassroots initiatives movements and other players in the solidarity economy ... seeking to team up their initiatives and scale out their democratic governance systems" (Moulaert et al. 2017, 19).

This "entrepreneurial/instrumental" interpretation of social enterprise as a welfare solution (Hulgård 2010) was "preparing social economy initiatives to reintegrate with the market" (Moulaert et al. 2017, 33). Successive UK inputs to various EU policy documents sought to cement this role by moving from "only a passive role to citizens, stakeholders and users" (Hubert and Bureau of European Policy Advisers 2015, 115). These approaches to social innovation are "interested in solutions to major social problems, based on entrepreneurial initiatives that emphasize philanthropy, individual responsibility, and the market more than the state" (Bouchard 2013, 7). Throughout this book, many TSOs are shown as small, fragmented and undercapitalised. Apart from their inability to meet increasing welfare expectations, many are collapsing in a funding regime dominated by procurement. Since largest numbers of UK social enterprises have turnovers of less than £100,000 and do not seek to participate in public sector tendering and procurement competitions, they now face significant difficulties. Despite these developments, the British Council continues to promote globally the latest variants of UK social enterprise (Catherall and Richardson 2014, 7).

Apart from recent social enterprise censi, the difficulties are highlighted in detail in a Convention of Scottish Local Authorities' Report for the National Community Planning Group (Garven et al. 2014, 25) which showed that of those surveyed "59% either no experience yet in contracting or feel that contracting is irrelevant to them". This means a gradual hollowing out the voluntary and community sector (Aiken and Harris 2017), within a policy framework which usually sets a precedent for social enterprises.

For the author, Rhodes, though writing in 1994, summarises the current situation (1994, 151):

> The process of hollowing out in British government is not another way of heralding the minimalist state of Thatcherite aims. It is more important; it is about redesigning governments to cope with scarcity and devising complex solutions to problems which defeat the simple-minded nostrums of both free markets and national plans.

Postscript

As a conclusion to this book, the author advocates policy prescriptions as an alternative to recent New Labour and Conservative developments. Since the 1980s and 1990s there has been a UK third sector history of the phasing out of grants, the introduction of loans and equity, a gradual infusion of external private investment and the prioritisation of impact measurement. Procurement, external investment and impact measurement are now dominant themes of social enterprise and third sector support. Initially, further research is needed on the effects of continuing these mechanisms and processes to support social enterprise and TSOs and their effect on their "hollowing out". As described throughout this book, the NVCO, Social Enterprise UK, Co-operatives UK, and other national TSOs have not only been willing participants but also policy entrepreneurs for these changes. Though latest developments involve Social Enterprise UK, Co-operatives UK and the Employee Ownership Association coming closer together to promote wider ownership, as part of their initiatives, governance frameworks for local community democratic accountability do not feature prominently.

Much local economic and social democracy has now disappeared. Apart from contributions above (Aiken and Harris 2017), others seek to describe consequences for the third sector and social capital (Roberts and Devine 2003, 315):

> [M]any advocates of social capital, advocates like Blair and Putnam, tend to downplay this historical context when they speak about civic renewal. As a result the inherent problems that accompany hollowing out processes, and which have a specific effect upon social capital, are also downplayed.

Much procurement has been dominated by a range of government proposals to use delivery by the third sector, whether knowingly or unwittingly, as an interim stage to promote the private sector. These include Article 77 of EU Procurement Directive 2014/24/EU, the Social Services and Wellbeing (Wales) Act 2014 and a range of proposals from the Co-operative Councils' Innovation Network, Co-ops UK, New Economics Foundation, NESTA and others to promote third sector structures in a highly competitive bidding process in a market which favours large private prime contracts, especially using payment by results. Since the Article 77 process will soon disappear under the UK government's "Tranforming Public Procurement" proposals (Cabinet Office 2020), preliminary indications are that public sector procurement will become an even more competitive market. Most of these market mechanisms lead to commissioning, procurement and contracts based on lowest price tenders, with a deteriorating standard of service. Many local councils now recognise that these policies are failing, with growing numbers of private and third sector providers "handing back" contracts because they cannot recruit or retain staff to deliver at the contract price. Little research is so far available on the results for social enterprises and TSOs from all of this.

The author believes that there are feasible and attainable policy prescriptions as an alternative. As an example, state support for accountable local community renewable energy, environmental and recycling initiatives would be more efficient and effective than exclusive reliance on corporate claims of their contributions to implementation of the UN Sustainable Development Goals. Selection and funding for new social enterprise and third sector initiatives should be prioritised for their restoration of local economic democracy rather than cut-price outsourcing. Through financial and other reasons not all of these organisations join in membership of NCVO, Social Enterprise UK, the Co-operative Party and Co-operatives UK.

There is a wealth of local development expertise among these organisations. But, instead of building on this, New Economics Foundation in its report to the Co-operative Party on "doubling the size of the cooperative economy" sought changes in the procurement market so that more co-operatives could compete (Lawrence, Pendleton and Mahmoud 2018). Many larger cities, including Greater Manchester, Plymouth, Sheffield and Preston have now established Co-operative Commissions or Community Wealth Building initiatives which will hopefully provide similar advice, funding expertise to that which was available following the 1978 Co-operative Development Agency Act. Sheffield and others are developing a series of "ownership hubs". There are also projects for the revival of a local social economy, as in the Liverpool Social Economy Forum, with its Kindred financial arm. But what is still missing from some – though not all – of these initiatives is the indigenous local community pressure which led to local structures in the 1970s and 1980s.

Within the health and care sector, further alternatives should be available to social enterprise and TSOs, as they are increasingly drawn into competition with the private sector for provision of Self-Directed Support, under some of whose models, the service recipient becomes both budget holder and service manager (Henderson et al. 2019). Other social enterprises have been drawn into delivery of social investment and social impact bond projects, though there is little evidence of any more funding stability under these programmes. Without the involvement of private investors, which seeks returns based on outcome payments, government departments and larger local authorities could set up Innovation Funds, into which bids could be invited from partnerships of public and TSOs – though these should be modelled on a different basis from the SRB and City Challenge in Chapter 4.

There are already precedents under Scottish Government programmes for Public Social Partnerships (PSPs), funded under previous EU EQUAL programmes. Under these, the public and third sectors jointly work on service delivery. Much of this approach was echoed in the Report of the Christie Commission on the Future Delivery of Public Services, which included (Christie Commission 2011, pt. 10):

> [P]ublic service organisations work together effectively to achieve outcomes – specifically, by delivering integrated services which help to secure improvements in the quality of life, and the social and economic wellbeing, of the people and communities of Scotland.

Between 2005 and 2007, three PSP pilots in Scotland were funded under the EU EQUAL Programme. In 2011, the Scottish Government funded a further ten pilots and in 2011 also published a detailed practical guide (Scottish Government 2011). Further funding programmes have sought to encourage collaborative provision of services and under the Developing Markets programme around 40 PSPs have been supported.

There are also UK government precedents. A worthwhile New Labour policy innovation was the "Better Government for Older People" (BGOP) programme (Younger-Ross 1998, 237). "Bids were encouraged from agencies interested in becoming pilot sites demonstrating or exploring positive engagement of older people" twenty-eight sites were chosen and activities were evaluated in reports from Warwick University (Jolley 2002, 90). BGOP was also promoted by the co-operative ChangeAgents (2015) and led to an Older People's Advisory Group to influence national and local policy and service provision for older people. This national action research initiative was steered by a consortium of six partners: Service First Unit in the Cabinet Office (Office of Public Service), Age Concern, Anchor Trust, Carnegie Third Age Programme, Help the Aged and Warwick University Local Authorities' Research Consortium. The Programme "developed ways to meet older people's needs better through improved information dissemination and different service delivery, including greater involvement of older people themselves" (Comptroller and Auditor General 2003, 23). These initiatives sought to change how they delivered services, leading to better transport provision and improved house design and repair services to help people stay in their homes. Some pilots undertook ground-breaking work on user-focused arrangements for joint care assessment and management (Comptroller and Auditor General 2003, 34).

Based on the approaches of the BGOP or PSPs, funding bids could be invited for Economic Democracy Projects. Together with service users, these should include statutory providers, trade unions and TSOs. Though a further £800mn has been projected by the Cabinet Office from pensions, insurance and securities dormant accounts under Labour's 2008 Dormant Bank Accounts Act (Weakley 2021) no further details have been provided. The Commission on Dormant Assets estimated that inclusion of further asset categories could lead to an extra £1–2bn of funding being transferred from "multiple financial services and non financial services products" for the "eventual benefit of good causes" (O'Donohoe and Dormant Assets Commission 2017, 6, 9).

There are also various public utility banking proposals which might initially be investigated at local rather than national level (Blackburn 2018, 14; Gowan 2009, 61; Mellor 2010, 29, 155; Meadway 2013, 29). Mondragon's Laboral Kutxa, its Caja Laboral credit union, German Sparkasse and other public or co-operative banks have all gradually evolved as banking systems rather than through one piece of legislation. Preston and other local initiatives are already exploring community investment banks. A further opportunity might be solutions based on enhancement of Co-operative and Community Finance (the former ICOF) and Community Development Finance Institutions, especially following a report on their sustainability for a previous Conservative government (Price Waterhouse Cooper 2015). Another possibility is a UK version of the US Community Reinvestment Act 1977 (Federal Deposit Insurance Corporation 2018), which requires deposit-taking institutions to meet credit needs of local communities.

The author hopes to continue projecting these alternatives beyond the publication of this book.

Appendix 1: Timeline of main literature contributions and events in the UK, North America and mainland Europe

Note: UK, **North America**, *Europe*.

Date	Event	Outcome
1968	Labour Government's first Urban Programmes spurred by Powell's "Rivers of Blood" speech. (Eileen) Younghusband Report funded by Calouste Gulbenkian Foundation.	Community Development Projects in 12 small scale areas. "Community Work and Social Change: A Report on Training". Report reviewed the value and purposes of community work and made recommendations on the training available and should be further developed.
1969	**Ladder of Participation.**	**Steps for levels of Community Involvement (Sherry Arnstein 1969).**
1969	Skeffington Report.	Recommended limited community participation in planning decisions (Arthur Skeffington MP and Ministry of Housing and Local Government, 1969).
1969	Calouste Gulbenkian Foundation funding for publication of initiatives for community development.	Beginning of recognition of need for direct community support.
1971	After formation of the Scott Bader Commonwealth in 1951, 1971 Industrial Common Ownership Movement (ICOM) "born out of the ashes of Democratic Integration in Industry (DEMINTRY)".	DEMINTRY had campaigned for twelve years for owners of businesses to convert their firms into "Common Ownerships" (Campbell 1983, 1). ICOM Working Party recommended Revolving Loan Fund.

Appendix 1 (Continued)

Date	Event	Outcome
1973	Workers' Occupation of Meriden and KME. Scottish Daily News.	Workers formed workers' cooperatives.
November 1973	Commission on Private Philanthropy and Public Needs (Filer Commission) – sought to regularise foundations' taxation exemptions and other problems. Death of John D. Rockefeller July 1978 stymied efforts of Filer report supporters. Rejected by US Treasury Secretary in Carter Administration.	To study role of philanthropic giving and make recommendations regarding ways to strengthen and increase effectiveness of voluntary sector. 19 recommendations in three main categories: – Broadening Base of Philanthropy – Improving Philanthropic Process – A Permanent Commission. Less significant 'Independent Sector' disbanded.
1973	Boyle Committee Report.	"Current Issues in Community Work". Reviewed major features of community work and suggested need to establish area resource centres, a national resource centre for community work, national forums and a national fund for community work projects.
1974	Labour Government. ICOM (Freer Spreckley 1981, 9).	Funding for Meriden, Kirkby Manufacturing Enterprises and Scottish Daily news. 13 Common Ownership firms registered with ICOM.
1976	Northern Federation of Wholefood Collectives (FNWC) Industrial Common Ownership Act.	30 separate wholefood collectives. 60 wholefood trading collectives by 1977. From David Watkins MP Private Members Bill. ICOM definition and £250,000 . ICOM Membership 50 by 1977 (Freer Spreckley 1981, 10).
1977	Peter Shore MP Inner Cities White Paper.	Beginning of more focused approach in inner cities.

Appendix 1 (Continued)

Date	Event	Outcome
1978	Wolfenden Committee Report. Cooperative Development Agency Act.	First detailed overall review of third sector. Mentions "a report published by the Calouste Gulbenkian Foundation, a Community Work Group under the chairmanship of Lord Boyle". Wolfenden questioned "whether the statutory sector can continue to grow as it has over the last three decades.... and whether even the existing allocation of resources between the statutory and non-statutory services is the most desirable one" (Wolfenden 1978, 24). Initial budget of £900,000 to support and promote cooperatives.
1978	Beechwood College, Leeds begins training for Cooperative Developments Agencies and social enterprises.	£170,000 initial funding from European Social Fund. "Social enterprise started in the late 1970s as a definition of good practice in cooperatives and commercial organisations that adopted Social Accounting and Audit as part of their normative annual measurement" (Freer Spreckley 2015, 2).
1979	*A Theory of Capitalist Regulation: the US Experience (Aglietta 1979).*	*Aglietta's earliest criticism of WISEs using Regulationist approach (Aglietta 1979, 444):* *"The employment and poverty traps that this array of assistance schemes creates are being denounced from all sides. The time has come for a political blueprint for a radical reform of the redistribution system."*
1979	ICOM (Campbell 1983, 2, 3).	138 new co-operatives registered. ICOM introduces new "company" model for common ownership, a development programme (funded by the EEC) aimed at persuading Local Authorities to use resources to assist common ownerships.

Appendix 1 (Continued)

Date	Event	Outcome
1980	Ashoka Foundation (Changemakers). Hansmann, Henry.	Encouragement for individual social entrepreneurs The Role of Nonprofit Enterprise (Hansmann 1980b, 89, 5).
1980	ICOM (Campbell 1983, 2, 3).	182 new firms register through ICOM. ICOM joins main worker co-operative federations in Italy, France and Holland in the formation of an EEC-wide Federation called CECOP. London ICOM employ staff with grant from GLC. One new cooperative formed every day.
June 1981	"Social Audit: A Management Tool for Cooperative Working". Basic definitions of social enterprise and guidance for future formations.	"To rely on fiscal control to redress the inequalities in the free market economy is like painting over rust in the hope it will disappear. ... The causes of inequality are primarily associated with the system of ownership" (Freer Spreckley 1981, 14). "The external element of the Social Enterprise Audit model is designed to open dialogue with the local community. This would include discussion of the currencies in use, the contribution or cost of the co-operative to the local community and an appreciation of alternative methods of measuring performance" (Freer Spreckley 1981, 18).
1981 and 1982	"Whose Business is Business". Centre for Employment Initiatives report on local community structures.	Wide survey of 1970s structures across the UK, which described "community companies (limited by guarantee or by shares), community co-operatives, workers co-operatives, neighbourhood co-operatives, and a variety of 'purpose-built' models" (Gostyn et al. 1981, 3). Like common ownership cooperatives, newer community controlled enterprises place far less emphasis on distribution of profits or gains to membership (Stares 1982, 14).

Appendix 1 (Continued)

Date	Event	Outcome
1980s	Rapid 1980s growth of co-ops.	60 Local Cooperative Development Agencies supported by local authorities provided start-up assistance. Over 10 years, triggered creation of 1,176 co-ops employing 6,900 people (Cornforth et al. 1988). Worker cooperative numbers rose from 73 in 1975 to 1200 in 1992 (Cornforth et al. 1988). As the main registration body, after 1976 ICOM registered over 2,700 cooperatives (Cooperative Commission 2001, 73). Many accounts of the development of cooperatives during the 1980s showed up to 1500 of these organisations across the UK. (Sawtell 2009b; 2009a; Cornforth et al. 1988; Cornforth 1983; Ridley-Duff 2009).
1981	*Aglietta, Lipietz and Regulationist advisers join Mitterrand "Union de la Gauche" Government.*	*Mitterrand French Government elected on similar manifesto to Labour Party's 1983 Manifesto.*
1982	Salamon and Abramson.	Called attention to dependence on government subsidy, with federal funding constituting between a third and three-quarters of organizational revenues (Salamon and Abramson 1992).
June 1983	Labour Party Election Manifesto.	Includes commitment on funding cooperatives. Based on 1980 NEC Working Group recommendations.
November 1983	*EU Commission Community Action to Combat Unemployment: The Contribution of Local Employment Initiatives: Communication of the Commission to the Council. COM (83) 662 final.*	*Major EU Commission initiative, based on Report on Local Employment Initiatives (LEIs), based on 22 public consultations and 7000 taking part. Considerable UK policy influence. OECD policy coordination. Written by Michael Young, Chris Brooks, in conjunction with OECD. Many LEIs were social enterprises.*

Appendix 1 (Continued)

Date	Event	Outcome
March 1984	*Report from of European Parliament Committee on Social Affairs and Employment on Communication from the Commission of the European Communities to the Council. COM (83) 662 final on Community Action to Combat Unemployment – the Contribution of Local Employment Initiatives.*	*European Parliament's endorsement of Commission's proposals with encouragement for Council of Ministers to adopt Commission Communication without delay.*
1985	Community Business described as social enterprise.	"Third sector enterprises are defined as those which release the talents and energy of the community to build its own future; pursue social objectives … a broadening of the intrinsically important common ownership concept beyond worker co-operatives alone, to include a range of "social" enterprises generically described as Community Business Ventures (CBVs)" (Murgatroyd and Smith 1985, 9).
1987	Salamon.	American welfare state a kind of "third-party government" in which federal programs were largely carried out through nongovernmental actors, they predicted that federal spending cuts would cripple non profits, rather than empower them" (Salamon 1987).
December 1988	*Revenu Minimum d'Insertion voted by National Assembly in France.*	*Implemented in 1992 and administered through local government system. Became main means tested benefit, claimed by 43% of working age population. RMI recipients received specific employment contracts for those in work and returning to work, forming basis for expansion of WISEs.*

Appendix 1 (Continued)

Date	Event	Outcome
January 1989	George Bush Snr Inauguration Address.	Conformation of voluntary and community sector role as "Thousand Points of Light" in Presidential Inaugural Address - "the programs that are the brighter points of light" (Bush 1989)
1990	*Report of the Walloon Social Economy Council (CWES) (Walloon Social Economy Council 1990).*	*Social Economy definition: organizations that share four characteristic features:* *– objective is to serve members or the community, not to make a profit* *– autonomous management* *– a democratic decision-making process* *– the pre-eminence of individuals and labour over capital in the distribution of income.*
1991	*Italian Social Cooperatives Law: A and B Cooperatives.*	*Social Cooperatives to deliver health and social care and work integration on local area basis.*
1991	Keltie and Meteyard: 'Organisations in the Social Economy'.	Definition of characteristics of social enterprise (Keltie and Meteyard 1991).
1992	*Jacques Delors' Presidency of European Commission from mid 1980s. European Social Chapter included Council Recommendation 92/441/EEC (European Council of Ministers 1992).*	*"Persons residing in the European Union (EU) should have access to sufficient resources and assistance to live in a manner compatible with human dignity."* *"This Recommendation defines the common principles for implementing this right in all the Member States in order to progressively cover all instances of exclusion."* UK Government Opt Out from Social Chapter, which was attached to 1992 EU Maastricht Treaty. Opt Out cancelled by Blair Government in 1997.
December 1992	New Labour Party Leader John Smith sets up Commission for Social Justice following April 1992 General Election defeat.	Commission publishes papers prefacing "Third Way" public service delivery, based on public sector enablement rather than delivery and increased personal responsibility.

Appendix 1 (Continued)

Date	Event	Outcome
1993	Salamon. Harvard Business School.	– "non profit organisations sucked increasingly into market type relations and for profit firms have steadily expanded their market niche" – "marketisation" of non profits before they were more widely described as "social enterprises" (Salamon 1993). – from 1977 to 1989, nearly 40% of growth of social service organization income and 51% of growth of civic organization income came from fees and other commercial sources (Salamon 1993). Launch of Social Enterprise Initiative.
1993	CENTRIS Report recommends "first and third" force. Public service delivery under contracts for first force. Third force grant dependent.	Definition with recognisable characteristics of social enterprise (Knight 1993, 74). In 1991 there were 150 community businesses and cooperatives with 8,400 members and shareholders, and an annual turnover of more than £15mn (Knight 1993, 181).
1993	*Protestant and Catholic coalition in Netherlands and Christian Democratic parties in Germany produced similar welfare patterns (Huber, Ragin and Stephens 1993; Van Kersbergen 2003).*	*Confirmation of third sector role in welfare delivery in Christian Democrat policies in several EU countries.*
1994	*Beginnings of 'L'Emergence de l'Entreprise Sociale en Europe' (EMES) Research Network.*	*Increasing focus on Work Integration Social Enterprises based on Revenu Minimum d'Insertion.*
1995	Mulgan and Landry: "The Other Invisible Hand". Demos publication.	Recommendation of looser governing structures for third sector organisations and taxation changes. Demos initial proposals for greater private investment for public service delivery.

Appendix 1 (Continued)

Date	Event	Outcome
June 1995	Quebec Women's "Bread and Roses" March on Poverty.	Laid foundations for participation in a Social and Economy Summit.
1996	Quebec Social Economy Summit.	Task Force representatives from state, market and civil society. In 1999 became the Chantier de l'economie sociale.
	Hansmann.	"The Ownership of Enterprise." "Non profits reduce transaction costs since nobody owns the firm so that its managers hold it in trust for its customer" (Hansmann 1996, 245).
1996	NCVO's Deakin Commission.	Recommends Compact between Voluntary Sector and Central Government.
1996	*Esping-Andersen (1996a).*	*Christian Democrat corporatist welfare approach "institutionalised familialism of supporting male breadwinner/female carer model with transfers".*
1997	School for Social Entrepreneurs formed. Rise of the Social Entrepreneur (Leadbeater 1997).	Formed by Michael Young, who had inspired European Commission 1983 Report on Local Employment Initiatives. Demos publication – social enterprise as a welfare reform mechanism, including private sector.
1997	Salamon estimate.	Social welfare cuts in 1970s and 1980s resulted in loss of $38bn for non profits outside health care (Salamon and Anheier 1997b).
1997	CIRIEC (Gelard 1997).	"50 years in the Life of CIRIEC" records approaches to UK academics to participate in discourse on social economy and UK failure to respond.
January 1998	Incorporation of Social Enterprise London.	Transformation from ICOM common ownership cooperatives and LCT to social enterprise promotion.
1998	Meaning of Social Entrepreneurship (Dees 1998b). USA Social Enterprise Alliance. Schwab Foundation.	Promotion of Social Entrepreneurship.

Appendix 1 (Continued)

Date	Event	Outcome
1998	Community Action Network formed (Nicholls 2010). Later grant from Millennium Commission.	Nicholls writes that CAN and others originators of UK social enterprise (Nicholls 2010, 618).
September 1998	*Martine Aubry Mission Letter to Alain Lipietz (Aubry 1998).*	*Seeking review of role of third sector.*
1999	Social Enterprise London first conference (January). Social Exclusion Unit.	Range of external speakers unconnected with Cooperative Movement. Policy Action Team Consultations and Reports. PAT 3, 9 and 16 recommendations on social enterprise and social entrepreneurship.
1999	*EU Commission "Concerted Strategy for Modernising Social Protection".*	*"The Commission feels that it Is now time to deepen the existing cooperation on the European level in order to assist Member States in successfully addressing the modernisation of social protection and to formulate a common political vision of Social Protection in the European Union" (European Commission 1999, 12). That the Council endorses a framework for closer cooperation in the field of social protection, based on the exchange of experiences, mutual concertation and evaluation of ongoing policy developments with a view to identifying best practices" (European Commission 1999, 16).*
April 2000	Gordon Brown as Chancellor asks Ronald Cohen to set up Social Investment Task Force.	Social Investment Task Force reports in 2001, 2003, 2005 and 2010 on private sector funding for public service delivery.
September 2000	*Lipietz Final Report on third sector to Martine Aubry.*	*"The Opportunity of a New Type of Society with a Social Vocation." Recommendation social economy structures and third sector programme which would be self financing.*

Appendix 1 (Continued)

Date	Event	Outcome
2001	*Lipietz Final Report published as book with others (Fourel et al. 2001).*	*"From the Societal Halo to the Third Sector: for a Framework Law on Socially Oriented Societies: Summary of Report submitted to Martine Aubry in September 2000" (Fourel et al. 2001).*
2001	DTI sets up Social Enterprise Unit (October). Paul Boateng MP, Finance Secretary to Treasury speech to voluntary sector (November).	Patricia Hewitt and ministers set out intentions on social enterprise delivery. Sets out intentions for public service delivery by third sector under contract.
2002	Yale Foundation Non Profits Survey. First survey of non profits moving towards social enterprise.	Less than half in profit. Outcomes mixed between ventures creating surpluses and those that lost money. 53% never operated revenue generating enterprise. Social motives limited (Massarksky and Beinhacker 2002, 10).
2002	Downing Street Breakfast Meeting with Cooperative Movement TUE 26 FEB 2002. DTI 'Strategy for Success' (Department of Trade and Industry, July 2002). Inaugural Meeting of Social Enterprise Coalition (July 2002). HM Treasury Cross Cutting Review of Third Sector delivery (HM Treasury, September, 2002). Cabinet Office, September (Cabinet Office, October 2002).	Blair personally explains social enterprise policy. First UK definition of social enterprise. UK nationwide structure to promote social enterprise. Recommends more direct contractual relationships (Osborne and McLaughlin 2004). Private Action, Public Benefit: Review of Charities and Not for Profit Sector: Strategy Unit Report'. Recommends changes to legal framework for voluntary and community sector, including social enterprise.
February and March 2003	Peter Lloyd's Consultancy Report to Social Enterprise Coalition and House of Lords Presentation.	Report and Presentation on moving social enterprise support to Regional Development Agencies which frames delivery outline framework for next 20 years.

Appendix 1 (Continued)

Date	Event	Outcome
2004	(Eikenberry, Kluver 2004).	Eikenberry and Kluver describe 'open market' process in North America. Less need to build networks and social capital. Non profits forced to compete.
2004	*EMES on WISEs (Davister, Defourny and Grégoire 2004).*	*"WISEs have existed in Europe for nearly 50 years, though many were born in the last 20 years in the framework of policies set up to fight unemployment (Davister, Defourny and Grégoire 2004, 22).*
2004	HM Government.	Companies (Audit, Investigations and Community Enterprise) Act 2004. Includes Community Interest Company legislation.
2005	*CIRIEC (Avila and Campos 2005)*	*Definition social economy from CIRIEC was the Charter of Principles of the Social Economy promoted by European Standing Conference on Co-operatives, Mutual Societies, Associations and Foundations.*
June 2006	Department of Health Social Enterprise Unit.	Department of Health sets up Social Enterprise Unit following White Paper "Our Health, Our Care, Our Say", extending contracting to third sector. Social Enterprise Investment Fund in April 2007.
2007	Yunus, Mohammed.	"Banker to the Poor". Initial outline of microfinance and Grameen (Yunus 2007).
April 2012	Big Society Capital.	Based on Dormant Bank Accounts Act 2008, BSC set up as Government's Social Investment wholesale bank, following reports of Social Investment Task Force.
2012	(Kickul et al. 2012).	Social Business Education: An Interview with Nobel Laureate Muhammad Yunus, Academy of Management Learning & Education, 11(3): 453-462.

Appendix 2: Co-operatives and social enterprises

1976 Common Ownership definition

1976 Industrial Common Ownership Act definition (Co-operatives UK 2009, 36):

> The term "common ownership" comes from the Industrial Common Ownership Act 1976 that sets out a number of conditions relating to ownership, in particular in the event of the winding up of the business, the members may not distribute residual assets amongst themselves but must pass them on to another common ownership enterprise or otherwise retain them within the sector or, failing either of these, donate them to charity.

> Enterprises set up under this act have to be owned and controlled by employees. The act was an attempt to avoid historical mistakes when previously successful businesses were wound up on the vote of non-employee members to distribute often quite considerable assets to the members. The term "common ownership" has been extended to apply to a range of structures where structures where the assets are held jointly and cannot be shared out among the members.

It is essential to understand the difference between co-operatives and social enterprises.

International Co-operative Alliance (ICA) definition

The general definition the ICA applies is as follows:

> A co-operative is an autonomous association of persons united voluntarily to meet their common economic, social and cultural needs and aspirations through a jointly-owned and democratically controlled enterprise.

Seven ICA principles:

- Voluntary and open membership

- Democratic member control
- Member economic participation
- Autonomy and independence
- Education, training and information
- Co-operation among co-operatives
- Concern for community.

Social Enterprise UK defines social enterprise as follows (Social Enterprise UK 2019):

- Your business has a clear social or environmental mission that is set out in its governing documents.
- You are an independent business and earn more than half of your income through trading (or are working towards this).
- You are controlled or owned in the interests of your social mission.
- You reinvest or give away at least half your profits or surpluses towards your social purpose.
- You are transparent about how you operate and the impact that you have.

SENSCOT: legal structures for the third sector

SENSCOT LEGAL

| | Unincorporated Association /Trust | Scottish Charitable Incorporated Organisation (SCIO) | Registered Society | | | Companies (Including Community Interest Companies (CICs)) | | | | |
| | | | Community Benefit Society | Co-operative | Pre-commence ment society | Guarantee | | Shares | | LLP |
						Company Ltd by Guarantee	CIC Ltd by Guarantee	Company Ltd by shares	CIC Ltd by shares	
Likely organisation	Unincorporated association: sports clubs, small community projects. Trusts: Small grant-making charity (low risk activities)	New charities, existing unincorporated charities	Democratic, community focused non-profit organisation (e.g. housing association, credit union, community development)	Community development finance intuitions (e.g. credit union) and more commercial social enterprises with members	Societies registered before the Co-operative and Community Benefit Societies Act 2014 (previously Industrial and Provident Societies)	Social enterprises/ charity/ community group – under right to buy	Specifically designed for social enterprises with protected social mission	Usually a commercial venture may be used for social purpose very rarely a charity. Used by charitable trading subsidiaries	Specifically designed for social enterprises with protected social mission	Joint venture project or consortia, particularly where see-through tax beneficial.
Social Purpose Protected	If charitable or constitutional requirement	Yes	FCA must approve any changes to rules.	FCA must approve any changes to rules.	FCA must approve any changes to rules.	If charitable or constitutional requirement	Yes	Only if constitutional requirement	Yes. Profit distribution allowed	If in members' agreement
Limited Liability	Unincorporated: No (members may be personally liable for debts) Trusts: degree of protection but trustees may be personally liable for debts	Yes	Yes	Yes	Yes	Yes	Yes	Yes	Yes	Yes

(Continued)

(*Continued*)

Tax treatment	No charitable tax breaks if non-charitable. If charitable, similar to SCIO	No corporation tax for charitable activities SDLT and CGT exemptions. Rates relief, gift aid on donations	If charitable, same as SCIO. Rates relief sometimes given if not charitable	Interest (similar to dividends) can be paid on shares which may also attract tax incentives	Depends on society's Rules	No charitable tax breaks if non-charitable, same as SCIO	No charitable tax breaks Rates and relief sometimes given	No particular tax reliefs unless trading subsidiary (shed profits through Gift Aid)	No charitable tax breaks. Rates and reliefs sometimes given	Tax charge on members profit share. No particular reliefs
Legal Personality	Unincorporated: No Trust: No	Yes – this is created when the SCIO is established	Yes	Yes	Yes	Yes		Yes	Yes	Yes
Purpose	If non-charity: any purposes If charity: must be charitable and for public benefit	Must be charitable and for public benefit	Benefit of the community – special reasons not to be a limited company	Benefits of its members. Cannot be charity	Depends on society's Rules	If non-charity: any. If charity: Charitable and for public benefit	Benefit of the community	Any	Benefit of the community	Any commercial purpose
Asset Lock	Only if charitable	Yes, statutory	Yes – specially drafted. If charitable - Yes	No	Depends on society's Rules	Usually – specially drafted, but definitely if charitable or CIC.	Yes, statutory	No (although can be drafted into it)	Yes – statutory	If in members agreement
Member voting rights	Unincorporated association: as set out in constitution. Usually one member one vote. Trusts do not have members	Usually one member, one vote. Members have duty of care towards charity.	One member one vote	One member one vote	One member one vote	Usually one member one vote	Usually one member one vote	Usually in proportion to shareholding	Usually in proportion to shareholding	As per members agreement

Debt Finance	Yes (bank/lender may require personal guarantee from trustee(s))	Yes	Yes (If charitable, ensure repayment terms are reasonable)	Yes.	Yes	Yes(If charitable, ensure repayment terms are reasonable)	Yes	Yes	Yes (caps on performance related interest (quasi equity))	Yes
Constitution	Constitution or Trust Deed	Constitution	Rules	Rules	Rules	Articles of Association	Articles of Association	Articles of Association	Articles of Association	Members' agreement.
Regulator	None/OSCR (if charitable)	OSCR only	Financial Conduct Authority	Financial Conduct Authority	Financial Conduct Authority	Companies house (and also OSCR if charitable or CIC Regulator if CIC)	Companies House + CIC regulator	Companies House	Companies House + CIC regulator	Companies House

Source: https://www.se-legal.net/.

References

6, Perri, and Diana Leat. 1997. 'Inventing the British Voluntary Sector by Committee: From Wolfenden to Deakin'. *Non-Profit Studies* 1 (2): 33–45.

ACEVO. 2009. 'Welfare to Work Reform: The Third Sector's Role: Final Report Third Sector Taskforce'. London: ACEVO.

Aglietta, Michel. 1979. *A Theory of Capitalist Regulation: The US Experience.* London: Verso.

Aiken, Mike, and Margaret Harris. 2017. 'The "Hollowing Out" of Smaller Third Sector Organisations?' *Voluntary Sector Review* 8 (3): 333–42. https://doi.org/10 .1332/204080517X15090106925654.

Aiken, Mike, Ben Cairns, and Stephen Thake. 2008. 'Community Ownership and Management of Assets'. York: Joseph Rowntree Foundation. www.jrf.org.uk/ report/community-ownership-and-management-assets.

Albo, Gregory, and Travis Fast. 2003. 'Varieties of Neoliberalism: Trajectories of Workfare in the Advanced Capitalist Countries'. In *Annual Meeting of the Canadian Political Science Association*, 30 May. Halifax, Nova Scotia: Canadian Political Science Association.

Alcock, Pete, and Jeremy Kendall. 2010. 'Constituting the Third Sector: Processes of Decontesation and Contention under UK Labour Governments in England'. TSRC Working Paper 42. Birmingham: University of Birmingham.

Alcock, Pete, Ross Millar, and Kelly Hall. 2012. 'Start-up and Growth: National Evaluation of the Social Enterprise Investment Fund (SEIF)'. Birmingham: Third Sector Research Centre. www.tsrc.ac.uk/LinkClick.aspx?fileticket=dllSde-27qNA%3D&tabid=969.

Alexander, Catherine. 2010. 'The Third Sector'. In *The Human Economy: A Citizen's Guide*, 213–24. Cambridge: Polity Press.

Amable, Bruno. 2000. 'Institutional Complementarity and Diversity of Social Systems of Innovation and Production'. *Review of International Political Economy* 7 (4): 645–87. www.tandfonline.com.proxy.idp.gcu.ac.uk/doi/pdf/ 10.1080/096922900750034572.

———. 2011. 'Morals and Politics in the Ideology of Neo-Liberalism'. *Socio-Economic Review* 9 (1): 3–30. http://ser.oxfordjournals.org/content/9/1/3.abstract.

Amin, Ash. 1994. *Post-Fordism: A Reader*. Oxford: Blackwell.

——— 2009 'Extraordinarily Ordinary: Working in the Social Economy' *Social Enterprise Journal* 5 (1): 30–49.

Amin, Ash, Angus Cameron, and Ray Hudson. 1999. 'Welfare as Work? The Potential of the UK Social Economy'. *Environment and Planning A* 31 (11): 2033–51. https://doi.org/10.1068/a312033.

————. 2002. *Placing the Social Economy*. London: Routledge.

————. 2003. 'The Alterity of the Social Economy'. In *Alternative Economic Spaces*, edited by Andrew Leyshon, Roger Lee, and Colin C. Williams, 27–54. London: Sage.

Anheier, Helmut K., Stefan Toepler, and S. Wojciech Sokolowski. 1997. 'The Implications of Government Funding for Non-profit Organizations: Three Propositions'. *International Journal of Public Sector Management* 10 (3): 190–213. http://search.proquest.com.gcu.idm.oclc.org/docview/234393070?pq-origsite=-summon.

Archambault, Edith. 1997. 'Chapter 5: France'. In *Defining the Nonprofit Sector: A Cross-National Analysis*, 103–27 *(Johns Hopkins, The State of Global Civil Society and Volunteering: Latest Findings from the Implementation of the UN Non-Profit Handbook)*. Baltimore: Johns Hopkins University.

Archer, Margaret S. 1982. 'Morphogenesis versus Structuration: On Combining Structure and Action'. *The British Journal of Sociology* 33 (4): 455–83. https://doi.org/10.2307/589357.

Archer, Margaret S., Roy Bhaskar, Andrew Collier, Tony Lawson, and Alan Norrie. 1998. *Critical Realism: Essential Readings*. London and New York: Routledge.

Arnstein, Sherry. 1969. 'A Ladder of Citizen Participation'. *Journal of the American Institute of Planners* 35 (4): 216–24. https://lithgow-schmidt.dk/sherry-arnstein/ladder-of-citizen-participation_en.pdf.

Atkinson, Rob. 2000. 'Narratives of Policy: The Construction of Urban Problems and Urban Policy in the Official Discourse of British Government 1968–1998'. *Critical Social Policy* 20 (2): 211–32.

Atkinson, Rob, and Simin Da Voudi. 2000. 'The Concept of Social Exclusion in the European Union: Context, Development and Possibilities'. *JCMS: Journal of Common Market Studies* 38 (3): 427–48. https://doi.org/10.1111/1468-5965.00229.

Atkinson, Rob, and Graham Moon. 1994. *Urban Policy in Britain: The City, the State and the Market*. London: Macmillan International Higher Education.

Aubrey, Carol, ed. 1994. *The Role of Subject Knowledge in the Early Years of Schooling*. London: The Falmer Press.

Aubry, Martine. 1998. 'Mission Letter of Martine Aubry, Minister of Employment and Solidarity to Alain Lipietz', 17 September.

Austin, James. 2006. 'Three Avenues for Social Entrepreneurship Research'. In *Social Entrepreneurship*, edited by Johanna Mair, Jeffrey Robinson, and Kai Hockerts, 22–33. Basingstoke: Palgrave Macmillan.

Austin, James, Howard Stevenson, and Jane Wei-Skillern. 2006. 'Social and Commercial Entrepreneurship: Same, Different, or Both?' *Entrepreneurship Theory and Practice* 30 (1): 1–22. https://doi.org/10.1111/j.1540–6520.2006.00107.x.

Avila, Rafael Chaves, and José Luis Monzón Campos. 2005. 'The Social Economy in the European Union'. Brussels: CIRIEC and EESC.

Bacchiega, Alberto, and Carlo Borzaga. 2001. 'Social Enterprises as Incentive Structures'. In *The Emergence of Social Enterprise*, edited by Carlo Borzaga, and Jacques Defourny, Vol. 3rd, 273–95. London and New York: Routledge.

Badelt, Christoph. 1997. 'Entrepreneurship Theories of the Non-Profit Sector'. *Voluntas* 8 (2): 162–78.

Bank of England. 2003. 'The Financing of Social Enterprises: A Special Report by the Bank of England'. London: Bank of England. www.bankofengland.co.uk/archive/Documents/historicpubs/news/2003/054.pdf.

Barbrook, Richard. 1990. 'Mistranslations: Lipietz in London and Paris'. *Science as Culture* 1 (8): 80–117. https://doi.org/10.1080/09505439009526273.

Bartlett, Will, and Julian Le Grand. 1993. 'The Theory of Quasi-Markets'. In *Quasi-Markets and Social Policy*, edited by Julian Le Grand and Will Bartlett, 13–34. London: Palgrave Macmillan UK.

Bastow, Steve, and James Martin. 2003. *Third Way Discourse: European Ideologies in the Twentieth Century*. Edinburgh: Edinburgh University Press.

Baumgartner, Frank R., and Bryan D. Jones. 1991. 'Agenda Dynamics and Policy Subsystems'. *Journal of Politics* 53 (4): 1044–74.

Benington, John. 1986. 'Local Economic Strategies: Paradigms for a Planned Economy?' *Local Economy* 1 (1): 7–24.

Bhaskar, Roy. 1978. *A Realist Theory of Science*, Vol. 2nd. Brighton: Harvester.

———. 1989. *Reclaiming Reality: A Critical Introduction to Contemporary Philosophy*. Abingdon: Routledge.

———. 2015. *The Possibility of Naturalism: A Philosophical Critique of the Contemporary Human Sciences*. Routledge.

Biewener, Carole. 2006. 'France and Quebec: The Progressive Visions Embodied in Different Social Economy Traditions'. In *Ethics and the Market: Insights from Social Economics*, edited by Betsy Jane Clary, Wilfred Dolfsma, and Deborah M. Figart, 126–39. Oxford: Routledge.

Big Society Capital. 2013. 'Big Society Capital First Annual Report'. London: Big Society Capital.

Birchall, Johnston. 2008. 'The "Mutualisation" of Public Services in Britain: A Critical Commentary'. *Journal of Co-Operative Studies* 41 (2): 5–16.

Birkhölzer, Karl. 2015. 'Social Enterprise in Germany: A Typology of Models'. ICSEM Working Papers No. 15. Liege: HEC University of Liege.

Birkhölzer, Karl, Nicole Ravensburg, Gunnar Sivertsen, Christian Lauterman, and Georg Mildenberger. 2015. 'Social Enterprise in Germany: Understanding Concepts and Context'. ICSEM Working Paper No. 14. Liege: HEC University of Liege.

Blackburn, Robin. 2018. 'The Corbyn Project'. *New Left Review* 111 (June): 5–32. https://newleftreview.org/II/111/robin-blackburn-the-corbyn-project.

Blair, Christopher. 2003. 'Co-Operatives and Community Benefit Societies Bill (Bill 40 of 2002/03)'. House of Commons Library Briefing Paper RP03–08. London: House of Commons. http://researchbriefings.parliament.uk/ResearchBriefing/Summary/RP03–08.

Blair, Tony. 1998. 'The Third Way: New Politics for the New Century'. Fabian Pamphlet No. 588. London: Fabian Society.

Bland, Jonathan. 2010. 'Social Enterprise Solutions for 21st Century Challenges: The UK Model of Social Enterprise and Experience'. Helsinki: Ministry of Employment and the Economy.

Blundel, Richard. 2007. 'Critical Realism: A Suitable Vehicle for Entrepreneurship Research?' In *Handbook of Qualitative Research Methods in Entrepreneurship*, edited by Helle Neergaard and John Parm Ulhoi, 1–23. Cheltenham: Edward Elgar Publishing. http://oro.open.ac.uk/28378/1/Blundel_-_critical_realism,_a_suitable_vehicle_for_entrepreneurship_research.pdf.

BMG Research. 2013. 'Social Enterprises: Market Trends: Based upon the BIS Small Business Survey 2012'. London: Cabinet Office. www.gov.uk/government/

uploads/system/uploads/attachment_data/file/205291/Social_Enterprises_ Market_Trends_-_report_v1.pdf.

———. 2017. 'The Future of Business: State of Social Enterprise Survey 2017'. London: Social Enterprise UK. www.socialenterprise.org.uk/Handlers/Download. ashx?IDMF=a1051b2c-21a4–461a-896c-aca6701cc441.

Boateng, Paul. 2001. 'Treasury Minister's Speech to Charities Aid Foundation Annual Conference, Thursday 08 November 2001'. *Guardian*, 8 November. https://www.theguardian.com/society/2001/nov/08/6

Bode, Ingo. 2006. 'Disorganized Welfare Mixes: Voluntary Agencies and New Governance Regimes in Western Europe'. *Journal of European Social Policy* 16 (4): 346–59. http://esp.sagepub.com/content/16/4/346.abstract.

Boltanski, Luc, and Eve Chiapello. 2005. 'The New Spirit of Capitalism'. *International Journal of Politics, Culture, and Society* 18 (3–4): 161–88. https://doi.org/10.1007/ s10767-006-9006-9.

Bornstein, David. 2004. *How to Change the World: Social Entrepreneurs and the Power of New Ideas*. Oxford: Oxford University Press. www.waynehoover.org/ transformativeactioncenter/docs/HowtoChangeTheWorld.pdf.

Borzaga, Carlo, and Jacques Defourny. 2001. 'Conclusions: Social Enterprises in Europe: A Diversity of Initiatives and Prospects'. In *The Emergence of Social Enterprise*, edited by Carlo Borzaga and Jacques Defourny, 43. London and New York: Routledge.

Borzaga, Carlo, Jacques Defourny, and Sophie Adam. 2001. *The Emergence of the Social Enterprise*. London: Routledge.

Boschee, Jeff, and Jim McClurg. 2003. 'Toward a Better Understanding of Social Entrepreneurship: Some Important Distinctions'. www.caledonia.org.uk/papers/ Social-Entrepreneurship.pdf.

Bouchard, Marie J. 2012. 'Social Innovation, an Analytical Grid for Understanding the Social Economy: The Example of the Quebec Housing Sector'. *Service Business* 6 (1): 47–59. https://doi.org/10.1007/s11628-011-0123-9.

———. 2013. 'The Social Economy in Quebec: A Laboratory of Social Innovation'. In *Innovation and the Social Economy: The Québec Experience*, 3–24. Toronto: University of Toronto Press.

Bourque, Gilles L., Margie Mendell Marguerite, and Ralph Rouzier. 2013. 'Solidarity Finance: History of an Emerging Practice'. In *Innovation and the Social Economy: The Québec Experience*, 180–205. Toronto: University of Toronto Press.

Boyle, Edward, George Wedell, Eileen Younghushand, and Community Work Group. 1973. *Current Issues in Community Work*. London: Routledge and Kegan Paul.

Brandsen, Taco, and Victor Pestoff. 2006. 'Co-Production, the Third Sector and the Delivery of Public Services'. *Public Management Review* 8 (4): 493–501. https:// doi.org/10.1080/14719030601022874.

Brandsen, Taco, Wim van de Donk, and Kim Putters. 2005. 'Griffins or Chameleons? Hybridity as a Permanent and Inevitable Characteristic of the Third Sector'. *International Journal of Public Administration* 28 (9): 749–65. www.tandfonline. com/doi/pdf/10.1081/PAD-200067320.

Brenner, Neil, and Nik Theodore. 2002. 'Cities and the Geographies of Actually Existing Neoliberalism?' *Antipode* 34 (3): 349–79. http://onlinelibrary.wiley.com. proxy.idp.gcu.ac.uk/doi/10.1111/1467–8330.00246/pdf.

Bristol, Terry, and Edward F. Fern. 2003. 'The Effects of Interaction on Consumers' Attitudes in Focus Groups'. *Psychology and Marketing* 20 (5): 433–54. https://doi.org/10.1002/mar.10080.

Brown, Jim. 2003. 'Defining Social Enterprise'. Paper presented at the Small Business and Entrepreneurship Development conference, 15 November, University of Surrey.

Brown, Wendy, 2006. 'American Nightmare: Neoliberalism, Neoconservatism, and De-Democratization'. *Political Theory* 34 (6): 690–714.

———. 2015. *Undoing the Demos? Neoliberalism's Stealth Revolution* (Near Futures series). New York: Zone Books.

Buchanan, Glen. 1986. 'Local Economic Development by Community Business'. *Local Economy* 1 (2): 17–28.

Bush, George. 1989. 'George Bush: Inaugural Address'. American Presidency Project, 20 January 1989. www.presidency.ucsb.edu/ws/index.php?pid=16610.

Cabinet Office. 2001a. 'Modernising the Legal and Regulatory Framework for Charities and the Voluntary Sector (Performance and Innovation Unit Review of Legal and Regulatory Framework for Charities and the Voluntary Sector)'. London: Cabinet Office.

———. 2001b. 'PIU Voluntary Sector Review: Organisational Forms for Social Enterprise'. London: Cabinet Office.

———. 2002. 'Private Action, Public Benefit: A Review of Charities and the Wider Not for Profit Sector: Strategy Unit Report'. London: Cabinet Office. http://webarchive.nationalarchives.gov.uk/+/http:/www.cabinetoffice.gov.uk/media/cabinetoffice/strategy/assets/strat%20data.pdf.

———. 2010. 'Modernising Commissioning: Increasing the Role of Charities, Social Enterprises, Mutuals and Cooperatives in Public Service Delivery'. London: Cabinet Office.

———. 2020. 'Transforming Public Procurement'. CP 353. https://assets.publishing.service.gov.uk/government/uploads/system/uploads/attachment_data/file/943946/Transforming_public_procurement.pdf.

Cabinet Office, and HM Government. 2011. 'Growing the Social Investment Market: A Vision and Strategy'. London: Cabinet Office.

Cabinet Office, and Office of the Third Sector. 2006. 'Social Enterprise Action Plan: Scaling New Heights'. London: HM Government. http://webarchive.nationalarchives.gov.uk/20070108124358/http://cabinetoffice.gov.uk/third_sector/documents/social_enterprise/se_action_plan_%202006.pdf.

CAG Consultants. 1997. 'CAG Report for London Cooperative Training and London ICOM Merger'. London: CAG Consultants.

Campbell, Gordon, and London Borough Grants. 1998. 'Letter from London Borough Grants about Reductions. Friday 24 April 1998'.

Campbell, Mike. 1983. 'ICOM: Note by Mike Campbell, Secretary'. Note Circulated to ICOM Members.

Campi, Sara, Jacques Defourny, and Olivier Grégoire. 2006. 'Work Integration Social Enterprises: Are They Multiple-Goal and Multi-Stakeholder Organizations?' In *The Emergence of Social Enterprise*, edited by Carlo Borzaga, and Jacques Defourny, Vol. 3rd, 29–49. London and New York: Routledge.

Carley, Michael, Paul Jenkins, and Harry Smith. 2001. *Urban Development and Civil Society. The Role of Communities in Sustainable Cities*. London and Sterling, VA: Earthscan Publications Ltd.

Carmel, Emma, and Jenny Harlock. 2008. 'Instituting the "Third Sector" as a Governable Terrain: Partnership, Procurement and Performance in the UK'. *Policy and Politics* 36 (2): 17. www.ingentaconnect.com/content/tpp/pap/2008/00000036/00000002/art00001#.

Carroll, Archie B. 1979. 'A Three-Dimensional Conceptual Model of Corporate Performance'. *Academy of Management Review* 4 (4): 497–505. https://doi.org/10.5465/amr.1979.4498296.

Carter, Bob, and Caroline New. 2004. 'Making Realism Work: Realist Social Theory and Empirical Research'. In *ESA Social Theory Conference*, 16–17 September. Paris: Routledge. https://doi.org/10.4324/9780203624289.

Catherall, Richard J., and Mark Richardson. 2014. 'What Will Social Enterprise Look like in Europe by 2020?' Manchester: British Council. www.britishcouncil.org/sites/default/files/what_will_social_enterprise_look_like_in_europe_by_2020_0.pdf.

Cattell, Charlie. 1999. 'Creating a Fairer Society: The Cooperative Contribution'. In *International Symposium on Workers' Cooperatives Legislation*, 1–14. Tokyo: UK Cooperative Council.

———. 2015. Interview with Former Senior ICOM/ICOF management.

Catterall, Bob, Alain Lipietz, Will Hutton, and Herbie Girardet. 1996. 'The Third Sector and the Stakeholder'. *City* 1 (5–6): 86–97. https://doi.org/10.1080/13604819608713461.

CDP Inter Project Editorial Team. 1977. 'Gilding the Ghetto: The State and Poverty Experiments'. London: Home Office.

Centre for Civil Society, and NCVO. 2001. 'Next Steps in Voluntary Action: An Analysis of Five Years of Developments in the Voluntary Sector in England, Northern Ireland, Scotland and Wales'. London: NCVO. http://eprints.lse.ac.uk/29403/1/Plowden_Report_2001.pdf.

ChangeAgents. 2015. 'Fair Care: The Three C's of Fair Care'. www.changeagents.coop/Change_AGEnts/Fair_Care.html.

Chapman, Tony, Deborah Forbes, and Judith Brown. 2007. '"They Have God on Their Side": The Impact of Public Sector Attitudes on the Development of Social Enterprise'. *Social Enterprise Journal* 3 (1): 78–89. www.rise.or.kr/RBS/Data/Files/fnAAN/research01/SEJ%202007-07.pdf.

Chiapello, Eve, and Gaëtan Godefroy. 2017. 'The Dual Function of Judgment Devices. Why Does the Plurality of Market Classifications Matter?' *Historical Social Research / Historische Sozialforschung* 42 (1 159)): 152–88. www.jstor.org/stable/44176028.

Christie Commission. 2011. 'Commission on Future Delivery of Public Services'. Edinburgh: Scottish Government. www.gov.scot/publications/commission-future-delivery-public-services/.

Clarke, Kenneth. 1987. 'Kenneth Clarke on Cooperatives'. *The New Cooperator. Journal of the Industrial Common Ownership Movement* Summer: 1.

Clift, Ben, and Jim Tomlinson. 2008. 'Negotiating Credibility: Britain and the International Monetary Fund, 1956–1976'. *Contemporary European History* 17 (4): 545–66. http://wrap.warwick.ac.uk/865/1/WRAP_Clift_negotiating_credibility.pdf.

Coase, R. H. 1937. 'The Nature of the Firm'. *Economica* 4 (16): 386–405. http://dx.doi.org/10.1111/j.1468-0335.1937.tb00002.x.

Coburn, Jonathan. 2015. 'Social Enterprise in Scotland: Census 2015'. Glasgow: Social Value Lab. www.socialenterprisescotland.org.uk/files/1a891c7099.pdf.

————. 2017. 'Social Enterprise in Scotland 2017'. Glasgow: Social Value Lab. www. socialvaluelab.org.uk/wp-content/uploads/2017/09/Census-2017-Main-Report. pdf?platform=hootsuite.

Coburn, Jonathan, and CEIS. 2019. 'Social Enterprise in Scotland: Census 2019'. www.ceis.org.uk/wp-content/uploads/2019/09/Social_Enterprise_in_Scotland_ Census_2019_Full_Report.pdf.

Cochrane, Allan. 1991. 'The Limits of Local Politics: Local Socialism and the Local Economy in the 1980s A Case Study of Sheffield's Economic Policies'. PhD Thesis, Milton Keynes: Open University.

————. 2007. *Understanding Urban Policy: A Critical Approach*. Oxford: Blackwell Publishing.

Colenutt, Bob, and Austin Cutten. 1994. 'Community Empowerment in Vogue or Vain?' *Local Economy: The Journal of the Local Economy Policy Unit* 9 (3): 236–50. http://journals.sagepub.com/doi/pdf/10.1080/02690949408726238.

Commission on Social Justice. 1994. 'Report of the Commission on Social Justice'. London: Institute for Public Policy Research.

Community Interest Company Regulator. 2019. 'Community Interest Companies Annual Report'. London: Office of the Regulator of Community Interest Companies (CIC). www.gov.uk/government/publications/cic-regulator-annual-report-2018-to-2019.

Comptroller and Auditor General. 2003. 'Development Effective Services for Older People'. National Audit Office, 26 March. www.nao.org.uk/wp-content/ uploads/2003/03/0203518.pdf.

Cooney, Kate. 2011. 'The Business of Job Creation: An Examination of the Social Enterprise Approach to Workforce Development'. *Journal of Poverty* 15 (1): 88–107. https://doi.org/10.1080/10875549.2011.539505.

Co-operative Commission. 2001. 'The Cooperative Advantage: Creating a Successful Family of Cooperative Businesses'. London: Cooperative Commission. www. uk.coop/sites/storage/public/downloads/coop-advantage.pdf.

Co-operative Party. 1997. 'Working for a Cooperative Future: Our Manifesto for the 1997 Election'. London: Co-operative Party.

Co-operative Union. 2001. 'Cooperative Union Policy Briefing: Cooperative Legal Framework'. Manchester: Cooperative Union.

————. 2002. 'Comments from The Cooperative Union, Incorporating ICOM, on Social Enterprise Unit Draft Strategy May 17 2002', 24 May. Cooperative Union.

Co-operatives Advisor I. 2015. Interview with Co-operatives Advisor I.

Co-operatives Advisor II. 2016. Interview with Co-operatives Advisor II.

Co-operatives Advisor III. 2016. Interview with Co-operatives Advisor III.

Co-operatives UK. 2009. 'Simply Legal: All You Need to Know about Legal Forms and Organisational Types for Community Enterprises'. Co-operatives UK. Manchester: Co-operatives UK. www.uk.coop/sites/storage/public/downloads/ simplylegal_0.pdf.

Coraggio, José, Philippe Eynaud, Adriane Ferrarini, Genauto Carvalho de França Filho, Luiz Inácio Gaiger, Isabelle Hillenkamp, Kenichi Kitajima, Jean-Louis Laville, Andrea Lemaitre, Youssef Sadik, Marilia Veronese, and Fernanda Wanderley. 2015. 'Theory of the Social Enterprise and Pluralism: The Social Enterprise of the Solidarity Type'. In *Civil Society, the Third Sector and Social Enterprise*, edited by Jean-Louis Laville, Dennis R. Young, and Philippe Eynaud, 234–9. Abingdon and New York: Routledge.

Corbett, Malcolm. 1999. 'Social Enterprise London: Report on Activities 1998–1999'.

Cornforth, Chris. 1983. 'Some Factors Affecting the Success or Failure of Worker Co-Operatives: A Review of Empirical Research in the United Kingdom'. *Economic and Industrial Democracy* 4 (2): 163–90. http://eid.sagepub.com/content/4/2/163.abstract.

———. 1984. 'The Role of Local Co-Operative Development Agencies in Promoting Worker Co-Operatives'. *Annals of Public and Cooperative Economics* 55 (3): 253–80. http://oro.open.ac.uk/15866/.

———. 1988. 'Can Entrepreneurship Be Institutionalised? The Case of Worker Co-Operatives'. *International Small Business Journal* 6 (4): 10–19. http://isb.sagepub.com/content/6/4/10.short.

———. 1989. 'The Role of Support Organisations in Developing Worker Cooperatives: A Model for Promoting Economic and Industrial Democracy?' In *The State, Trade Unions and Self-Management: Issues of Competence and Control* (Business and Economics series), Vol. 1st, 107–25. Berlin: Walter de Gruyter GmbH & Co KG.

Cornforth, Chris, and Alan Thomas. 1991. 'Cooperative Development: Barriers, Support Structures and Cultural Factors'. *Economic and Industrial Democracy* 11 (4): 451–61. https://journals.sagepub.com/doi/pdf/10.1177/014383 1X9001100401.

Cornforth, Chris, Alan Thomas, Roger Spear, and Jenny Lewis. 1988. *Developing Successful Worker Co-Operatives*. London: Sage.

Crainer, Stuart. 2013. 'Profile: Charles Handy, Social Philosopher'. London Business School, 1 May. www.london.edu/think/profile-charles-handy-social-philosopher.

Crimmins, J. C., and M. Keil. 1983. *Enterprise in the Non Profit Sector*. New York: Rockefeller Brothers Fund.

Cripps, Francis. 1981. 'Government Planning as a Means to Economic Recovery in the UK'. *Cambridge Journal of Economics* 5 (1): 95–106.

Crouch, Colin. 2005. *Capitalist Diversity and Change: Recombinant Governance and Institutional Entrepreneurs*. Oxford: Oxford University Press.

Daft, Richard L., and Arie Y. Lewin. 1990. 'Can Organisation Studies Begin to Break out of the Normal Sciences Straitjacket? An Editorial Essay'. *Organisation Science* 1 (1): 1–9.

Daigneault, Pierre-Marc. 2014. 'Reassessing the Concept of Policy Paradigm: Aligning Ontology and Methodology in Policy Studies. *Journal of European Public Policy* 21 (3): 453–69.

Dancuse, Luc, Marie J. Bouchard, and Richard Morin. 2013. 'Governance and the Associative Sector of the Social Economy: The Partnership between the State and Civil Society in Question'. In *Innovation and the Social Economy: The Québec Experience*. 97–126. Toronto: University of Toronto Press.

Danermark, Berth, Mats Ekstrom, Liselotte Jakobsen, and Jan Ch. Karlsson. 2002. *Explaining Society. Critical Realism in the Social Sciences* (Routledge Studies in Critical Realism). Milton Keynes: Routledge.

Dart, Raymond. 2004. 'The Legitimacy of Social Enterprise'. *Non-profit Management and Leadership* 14 (4): 411–24.

Davister, Catherine, Jacques Defourny, and Olivier Grégoire. 2004. 'Work Integration Social Enterprises in the European Union: An Overview of Existing Models', EMES Working Paper WP No. 04/04: 2–20. www.joseacontreras.net/econom/Economia/Economia_Social_CIES/pdf/economiasocial/investigacion/PERSE%20Work%20Integration.pdf.

De Cuyper, Peter, Laura Jacobs, and Caroline Gijselinckx. 2015. 'More than Work Integration Strategy for the Delimitation of a Population of Social Economy Actors for a Monitor of the Social Economy in Flanders'. *Annals of Public and Cooperative Economics* 86 (2): 267–90. https://doi.org/10.1111/apce.12081.

Deakin, Nicholas. 1996. 'Meeting the Challenge of Change: Voluntary Action into the 21st Century: Report of the Commission on the Future of the Voluntary Sector in England'. London: NCVO.

———. 2001. 'Public Policy, Social Policy and Voluntary Organisations'. In *Voluntary Organisations and Social Policy in Britain*, edited by Margaret Harris and Colin Rochester, 21–36. Basingstoke: Palgrave Macmillan.

Dees, J. Gregory. 1998a. 'Enterprising Nonprofits: What Do You Do When Traditional Sources of Funding Fall Short?' *Harvard Business Review*, January/February: 55–67. https://centers.fuqua.duke.edu/case/wp-content/uploads/sites/7/2015/03/Article_Dees_EnterprisingNonprofits_1998.pdf.

———. 1998b. 'The Meaning of "Social Entrepreneurship"'. Paper for Centre for the Advancement of Social Entrepreneurship at Duke University School of Business, revised 30 May: 1–5. www.caseatduke.org/documents/dees_sedef.pdf.

———. 2003. 'Social Entrepreneurship Is About Innovation and Impact, Not Income'. Skoll Foundation's *Social Edge*, September. www.caseatduke.org/articles/1004/corner.htm.

Dees, J. Gregory, and Beth Battle Anderson. 2006. 'Framing a Theory of Social Entrepreneurship: Building on Two Schools of Practice and Thought'. *ARNOVA Occasional Paper Series* 1 (3): 39–66. www.caseatduke.org/articles/0806knowledge/index.html.

Defourny, Jacques. 2001. 'From Third Sector to Social Enterprise'. In *The Emergence of Social Enterprise*, edited by Carlo Borzaga and Jacques Defourny, 1–18. London and New York: Routledge. http://orbi.ulg.ac.be/bitstream/2268/90501/1/From%20Third%20Sector%20to%20Social%20Enterprise.pdf.

Defourny, Jacques, and Jose Luis Monzón Campos. 1992. *Economie Sociale. Entre Économie Capitaliste et Économie Publique*. Bruxelles-Paris: De Boeck.

Defourny, Jacques, Patrick Develtere, and Bénédicte Fonteneau. 1999. 'The Social Economy: The Worldwide Making of a Third Sector'. In *L'Économie Sociale Au Nord et Au Sud*. Centre d'Économie Sociale, University of Liege: De Boeck. https://emes.net/publications/members-publications/leconomie-sociale-au-nord-et-au-sud/.

Defourny, Jacques, and Patrick Develtere. 1999. 'The Social Economy: The Worldwide Making of a Third Sector'. University of Liege and University of Leuven, 1038. http://citeseerx.ist.psu.edu/viewdoc/download?doi=10.1.1.903.5390&rep=rep1&type=pdf.

Defourny, Jacques, and Marthe Nyssens. 2006. 'Defining Social Enterprise'. In *Social Enterprise in Europe: At the Crossroads of Market, Public Policies and Third Sector* (Routledge Studies in the Management of Voluntary and Non-Profit Organisations). Abingdon: Routledge.

———. 2008. 'Social Enterprise in Europe: Recent Trends and Developments'. *Social Enterprise Journal* 4 (3): 202–28.

———. 2010a. 'Conceptions of Social Enterprise and Social Entrepreneurship in Europe and the United States: Convergences and Divergences'. *Journal of Social Entrepreneurship* 1 (1): 32–53. www.tandfonline.com/doi/pdf/10.1080/19420670903442053?needAccess=true&instName=Glasgow+Caledonian+University.

———. 2010b. 'Social Enterprise'. In *The Human Economy: A Citizen's Guide*, 285–92. Cambridge: Polity Press.

————. 2010c. 'Conceptions of Social Enterprise and Social Entrepreneurship in Europe and the United States: Convergences and Divergences'. *Journal of Social Entrepreneurship* 1 (1): 32–53. https://doi.org/10.1080/19420670903442053.

————. 2013. 'Social Innovation, Social Economy and Social Enterprise: What Can the European Debate Tell Us?' In *The International Handbook of Social Innovation: Collective Action, Social Learning and Transdisiplinary Research*, 40–52. Cheltenham: Edward Elgar Publishing. http://orbi.ulg.ac.be/bitstream/2268/162368/1/Defourny%20Nyssens%202013%20Social%20Innovation.pdf.

Defourny, Jacques, Marthe Nyssens, and EMES. 2012. 'The EMES Approach of Social Enterprise in a Comparative Perspective'. European Research Network Working Paper No. 12/03. Louvain: Catholic University of Louvain. https://dial.uclouvain.be/pr/boreal/object/boreal%3A114773/datastream/PDF_01/view.

Defourny, Jacques, Victor Pestoff, and EMES. 2008. 'Images and Concepts of the Third Sector in Europe'. European Research Network EMES Working Paper. Liege: European Research Network EMES.

Defourny, Jacques, and Shin-Yang Kim. 2011. 'Emerging Models of Social Enterprise in Eastern Asia: A Cross-country Analysis'. *Social Enterprise Journal* 7 (1): 86–111. www.emeraldinsight.com/doi/pdfplus/10.1108/17508611111130176.

Demoustier, Danièle. 2001. *L'économie Sociale et Solidaire, S'associer pour Entreprendre Autrement*. Paris: Syros.

Demoustier, Danièle, and Damien Rousselière. 2004. 'Social Economy as Social Science and Practice: Historical Perspectives on France 1'. *EMOI CAHIER de RECHERCHE* 6: 1–27.

Demoustier, Danièle, Damien Rousselière, Betsy Jane Clary, Wilfred Dolfsma, and Deborah M. Figart. 2006. 'Social Economy as Social Science and Practice'. In *Ethics and the Market: Insights from Social Economics*, edited by Danièle Demoustier and Damien Rousselière. Abingdon and New York: Routledge.

Demsetz, Harold. 1997. 'The Firm in Economic Theory: A Quiet Revolution'. *The American Economic Review: Papers and Proceedings of the Hundred and Fourth Annual Meeting of the American Economic Association* 87 (2): 426–29. www.jstor.org/stable/2950959.

Denord, François. 2017. 'The Long Road of French Neoliberalism'. In *Postwar Conservatism, A Transnational Investigation*, edited by Clarisse Berthezène and Jean-Christian Vinel, 79–94. Springer International Publishing. https://doi.org/10.1007/978-3-319-40271-0_4.

Department of the Environment. 1997. '*Good Practice Guide: Development Effective Forward Strategies*'. London: Department of the Environment.

Department of Environment, Transport and the Regions, and Murray Stewart. 2000. 'Collaboration and Coordination in Area Based Initiatives: Second Research Working Paper'. London: Department of Environment, Transport and the Regions.

Department of Health. 2006. 'Our Health, Our Care, Our Say: A New Direction for Community Services'. London: Department of Health.

Department of Health Social Enterprise Unit. 2007. 'Welcoming Social Enterprise into Health and Social Care: A Resource Pack for Social Enterprise Providers and Commissioners'. Leeds: Department of Health Social Enterprise Unit.

Department of Land Economy, and University of Cambridge. 2002. 'Lessons and Evaluation Evidence from Ten Single Regeneration Budget Case Studies: Mid Term Report'. London: Department of Transport, Local Government and the Regions.

Department of Trade and Industry. 2002. 'Social Enterprise: A Strategy for Success'. London: Department of Trade and Industry.

———. 2003. 'Enterprise for Communities: Proposals for a Community Interest Company'. Gov UK Web Archive, March. https://webarchive.nationalarchives.gov.uk/20060214080654/www.dti.gov.uk/cics/pdfs/condoc.pdf.

———. 2004. 'Companies (Audit, Investigations and Community Enterprise) Act 2004'. www.legislation.gov.uk/ukpga/2004/27/pdfs/ukpga_20040027_en.pdf.

Depedri, Sara. 2014. 'Public Programs Supporting Work Integration in the Trento Province – Intervento 18'. Trento, Italy: Euricse – European Research Institute on Cooperative and Social Enterprises. http://socialeconomy.pl/node/99.

Deraedt, Eva, and Wim Van Opstal. 2009. 'Een Monitor Voor de Sociale Inschakelingseconomie in Vlaanderen. Methodologierapport'. Leuven: HIVA-KU Leuven.

Derrick, Paul. 1981. 'How to Form a Common Ownership Enterprise. What Is Common Ownership?' Leeds: Industrial Common Ownership Movement.

Desroche, Henri. 1983. *Pour un Traité d'économie Sociale*. Paris: CIEM.

Dickinson, Helen, Kerry Allen, Pete Alcock, Rob Macmillan, and Jon Glasby. 2012. 'The Role of the Third Sector in Delivering Social Care'. National Institute for Health Research. London: London School of Economics.

DiMaggio, Paul J., and Walter W. Powell. 1983. 'The Iron Cage Revisited: Institutional Isomorphism and Collective Rationality in Organizational Fields'. *American Sociological Review* 48 (2): 147–60.

Director of London ICOM. 1997. 'Director's Resignation Letter of September 18 1997', 18 September.

Dobkin Hall, Peter. 2001. *'Inventing the Non-profit Sector' and Other Essays on Philanthropy, Voluntarism, and Non-profit Organizations*. JHU Press.

———. 2006. 'A Historical Overview of Philanthropy, Voluntary Associations, and Non-profit Organizations in the United States, 1600–2000'. In *The Non-profit Sector: A Research Handbook – Second Edition*, Vol. 2nd. New Haven, CT: Yale University Press. www.hks.harvard.edu/fs/phall/Powell%20Essay-Final%20-%20rev.pdf.

———. 2013. 'Philanthropy, the Non-Profit Sector and the Democratic Dilemma'. Daedulus. https://sites.hks.harvard.edu/fs/phall/PDH-Daedalus.pdf.

Doherty, Bob, Helen Haugh, and Fergus Lyon. 2014. 'Social Enterprises as Hybrid Organizations: A Review and Research Agenda'. *International Journal of Management Reviews* 16: 417–36. http://dx.doi.org/10.1111/ijmr.12028.

Dowling, Emma, and David Harvie. 2014. 'Harnessing the Social: State, Crisis and (Big) Society'. *Sociology* 48 (5): 869–86. http://soc.sagepub.com/content/48/5/869.short.

Draperi, Jean-François. 2009. 'L'entrepreneuriat Social, un Mouvement de Pensee Inscrit dans le Capitalisme'. *RECMA Revue internationale de l'économie sociale*. http://www.recma.org/actualite/lentrepreneuriat-social-un-mouvement-de-pensee-inscrit-dans-le-capitalisme-j-f-draperi.

Drucker, Peter F. 1985. 'Innovation and Entrepreneurship: Practice and Principles'. University of Illinois at Urbana-Champaign's Academy for Entrepreneurial Leadership Historical Research Reference in Entrepreneurship. https://ssrn.com/abstract=1496169.

Dunford, M. 1990. 'Theories of Regulation'. *Environment and Planning D: Society and Space* 8 (3): 297 321. https://doi.org/10.1068/d080297.

Easterby-Smith, Mark, Richard Thorpe, and Paul Jackson. 2012. *Management Research*, Vol. 4th. London: Sage.

Edmiston, Daniel. 2016a. 'Social Impact Bonds: Opportunities and Challenges for Social Innovation'. Report on CRESSI Practitioner Seminar. Oxford: CRESSI.

———. 2016b. 'The UK Social Innovation Policy Agenda', 2016. http://eureka.sbs. ox.ac.uk/5950/1/CRESSI_Working_Paper_19_UK_Social_Innovation_Policy_ Edmiston.pdf.

Edmiston, Daniel, and Alex Nicholls. 2017. 'Social Impact Bonds: The Role of Private Capital in Outcome-Based Commissioning'. *Journal of Social Policy*, April: 1–20. https://doi.org/10.1017/S0047279417000125.

Edwards, Paul K., Joe O'Mahoney, and Steve Vincent. 2014. 'Critical Realism and Ethnography'. In *Studying Organizations Using Critical Realism: A Practical Guide*, edited by Paul K. Edwards, Joe O'Mahoney, and Steve Vincent. Oxford: Oxford University Press. www.oxfordscholarship.com.gcu.idm.oclc.org/view/10.1093/acpro f:oso/9780199665525.001.0001/acprof-9780199665525-chapter-7.

Eikenberry, Angela M. 2009. 'Refusing the Market: A Democratic Discourse for Voluntary and Nonprofit Organizations'. *Nonprofit and Voluntary Sector Quarterly* 38 (4): 582–96.

Eikenberry, Angela M., and Jodie Drapal Kluver. 2004. 'The Marketization of the Non-profit Sector: Civil Society at Risk?' *Public Administration Review* 64 (2): 132–40. http://search.proquest.com/docview/197173538/fulltextPDF?accoun-tid=15977#.

EKOS Consulting Ltd and Scottish Government Social Research. 2008. 'Evaluation of the Futurebuilders Scotland Funding Programme'. Edinburgh: Scottish Government Social Research. www.webarchive.org.uk/wayback/archive/ 20170401200404/www.gov.scot/Publications/2008/07/01091406/0.

Elkington, John, and Pamela Hartigan. 2008. *The Power of Unreasonable People: How Social Entrepreneurs Create Markets That Change the World*. Vol. 1st. Boston, MA: Harvard Business Press.

Emerson, Jed, and Fay Twersky. 1996. 'New Social Entrepreneurs: The Success, Challenge and Lessons of Non-Profit Enterprise Creation'. San Francisco: Roberts Foundation: Homeless Economic Development Fund. http://community-wealth.org/_pdfs/articles-publications/social/report-redf96-intro.pdf.

Esping-Andersen, Gosta. 1990. *The Three Worlds of Welfare Capitalism*, Vol. 2013. Cambridge: Polity.

———. 1996a. 'After the Golden Age? Welfare State Dilemmas in a Global Economy'. In *Welfare States in Transition: National Adaptations in Global Economies*, edited by Gosta Esping-Andersen, Vol. 1st, 1–31. London: Sage.

———. 1996b. 'Welfare States without Work: The Impasse of Labour Shedding and Familialism in Continental European Social Policy'. In *Welfare States in Transition: National Adaptations in Global Economics*, edited by Gosta Esping-Andersen, 66–76. London: Sage.

———. 1999. *Social Foundations of Post Industrial Economies*. Oxford: Oxford University Press.

European Commission. 1983. 'Community Action to Combat Unemployment: The Contribution of Local Employment Initiatives: Communication of the Commission to the Council. COM(83) 662 Final'. Brussels: European Commission.

———. 1997. 'Promoting the Role of Voluntary Organisations and Foundations in Europe'. Brussels: European Commission. http://eur-lex.europa.eu/legal-content/ EN/TXT/HTML/?uri=URISERV:c10714&from=EN.

———. 1999. 'Communication from the Commission: A Concerted Strategy for Modernising Social Protection'. Brussels: European Commission.

———. 2000. 'Communication from the Commission of 1 March 2000, Building an Inclusive Europe'. Communication from European Commission: The Challenge of Social Exclusion-Operational Tools under the New Provisions of the Amsterdam Treaty. http://europa.eu/legislation_summaries/employment_and_social_policy/social_inclusion_fight_against_poverty/c10621_en.htm.

——. 2013. 'Regulation (EU) No 1301/2013 of the European Parliament and of the Council of 17 December 2013 on the European Regional Development Fund and on Specific Provisions Concerning the Investment for Growth and Jobs Goal and Repealing Regulation (EC) No 1080/2006'. http://eur-lex.europa.eu/legal-content/EN/TXT/PDF/?uri=CELEX:32013R1301&from=EN.

European Council of Ministers. 1992. 'Council Recommendation 92/441/EEC of 24 June 1992 on Common Criteria Concerning Sufficient Resources and Social Assistance in Social Protection Systems. *Official Journal of the European Communities* L245, 26 August. http://europa.eu/legislation_summaries/employment_and_social_policy/social_inclusion_fight_against_poverty/c10609_en.htm.

European Trade Union Congress. 2019. 'ETUC Action Programme 2019-2023'. www.etuc.org/sites/default/files/page/file/2019-06/20190621%20Action%20Programme.pdf.

Evers, Adalbert. 1995. 'Part of the Welfare Mix: The Third Sector as an Intermediate Area'. *Voluntas*, 6 (2): 119–39.

Evers, Adalbert, and Jean-Louis Laville. 2004. 'Defining the Third Sector in Europe'. In *The Third Sector in Europe*, 11–42. Cheltenham: Edward Elgar Publishing.

——. eds. 2005. 'Social Services by Social Enterprises: On the Possible Contributions of Hybrid Organizations and a Civil Society'. In *The Third Sector in Europe* (Globalization and Welfare series), 237–52. Cheltenham: Edward Elgar Publishing.

Farnsworth, John, and Bronwyn Boon. 2010. 'Analysing Group Dynamics within the Focus Group'. *Qualitative Research* 10 (5): 605–24. https://doi.org/10.1177/1468794110375223.

Fauquet, G., and Maurice Colombain. 1965. 'Oeuvres-Le Secteur Coopératif. Regards sur le Mouvement Coopératif. Organisation du Travail par Équipes Coopératives'. In *Oeuvres Complètes*. Paris: Editions de l'Institut des études coopératives.

Fecher, Fabienne, and Benoît Lévesque. 2008. 'The Public Sector and the Social Economy in the Annals (1975–2007): Towards a New Paradigm'. *Annals of Public and Cooperative Economics* 79 (3–4): 679–727.

——. 2015. 'Presentation: Some Current Issues and Challenges in the Social Economy'. *Annals of Public and Cooperative Economics* 86 (2): 179–89. https://doi.org/10.1111/apce.12087.

Federal Deposit Insurance Corporation. 2018. 'FDIC: Community Reinvestment Act (CRA)'. www.fdic.gov/regulations/cra/.

Ferlie, Ewan, Lynn Ashburner, Louise Fitzgerald, and Andrew Pettigrew. 1996. *The New Public Management in Action*. Oxford: Oxford University Press. www.oxfordscholarship.com.gcu.idm.oclc.org/view/10.1093/acprof:oso/9780198289029.001.0001/acprof-9780198289029.

Ferrera, Maurizio, Manos Matsaganis, and Stefano Sacchi. 2002. 'Open Coordination against Poverty: The New EU "Social Inclusion Process"'. *Journal of European Social Policy* 12 (3): 227–39. http://esp.sagepub.com/content/12/3/227.full.pdf+html.

Filer Commission on Private Philanthropy and Public Needs. 1975. 'Giving in America: Toward a Stronger Voluntary Sector'. https://archives.iupui.edu/bitstream/handle/2450/889/giving.pdf?sequence=1.

Financial Conduct Authority, Companies House. 2002. 'Memorandum and Articles of Social Enterprise Coalition'.

Finn, Dan, and Dave Simmons. 2003. 'Intermediate Labour Markets in Britain and an International Review of Transitional Employment Programmes'. University of Portsmouth: Department of Work and Pensions.

Fischer, Frank. 2003. *Reframing Public Policy: Discursive Politics and Deliberative Practices: Discursive Politics and Deliberative Practices*. Oxford: Oxford University Press.

Fisher, Lawrence M. 2003. 'The Paradox of Charles Handy'. Strategy and Business. www.strategy-business.com/article/03309?gko=4d780.

Fleetwood, S. 2006. 'Re-Thinking Labour Markets: A Critical Realist-Socioeconomic Perspective'. *Capital & Class* 30 (2): 59–89. http://journals.sagepub.com/doi/abs/10.1177/030981680608900103.

Fleetwood, Steve. 2004. 'The Ontology of Organisation and Management Studies'. In *Realist Applications in Organisation and Management Studies*. London: Routledge. http://eprints.uwe.ac.uk/16278/2/Download.pdf.

Fletcher, Amber J. 2016. 'Applying Critical Realism in Qualitative Research: Methodology Meets Method'. *International Journal of Social Research Methodology* 20 (2): 181–94. www.tandfonline.com/doi/pdf/10.1080/13645579.2016.1144401?needAccess=true.

———. 2020. 'Critical Realism: Philosophical And Methodological Considerations'. In *Qualitative Analysis: Eight Approaches for the Social Sciences*. Sage.

Focus Group Voice 1. 2016. 'Did Organisations on the Ground Recognise What Was Happening?' Focus Group WED 21 SEP 2016. Reaction to DTI Definition, Private Action Public Benefit and Cross Cutting Review.

Focus Group Voice 2. 2016. 'How Much Discussion about Wider Development of Social Enterprise?' Focus Group WED 21 SEP 2016.

Focus Group Voice 4. 2016. 'Did Social Enterprise London Precede or Reflect Changes Taking Place on the Ground?' Focus Group WED 21 SEP 2016.

Focus Group Voice 5. 2016. 'Did These Developments Reflect What People Were Thinking?' Focus Group WED 21 SEP 2016.

Fordham, Geoff. 1993. 'Sustaining Local Involvement'. *Community Development Journal* 28 (4): 299–304. www.jstor.org/stable/44257107?seq=1#page_scan_tab_contents.

———. 1995. 'Made to Last: Creating Sustainable Neighbourhood and Estate Regeneration'. York: Joseph Rowntree Foundation.

Fordham, Geoff, Jo Hutchinson, and Paul Foley. 1999. 'Strategic Approaches to Local Regeneration: The Single Regeneration Budget Challenge Fund'. *Regional Studies* 33 (2): 131–41. https://doi.org/10.1080/00343409950122936.

Fordham, Geoff and Victor Hausner and Associates. 1991. 'Small Area Based Urban Initiatives. A Review of Recent Experience. Volume 1: Main Report'. London: Department of Trade and Industry.

Former Government Advisor I. 2015. Interview with former Government Advisor.

Former Government Advisor II. 2016. Interview with former Government Advisor II.

Former London ICOM Members. 2016. Interview with Former London ICOM Members.

Former Senior Civil Servant I. 2016. The Development of Urban Policy 1968–1997: Paper from Interview.

Former Senior Civil Servant II. 2015. Interview with Former Senior Civil Servant II.

Former Senior Civil Servant III. 2016. Interview with Former Senior Civil Servant III.

Former Senior Civil Servant IV. 2015. Interview with Former Senior Civil Servant IV.

Former Senior Civil Servant V. 2017. Interview with Former Senior Civil Servant V.

Former Senior Co-operative Movement representative. 2016. Interview with Former Senior Co-operative Movement Representative.

Former Senior Co-operative Movement Representative II. 2016. Interview with Former Senior Co-operative Movement representative II.

Former Senior ICOM/ICOF Management. 2015. Interview with Former Senior ICOM/ICOF Management.

Former Senior ICOM/ICOF Management II. 2015. Interview with Former Senior ICOM/ICOF Management.

Former Senior Management, Grant Awarding Body. 2015. Interview with Former Senior Management, Grant Awarding Body.

Former Senior Social Enterprise London Representative. 2016. Interview with Former Senior Social Enterprise Representative.

Former Social Enterprise Board Member IV. 2015. Interview with Former Social Enterprise London Board Member IV.

Former Social Enterprise Board Member V. 2016. Interview with former Social Enterprise London Board Member V.

Former Social Enterprise Board Member VI. 2016. Written Note of Interview with former Social Enterprise London Board Member VI.

Former Social Enterprise London Board Member. 2015. Interview with former Social Enterprise London Board Member.

Former Social Enterprise London Board Member II. 2015. Interview with Former Social Enterprise London Board Member II.

Former Social Enterprise London Board Member III. 2015. Interview with former Social Enterprise London Board Member III.

Former Social Enterprise London Board Member V. 2016. Interview with former Social Enterprise London Board Member V.

Fourel, Christope, Alain Lipietz, Edith Arnoult Brill, Jean-Louis Laville, Jean Christophe Le Dulgou, and Sibille Hugues. 2001. 'From the Societal Halo to the Third Sector: for a Framework Law on Socially Oriented Societies: Summary of Report submitted to Martine Aubry in September 2000'. Paris: Syros: Alternatives Economiques.

Fuller, Crispian, and Mike Geddes. 2008. 'Urban Governance Under Neoliberalism: New Labour and the Restructuring of State-Space'. *Antipode* 40 (2): 252–82. http://onlinelibrary.wiley.com.proxy.idp.gcu.ac.uk/doi/10.1111/j.1467–8330.2008.00591.x/pdf.

Fyfe, Nicholas R. 2005. 'Making Space for "Neo-Communitarianism": The Third Sector, State and Civil Society in the UK'. *Antipode* 37 (3): 536–57. http://onlinelibrary.wiley.com.proxy.idp.gcu.ac.uk/doi/10.1111/j.0066–4812.2005.00510.x/abstract.

Galera, Giulia, and Carlo Borzaga. 2009. 'Social Enterprise: An International Overview of Its Conceptual Evolution and Legal Implementation'. *Social Enterprise Journal* 5 (3): 210–28. https://doi.org/10.1108/17508610911004313.

Garven, Fiona, Alistair Grimes, James Mitchell, and Geoff Whittam. 2014. 'Community Engagement and Co-Production: Report (Draft) to the National Community Planning Group'. Edinburgh: COSLA National Community Planning Group.

Gelard, Yvonne. 1997. '1947 1997: 50 Years in the Life of CIRIEC'. CIRIEC. www.ciriec.ulg.ac.be/wp-content/uploads/2016/01/EN_BrochureCIRIEC_1947–1997.pdf.

Gianfaldoni, Patrick, and Pierre-Henri Morand. 2015. 'Incentives, Procurement and Regulation of Work Integration Social Enterprises In France: Old Ideas for New Firms?' *Annals of Public and Cooperative Economics* 86 (2): 199–219.

Giddens, Anthony. 1984. *The Constitution of Society*. Oxford: Polity Press.
———. 1998. *The Third Way*. Cambridge: Polity Press.
Gijselinckx, Caroline, and Patrick Develtere. 2008. 'The Cooperative Trilemma: Co-Operatives between Market, State and Civil Society'. SSRN Scholarly Paper ID 1330375. Rochester, NY: Social Science Research Network. https://papers. ssrn.com/abstract=1330375.
Global Social Impact Investment Steering Group. 2015. 'Summary of the First Meeting of the Global Social Impact Investment Steering Group Teleconference: 2nd September'. London: Global Social Impact Investment Steering Group.
Global Steering Group for Impact Investment. 2020. 'Leaders' Declaration for a Just and Sustainable Future – GSG'. https://gsgii.org/leaders-declaration-for-a-just-and-sustainable-future/.
Godley, Wynne, and Robert M May. 1977. 'The Macroeconomic Implications of Devaluation and Import Restriction'. *Economic Policy Review*, Cambridge Economic Policy Group: 11.
Gonçalves, Claudinei Pereira, Kester Carrara, and Richardson Moro Schmittel. 2015. 'The Phenomenon of Social Enterprises: Are We Keeping Watch on This Cultural Practice?' *VOLUNTAS: International Journal of Voluntary and Non-profit Organizations*, April: 1–26. http://link.springer.com/article/10.1007/s11266-015-9624-9/fulltext.html.
Gorsky, Martin, John Mohan, and Tim Willis. 2005. 'From Hospital Contributory Schemes to Health Cash Plans: The Mutual Ideal in British Health Care after 1948'. *Journal of Social Policy* 34 (03): 447–67.
Gostyn, Penny, Sonya Hudson, Rodney Stares, Colin Ball, and Community Ventures Business Unit. 1981. 'Whose Business Is Business?' London: Calouste Gulbenkian Foundation.
Gowan, Peter. 2009. 'Crisis in the Heartland'. *New Left Review* II (55): 5–29.
Graefe, Peter. 2005. 'Roll Out Neoliberalism and the Social Economy (Draft)'. McMaster University. www.cpsa-acsp.ca/papers-2005/Graefe.pdf.
Graziano, Paolo R., Sophie Jacquot, and Bruno Palier. 2011. 'Domestic Reconciliation Policies and the Usages of Europe'. *European Journal of Social Security* 13 (1): 3–25.
Grenier, Paola. 2002. 'The Function of Social Entrepreneurship in the UK'. In *ISTR Conference*, 1–27, 7–10 July. Cape Town: LSE. http://citeseerx.ist.psu.edu/viewdoc/download?doi=10.1.1.198.9090&rep=rep1&type=pdf.
———. 2006. 'Social Entrepreneurship: Agency in a Globalizing World'. In *Social Entrepreneurship: New Paradigms of Sustainable Social Change*, edited by Alex Nicholls, 119–43. Oxford: Oxford University Press.
———. 2009. 'The Role of the "Social Entrepreneur" in UK Social Policy: Discourse and Practice'. PhD Thesis.
Granovetter, Mark. 1985. 'Economic Action and Social Structure: The Problem of Embeddedness'. *American Journal of Sociology* 91 (3): 481–510.
Gurney, Peter. 2015. '"The Curse of the Co-Ops": Co-Operation, the Mass Press and the Market in Interwar Britain'. *The English Historical Review* 130 (547): 1479–512. https://doi.org/10.1093/ehr/cev301.
Haddon, Catherine. 2012. 'Making Policy in Opposition: The Commission on Social Justice, 1992–1994'. London: Institute for Government. www.instituteforgovernment.org.uk/sites/default/files/publications/CSJ%20final_0.pdf.
Hall, Peter A. 1993. 'Policy Paradigms, Social Learning, and the State: The Case of Economic Policymaking in Britain'. *Comparative Politics* 25 (3): 275–96. www.jstor.org/stable/422246?seq=1#page_scan_tab_contents.

Hall, Peter A., and David Soskice. 2001a. 'An Introduction to Varieties of Capitalism'. www.people.fas.harvard.edu/~phall/VofCIntro.pdf.

———. 2001b. 'An Introduction to Varieties of Capitalism'. In *Varieties of Capitalism: The International Foundations of Comparative Advantage*. Oxford: Oxford University Press.

Hall, Stephen. 2003. 'The "Third Way" Revisited: "New" Labour, Spatial Policy and the National Strategy for Neighbourhood Renewal'. *Planning, Practice & Research* 18 (4): 265–77.

Handy, Charles. 1989. *The Age of Unreason: New Thinking for a New World*. London: Random House Business Books.

Hansmann, Henry. 1980a. 'The Role of Non-profit Enterprise'. *Yale Law Journal* 89 (5): 835–901. www.law.yale.edu/documents/pdf/faculty/hansmanntheroleofnon-profitenterprise.pdf.

———. 1980b. 'The Role of Non-profit Enterprise'. *The Yale Law Journal* 89 (5): 835–901. https://doi.org/10.2307/796089.

———. 1987. 'Economic Theories of Nonprofit Organizations'. In *The Non Profit Sector: Research Handbook*, 27–42. New Haven, CT: Yale University Press.

———. 1996. *The Ownership of Enterprise*. Cambridge, MA: Harvard University Press.

Hargreaves, Ian. 1999. *New Mutualism: In from the Cold : The Co-Operative Revival and Social Exclusion*. London: Co-operative Party in conjunction with the United Kingdom Co-operative Council.

Harlock, Jenny. 2012. 'The Third Sector as a Public Service Provider'. Third Sector Research Centre, October 22, 13–4. www.bristol.ac.uk/media-library/sites/cmpo/migrated/documents/thirdsectoraspublicserviceprovider.pdf.

Harris, Bernard. 2010. 'Voluntary Action and the State in Historical Perspective'. *Voluntary Sector Review* 1 (1): 25–40.

Harris, Margaret. 2001. 'Voluntary Organisations in a Changing Social Policy Environment'. In *Voluntary Organisations and Social Policy in Britain*, edited by Margaret Harris and Colin Rochester, Vol. 1st, 213–28. Basingstoke: Palgrave.

Harvey, David. 1987. 'Flexible Accumulation through Urbanization: Reflections on "Post-Modernism" in the American City'. *Antipode* 19 (3): 260–86. https://onlinelibrary.wiley.com/doi/abs/10.1111/j.1467–8330.1987.tb00375.x.

Haugh, Helen. 2005. 'A Research Agenda for Social Entrepreneurship'. *Social Enterprise Journal* 1 (1): 1–12. www.socialenterprisecanada.ca/webconcepteurcontent63/000024540000/upload/Resources/SE%20Journal%20March%20 2005%20V1%20I1.pdf#page=5.

Haugh, Helen, and Michael Kitson. 2007. 'The Third Way and the Third Sector: New Labour's Economic Policy and the Social Economy'. *Cambridge Journal of Economics* 31 (6): 973–94.

Hausner, Victor. 1987. 'Urban Economic Change: Five English Cities. Introduction'. In *Urban Economic Change: Five English Cities*, edited by Victor Hausner, 1–43. Oxford: Clarendon Press.

———. 1988. 'Capacity Building and Task Force Exit Strategies. Programme Paper No 10'. London: Victor Hausner and Associates.

Haynes, Paul. 2012. 'The Social of Social Entrepreneurship: Building a New Field Using a New Paradigm'. *American Journal of Entrepreneurship* 5 (1): 57–69.

Hayton, Keith. 1996. 'A Critical Examination of the Role of Community Business in Urban Regeneration'. *Town Planning Review* 67 (1): 1–18.

Hazenberg, Richard, Meanu Bajwa-Patel, Michael J. Roy, Micaela Mazzei, and Simone Baglioni. 2016. 'A Comparative Overview of Social Enterprise

"Ecosystems" in Scotland and England: An Evolutionary Perspective'. *International Review of Sociology* 26 (2): 205–22. https://doi.org/10.1080/03906701.20 16.1181395.

Henderson, Fiona, Kelly Hall, Audrey Mutongi, and Geoff Whittam. 2019. 'Social Enterprise, Social Innovation and Self-Directed Care: Lessons from Scotland'. *Social Enterprise Journal* May: 19. https://doi.org/10.1108/SEJ-12-2018-0080.

Henderson, James. 2015. 'Community Anchors'. Edinburgh: What Works Scotland. https://whatworksscotland.ac.uk/publications/community-anchors/

Henderson, James, and Christopher McWilliams. 2017. 'The UK Community Anchor Model and Its Challenges for Community Sector Theory and Practice'. *Urban Studies* 54 (16). https://doi.org/10.1177/0042098016684733.

Heseltine, Michael. 1981. 'Heseltine Report to Margaret Thatcher: "It Took a Riot"'. London: Margaret Thatcher Foundation and Department of Environment.

HM Government. 2011. 'Open Public Services White Paper'. London: Cabinet Office. www.gov.uk/government/uploads/system/uploads/attachment_data/file/255288/OpenPublicServices-WhitePaper.pdf.

HM Treasury. 1999. 'Enterprise and Social Exclusion: National Strategy for Neighbourhood Renewal: Policy Action Team 3'. London: HM Treasury; http://webarchive.nationalarchives.gov.uk/20130128101412/www.cabinetoffice.gov.uk/media/cabinetoffice/social_exclusion_task_force/assets/publications_1997_to_2006/pat_report_3.pdf.

———. 2002. 'The Role of the Voluntary and Community Sector in Service Delivery: A Cross Cutting Review'. London: HM Treasury. www.oneeastmidlands.org.uk/sites/default/files/library/RoleofVCSinServiceDelivery-CrossCuttingReview.pdf.

———. 2009. 'Pre-Budget Report: Securing the Recovers; Growth and Opportunity'. Pre-Budget Report CM 7747. London: Stationery Office. https://assets.publishing.service.gov.uk/government/uploads/system/uploads/attachment_data/file/238510/7747.pdf.

Hodgson, Geoffrey M. 2017. 'Karl Polanyi on Economy and Society: A Critical Analysis of Core Concepts'. *Review of Social Economy* 75 (1): 1–25. https://doi.org/10.1080/00346764.2016.1171385.

Home Office. 2005. 'Strengthening Partnerships: Next Steps for Compact. The Relationship between the Government and the Voluntary and Community Sector'. London: Home Office.

House of Commons Public Accounts Committee. 2006. 'Working with the Voluntary Sector'. London: House of Commons Public Accounts Committee. www.publications.parliament.uk/pa/cm200506/cmselect/cmpubacc/717/717.pdf.

———. 2009. 'Building the Capacity of the Third Sector'. London: House of Commons. www.publications.parliament.uk/pa/cm200809/cmselect/cmpubacc/436/436.pdf.

House of Lords Parliamentary Report. 1978. 'Debate on Voluntary Organisations: Wolfenden Report'. http://hansard.millbanksystems.com/lords/1978/jan/18/voluntary-organisations-wolfenden-report.

Howland, Lydia, Louise Humphrey, Charles Tims, Adam Hart, and Mike Crook. 2003. 'Community into Business: Growing Hackney through Social Enterprise'. Report for Hackney Cooperative Developments. Hackney, London: Demos.

Huber, Evelyne, Charles Ragin, and John D. Stephens. 1993. 'Social Democracy, Christian Democracy, Constitutional Structure, and the Welfare State'. *American Journal of Sociology* 99 (3): 711–49. www.jstor.org/stable/2781288?seq=1.

Hubert, Agnes, and Bureau of European Policy Advisers. 2015. 'Empowering People, Driving Change: Social Innovation in the European Union'. Europa, 28 October.

Hudson, Ray. 1989. 'Labour-Market Changes and New Forms of Work in Old Industrial Regions: Maybe Flexibility for Some but Not Flexible Accumulation'. *Environment and Planning D: Society and Space* 7 (1): 5–30. https://doi.org/10.1068/d070005.

———. 2002. 'New Geographies and Forms of Work and Unemployment and Public Policy Innovation in Europe'. *Tijdschrift Voor Economische En Sociale Geografie* 93 (3): 316–35. https://doi.org/10.1111/1467-9663.00205.

———. 2010. 'The Changing Geography of Manufacturing and Work: Made in the UK?' In *The Economic Geography of the UK*, edited by N. Coe and A. Jones, 139–52. London: Sage.

Hulgård, Lars. 2010. 'Social Enterprise'. In *The Human Economy: A Citizen's Guide*, 293–300. Cambridge: Polity Press.

Huybrechts, Benjamin, and Alex Nicholls. 2012. 'Social Entrepreneurship: Definitions, Drivers and Challenges'. In *Social Entrepreneurship and Social Business*, 31–48. Gabler Verlag. https://link.springer.com/chapter/10.1007/978-3-8349-7093-0_2.

Industrial Common Ownership Movement (ICOM). 1985. 'ICOM Annual Report 1985'. Leeds: ICOM.

———. 1987. 'Bespoke Service on Rules'. *The New Cooperator. Journal of the Industrial Common Ownership Movement* 30 (2): 2.

———. 1996. 'Creating a Social Economy: Why a Labour Government Should Support the Development of Cooperative Enterprises'.

ICOM Working Party. 1971. 'ICOM Working Party Note – Revolving Loan Fund'. 28 November. London: ICOM.

ICOM/ICOF. 1996. 'Cooperative Opportunity for All: A National Strategy for Cooperative Development (Executive Summary)'.

ICOM/ICOF Policy and Promotion Committee. 1999. 'Minutes of Meeting of Monday 15 March 1999'.

IDOX Group from Planning Exchange. 2017. 'Regeneration Examples from "LEDIS" List Sent to IDOX on THU 07 SEP 2017', 10 November.

Implementation SubGroup, Social Enterprise Coalition. 2002. 'Implementation SubGroup SEC Note of Meeting on June 07 2002. (House of Lords)'.

Iversen, Torben, and Thomas R. Cusack. 2000. 'The Causes of Welfare State Expansion: Deindustrialization or Globalization?' *World Politics* 52 (3): 313–49. https://doi.org/10.1017/S0043887100016567.

Jacobs, Laura, and Caroline Gijselinckx. 2013. 'WISE's in Flanders: Steppingstones to Sustainable Work?' In *18. EMES-SOCENT Conference, Selected Papers, no. LG13-52*. Liege. https://emes.net/content/uploads/publications/Jacobs__Gijselinckx_ECSP-LG13-52.pdf.

Jacobs, Laura, V. Heylen, Caroline Gijselinckx, and B. Capeau. 2012. 'Doorstroom van Doelgroepwerknemers Uit de Sociale Inschakelingseconomie'. Steunpunt Werk. www.steunpuntwerk.be/node/2300.

Jacquot, Sophie, Clemence Ledoux, and Bruno Palier. 2011. 'Means to a Changing End – European Resources, The EU and the Reconciliation of Paid Work and Private Life'. *European Journal of Social Security* 13 (1): 26–43. http://journals.sagepub.com/doi/pdf/10.1177/138826271101300102.

Jessop, Bob. 1997. 'Twenty Years of the (Parisian) Regulation Approach: The Paradox of Success and Failure at Home and Abroad'. *New Political Economy* 2 (3): 503–26. https://doi.org/10.1080/13563469708406326.

———. 2002. 'Liberalism, Neoliberalism, and Urban Governance: A State Theoretical Perspective'. *Antipode* 34 (3): 452–72.

———. 2005. 'Critical Realism and the Strategic-Relational Approach'. *New Formations* 56: 40–53.

Jessop, Bob, Kevin Bonnett, Simon Bromley, and Tom Ling. 1988. *Thatcherism: A Tale of Two Nations*. Cambridge: Polity Press.

Johnson, David. 1988. 'An Evaluation of the Urban Development Grant Programme'. *Local Economy: The Journal of the Local Economy Policy Unit* 2 (4): 251–70. https://doi.org/10.1080/02690948808725909.

Johnson, Norman. 1989. 'The Privatization of Welfare'. *Social Policy & Administration* 23 (1): 17–30. https://doi.org/10.1111/j.1467-9515.1989.tb00493.x.

———. 1992. 'The Changing Role of the Voluntary Sector in Britain from 1945 to the Present Day'. In *Government and Voluntary Organizations: A Relational Perspective*. Avebury.

Johnson, Sherrill. 2000. 'Literature Review of Social Entrepreneurship'. www.researchgate.net/publication/246704544_Literature_Review_Of_Social_Entrepreneurship.

Johnson, Toby. 2007. 'Handling Exclusion through Social Firms: EQUAL Community Initiative Policy Brief'. Brussels: AEIDL.

Jolley, D. 2002. 'Better Government for Older People'. *International Journal of Geriatric Psychiatry* 17 (1): 90. https://doi.org/10.1002/gps.531.

Jones, Martin, and Kevin Ward. 2002. 'Excavating the Logic of British Urban Policy: Neoliberalism as the "Crisis of Crisis Management?"' *Antipode* 34 (3): 473–94. http://onlinelibrary.wiley.com.proxy.idp.gcu.ac.uk/doi/10.1111/1467-8330.00251/pdf.

JURUE Division of ECOTEC Research and Consulting. 1986. 'Inner Cities Research Programme: Assessment of the Employment Effects of Economic Development Projects Funded under the Urban Programme' (Inner Cities Research Series). London: Department of the Environment.

Kay, Alan, and Community Business Scotland Network. 2003. 'General Paper on Social Enterprise and Its Possible Future Role in Western Society – for the Department Of Humanities, Sapporo Gakuin University, Japan'. Edinburgh: Community Business Scotland Network.

Keil, Roger. 2009. 'The Urban Politics of Roll-with-it Neoliberalization'. *City* 13 (2–3): 230–45. https://doi.org/10.1080/13604810902986848.

Keltie, Dave, and Martin Meteyard. 1991. 'Organisations in the Social Market Economy'. *Community Business News*.

Kendall, Jeremy. 2000. 'The Mainstreaming of the Third Sector into Public Policy in England in the Late 1990s: Whys and Wherefores'. *Policy & Politics* 28 (4): 541–62. https://doi.org/10.1332/0305573002501135.

———. 2003. *The Voluntary Sector: Comparative Perspectives in the UK*. London: Routledge.

———. 2004. 'The Mainstreaming of the Third Sector'. In *Strategy Mix for Non-Profit Organisations: Vehicles for Social and Labour Market Integrations* (Nonprofit and Civil Society Studies), edited by Zimmer Annette and Christina Stecker, 41–71. New York: Kluwer Academic/Plenum Publishers.

Kendall, Jeremy, and Martin Knapp. 1995. 'A Loose and Baggy Monster'. In *An Introduction to the Voluntary Sector*, edited by Justin Davis Smith, Colin Rochester, and Rodney Hedley, 66–95. London: Routledge.

Kenyon, Maria, and Joanna Crellin. 2001. 'Social Enterprise Seminar Thursday 09 October 2001'. Summary of Social Enterprise Policy progress. London: Department of Trade and Industry.

Kerlin, Janelle A. 2006. 'Social Enterprise in the United States and Europe: Understanding and Learning from the Differences'. *Voluntas: International Journal of Voluntary and Non-profit Organizations* 17 (3): 246. https://doi.org/10.1007/s11266-006-9016-2.

———. 2010. 'A Comparative Analysis of the Global Emergence of Social Enterprise'. *Voluntas: International Journal of Voluntary and Nonprofit Organizations* 21 (2): 162–79.

Kickul, Jill, Siri Terjesen, Sophie Bacq, and Mark Griffiths. 2012. 'Social Business Education: An Interview with Nobel Laureate Muhammad Yunus'. *Academy of Management Learning & Education* 11 (3): 453–62.

Kingdon, John W. 2011. *Agendas, Alternatives and Public Policies* (Longman Classics in Political Science). Updated 2nd edition. Boston, MA: Longman.

Klein, Juan Luis, and Tremblay, Pierre-Andre. 2013. 'The Social Economy: A Springboard for Local Development Projects'. In *Innovation and the Social Economy: The Québec Experience*, 229–54. Toronto: University of Toronto Press.

Kleinman, Mark, and David Piachaud. 1993. 'European Social Policy: Conceptions and Choices'. *Journal of European Social Policy* 3 (1): 1–19. http://esp.sagepub.com/content/3/1/1.abstract.

Knight, Barry. 1993. 'Voluntary Action: The CENTRIS Report'. Newcastle: CENTRIS.

Knight, Barry, and Ruth Hayes. 1981. 'Self Help in the Inner City'. London: London Voluntary Service Council.

———. 1982. 'The Self Help Economy: Social and Economic Development in the Inner City'. 0 901171 33 6. London: London Voluntary Service Council.

Korpi, Walter. 2008. 'Origins of Welfare States: Changing Class Structures, Social Democracy, and Christian Democracy'. Stockholm, 1–36. http://citeseerx.ist.psu.edu/viewdoc/download?doi=10.1.1.613.4862&rep=rep1&type=pdf.

Korpi, Walter, and Joakim Palme. 1998. 'The Paradox of Redistribution and Strategies of Equality: Welfare State Institutions, Inequality, and Poverty in the Western Countries'. *American Sociological Review* 63 (5): 661–87. www.jstor.org/stable/pdfplus/2657333.pdf?acceptTC=true&jpdConfirm=true.

Kramer, Ralph. 1992. 'Chapter Two: The Role of Voluntary Social Service Organisations in Four European States: Policies and Trends in England, the Netherlands, Italy and Norway'. In *Government and Voluntary Organizations: A Relational Perspective*. Avebury.

Kuhn, Thomas S. 1962. *The Structure of Scientific Revolutions*. Chicago: University of Chicago Press. www.marxists.org/reference/subject/philosophy/works/us/kuhn.htm.

Kuhnle, Stein, and Per Selle. 1992. 'Government and Voluntary Organisations: A Relational Perspective'. In *Government and Voluntary Organizations: A Relational Perspective*. Avebury.

Labour Government. 1976. 'Industrial Common Ownership Act 1976'. www.legislation.gov.uk/ukpga/1976/78/section/2/england/2009–10–01#section-2–1-a-ii.

Labour Party. 1983. 'New Hope for Britain'. London: Labour Party.

———. 1997. 'Building The Future Together: Labour's Policies for Partnership between Government and the Voluntary Sector'. London: Labour Party.

———. 2017. 'For the Many. Not the Few'. London: The Labour Party. https://labour.org.uk/wp-content/uploads/2017/10/labour-manifesto-2017.pdf.

———. 2018. 'Labour Party Rule Book 2018'. London: Labour Party. http://labour.org.uk/wp-content/uploads/2018/04/2018-RULE-BOOK.pdf.

———. 2019. 'It's Time for Real Change'. https://labour.org.uk/manifesto-2019/.

Laville, Jean-Louis. 1996. 'Economy and Solidarity: Exploring the Issues'. Paris. www.jeanlouislaville.fr/wp-content/uploads/1996/06/Economy-and-solidarity-exploring-the-issue.pdf.

———. 2003. 'A New European Socioeconomic Perspective'. *Review of Social Economy* 61 (3): 389–405. https://doi.org/10.1080/0034676032000115831.

———. 2010a. 'Plural Economy'. In *The Human Economy: A Citizen's Guide*, 77–83. Cambridge: Polity Press.

———. 2010b. 'Solidarity Economy'. In *International Encyclopedia of Civil Society*, edited by Helmut K. Anheier and Stefan Toepler, 1464–70. New York: Springer US.

———. 2010c. 'Solidarity Economy (Economie Solidaire)'. In *The Human Economy: A Citizen's Guide*, 225–33. Cambridge: Polity Press.

———. 2011. 'What Is the Third Sector? From the Non-Profit Sector to the Social and Solidarity Economy – Theoretical Debate and European Reality: EMES Working Papers 11/01'. Louvain.

———. 2013. 'The Social and Solidarity Economy: A Theoretical and Plural Framework'. In *Potential and Limits of Social and Solidarity Economy* conference, 6–8 May. United Nations Research Institute for Social Development.

Laville, Jean-Louis, Carlo Borzaga, Jacques Defourny, Adalbert Evers, Jane Lewis, Marthe Nyssens, and Victor Pestoff. 1999. 'Third System: A European Definition'. Brussels: European Commission.

Laville, Jean-Louis, and Marthe Nyssens. 2000. 'Solidarity-Based Third Sector Organizations in the "Proximity Services" Field: A European Francophone Perspective'. *Voluntas: International Journal of Voluntary and Nonprofit Organizations* 11 (1): 67–84. https://doi.org/10.1023/A:1008955016464.

Laville, Jean-Louis, Carlo Borzaga, Jacques Defourny, Adalbert Evers, Jane Lewis, Marthe Nyssens, and Victor Pestoff. 2000. 'The Third System: A European Definition'. In *The Enterprises and Organisations of the Third System: A Strategic Challenge for Employment*, 116–42. Pilot Action 'Third System and Employment' of the European Commission. Brussels: CIREC. www.ciriec.ulg.ac.be/en/publications/etudesrapports/les-entreprises-et-organisations-du-troisieme-systeme-un-enjeu-strategique-pour-lemploi-2000/.

Laville, Jean-Louis, Andreia Lemaître, and Marthe Nyssens. 2006. 'Public Policies and Social Enterprise in Europe: The Challenge of Institutionalization'. In *Social Enterprise*, edited by Marthe Nyssens, 272–95. London: Routledge.

Laville, Jean-Louis, Benoît Lévesque, and Marguerite Mendell. 2005. 'Diverse Approaches and Practices in Europe and Canada'. In *The Social Economy: Building Inclusive Economies*, 155–87. Paris: OECD Publishing. https://doi.org/10.1787/9789264039889-7-en.

Laville, Jean-Louis, Dennis Young, and Philippe Eynaud, eds. 2015. *Civil Society, the Third Sector and Social Enterprise*. Routledge.

Lawless, Paul. 1989. *Britain's Inner Cities*, Vol. 1989. London: Paul Chapman Publishing.

Lawless, Paul, and Frank Brown. 1986. *Urban Growth and Change in Britain: An Introduction*. London: Harper and Row.

Lawrence, Matthew, Andrew Pendleton, and Sara Mahmoud. 2018. 'Co-Operatives Unleashed'. London: New Economics Foundation. https://neweconomics.org/2018/07/co-operatives-unleashed.

Laycock, Emma, and Co-operatives UK. 2017. 'ICOM Registration Details'. Manchester: Co-operatives UK.

Leadbeater, Charles. 1997. 'The Rise of the Social Entrepreneur'. London: Demos Independent Think Tank. www.demos.co.uk/files/theriseofthesocialentrepreneur.pdf.

Leadbeater, Charles, and Ian Christie. 1999. *To Our Mutual Advantage*. London: Demos.

Leborgne, Daniele, and Alain Lipietz. 1988. 'New Technologies, New Modes of Regulation: Some Spatial Implications'. *Environment and Planning D: Society and Space* 6 (3): 263–80. https://doi.org/10.1068/d060263.

Le Grand, Julian. 1991. 'Quasi-Markets and Social Policy'. *The Economic Journal* 101 (408): 1256–67. www.jstor.org/stable/2234441.

———. 2013. 'The Public Service Mutual: A Revolution in the Making? In *Making It Mutual: The Ownership Revolution That Britain Needs*. ResPublica. www.the-news.coop/39452/news/co-operatives/public-service-mutual-revolution-making/.

Le Grand, Julian, and Ray Robinson. 1984. 'The Market and the State'. In *Economics of Social Problems*, 1–286. London: Palgrave Macmillan.

Le Grand, Julian, and Saul Estrin, eds. 1989. *Market Socialism*. Oxford: Clarendon Press.

Legros, Michel. 2009. 'France: Minimum Income Schemes. From Crisis to Another. The French Experience of Means Tested Benefits'. Brussels: European Commission. http://ec.europa.eu/social/BlobServlet?docId=9028&langId=en.

Lévesque, Benoît. 1999. 'Le développement local et l'économie sociale: deux éléments devenus incontournables du nouvel environnement'. Montreal: Center for Research on Social Innovations (CRISES). http://crises.uqam.ca/upload/files/publications/etudes-theoriques/ET9905.pdf.

———. 2013. 'How the Social Economy Won Recognition in Quebec at the End of the Twentieth Century'. In *Innovation and the Social Economy: The Québec Experience*, 25–70. Toronto: University of Toronto Press.

Lewis, David. 2010. 'Political Ideologies and Non-Governmental Organizations: An Anthropological Perspective'. *Journal of Political Ideologies* 15 (3): 333–45. www.tandfonline.com/doi/pdf/10.1080/13569317.2010.513877.

Lewis, Jane. 1993. 'Developing the Mixed Economy of Care: Emerging Issues for Voluntary Organisations'. *Journal of Social Policy* 22 (2): 173–92. http://dx.doi.org/10.1017/S0047279400019292.

———. 1999. 'Reviewing the Relationship Between the Voluntary Sector and the State in Britain in the 1990s'. *Voluntas; Baltimore* 10 (3): 255–70.

———. 2004. 'The State and the Third Sector in Modern Welfare States: Independence, Instrumentality, Partnership'. In *The Third Sector in Europe* (Globalization and Welfare series), edited by Adalbert Evers and Jean-Louis Laville. Cheltenham: Edward Elgar Publishing.

Light, Paul C. 2006. 'Reshaping Social Entrepreneurship'. *Stanford Social Innovation Review* 4 (3): 47–51. https://pdfs.semanticscholar.org/00c8/71d9c22f88a86bc-2173cb9add2dee47ae2d2.pdf.

Lipietz, Alain. 1988. 'Reflections on a Tale: The Marxist Foundations of the Concepts of Regulation and Accumulation'. *Studies in Political Economy* 26 (0): 7–33. http://spe.library.utoronto.ca/index.php/spe/article/download/13195.

———. 1989. 'The Regulation Approach and the Problems of Current Capitalist Crisis'. In *IFES Marxism and the Global Society*, 1–40. Seoul and Paris: CEPREMAP. http://lipietz.net/spip.php?article629.

———. 1992. *Towards a New Economic Order: Postfordism, Ecology and Democracy*, Vol. 1992. Cambridge: Polity Press.

———. 1996. 'The Third Sector: Resolving the Crisis of the Welfare State'. *City* 1 (1–2): 141–4. https://doi.org/10.1080/13604819608900033.

———. 1997. 'The Post-Fordist World: Labour Relations, International Hierarchy and Global Ecology'. *Review of International Political Economy* 4 (1): 1–41. https://doi.org/10.1080/096922997347841.

———. 1999. 'Progress Report to Mission Letter of Minister of Employment and Solidarity, Mme Martine Aubry'. https://translate.google.co.uk/translate?hl=en&sl=fr&u=http://lipietz.net/Rapport-final-sur-l-entreprise-a-but-social-et-le-tiers-secteur&prev=search.

Lipietz, Alain, and Jane Jenson. 1987. 'Rebel Sons: The Regulation School'. http://lipietz.net/IMG/article_PDF/article_750.pdf.

Lipietz, Alain, Andrew Glyn, Stephen A. Marglin, Alan Hughes, and Ajit Singh. 1990. 'The Golden Age of Capitalism: Reinterpreting the Postwar Experience'. *Studies in Development Economics*. Oxford: Clarendon Press. http://lipietz.net/ALPC/EGM/EGM_1986j-en1.pdf.

Litchfield, Richard. 2019. 'Is Big Society Capital a Big Problem?' *Pioneers Post*, 16 October. www.pioneerspost.com/news-views/20191016/big-society-capital-big-problem.

Lloyd, P. 2002. 'Tackling Social Exclusion with Social Enterprise Organisations'. In *SME Seminar Series*, Kingston University.

Lloyd, Peter. 2003a. 'Social Enterprise in the English RDAs and in Wales, Scotland and Northern Ireland: Report to Social Enterprise Coalition'. London: University of Liverpool.

———. 2003b. 'Social Enterprise in the English RDAs, and In Wales, Scotland and Northern Ireland'. London: House of Lords.

———. 2005. 'The European Union and Its Programmes Related to the Third System'. In *The Third Sector in Europe* (Globalization and Welfare series), edited by Adalbert Evers and Jean-Louis Laville. Cheltenham: Edward Elgar Publishing.

Lloyd, Stephen. 2010. 'Creating the CIC'. *Vermont Law Review* 35 (1): 31–43. http://lawreview.vermontlaw.edu/wp-content/uploads/2012/02/13-LLoyd-Book-1-Vol.-35.pdf.

Locke, John. 1959. 'Epistle to the Reader'. In *An Essay Concerning Human Understanding*, edited by Alexander Campbell Fraser, Vol. 1st. New York.

London Cooperative Training Secretary. 1997. 'Letter from London Cooperative Training and London ICOM about First Meeting of Social Enterprise London Steering Committee on Friday 10 October 1997'.

London ICOM. 1993. 'London Directory of Worker Coops 1993'. London: London ICOM.

———. 1996. 'London ICOM 14th Annual Report 1996'. London: London ICOM.

———. 1997a. 'London ICOM Fifteenth Annual Report'. London: London ICOM.

———. 1997b. 'London ICOM Strategy Day. Research Brief, Appendices and Other Papers Considered'. London: London ICOM.

———. 1997c. '"Future of London ICOM". ExtraOrdinary General Meeting. Thursday 3 April 1997'. London: London ICOM.

———. 1997d. 'London ICOM Emergency Staff SubCommittee Meeting on Wednesday 17 September 1997'. London: London ICOM.

Lounsbury, M., and D. Strang. 2009. 'Social Entrepreneurship. Success Stories and Logic Construction'. In *Globalisation, Philanthropy and Civil Society: Projecting Institutional Logics Abroad*, edited by D. Hammack and S. Heydemann, 71–94. Bloomington, IN: Indiana University Press.

Lupton, Ruth, Alex Fenton, and Amanda Fitzgerald. 2013. 'Labour's Record on Neighbourhood Renewal in England: Policy, Spending and Outcomes 1997–2010'. Centre for Analysis of Social Exclusion (CASE) Social Policy in a Cold Climate Working Paper 6 July. http://sticerd.lse.ac.uk/dps/case/spcc/wp06.pdf.

Lynch, Julia. 2009. 'Italy: A Christian Democratic or Clientelist Welfare State?' In *Religion, Class Coalitions and Welfare States*, 91–118. Cambridge: Cambridge University Press.

MacLeod, Gordon, and Martin Jones. 1999. 'Reregulating a Regional Rustbelt: Institutional Fixes, Entrepreneurial Discourse, and the "Politics of Representation"'. *Environment and Planning D: Society and Space* 17 (5): 575–605. https://doi.org/10.1068/d170575.

Macmillan, Rob. 2011. '"Supporting" the Voluntary Sector in an Age of Austerity: The UK Coalition Government's Consultation on Improving Support for Frontline Civil Society Organisations in England'. *Voluntary Sector Review* 2 (1): 115–24.

Mahoney, Christine, and Michael J. Beckstrand. 2011. 'Following the Money: European Union Funding of Civil Society Organizations'. *JCMS: Journal of Common Market Studies* 49 (6): 1339–61.

Mair, Johanna, and Ignasi Marti. 2006. 'Social Entrepreneurship Research: A Source of Explanation, Prediction, and Delight'. *Journal of World Business* 41: 36–42.

Mansfield, Claire, and Dan Gregory. 2019. 'Capitalism in Crisis? Transforming Our Economy for People and Planet – SOSE 2019'. Social Enterprise UK, 24 February. www.socialenterprise.org.uk/state-of-social-enterprise-reports/capitalism-in-crisis-transforming-our-economy-for-people-and-planet/.

Margaret Thatcher Foundation. 2014. 'The Bruges Speech, 20 September 1988'. www.margaretthatcher.org/archive/Bruges.asp.

Martin, John P., and David Grubb. 2001. 'What Works and for Whom: A Review of OECD Countries' Experiences with Active Labour Market Policies'. Working Paper, IFAU – Institute for Labour Market Policy Evaluation No. 14: 1–53. www.econstor.eu/dspace/bitstream/10419/82211/1/wp01–14.pdf.

Martin, Roger L., and Sally Osberg. 2007. 'Social Entrepreneurship: The Case for Definition'. *Stanford Social Innovation Review*, Spring.

Martin, Ron. 1989. 'The New Regional Economics and the Politics of Regional Restructuring'. In *Regional Policy and the Crossroads: European Perspectives*, edited by E. Swyngedouw, L. Albrechts, F. Moulaert, and P. Roberts, 27–51. London: Jessica Kingsley.

Martinelli, Flavia, Frank Moulaert, Erik Swyngedouw, and Oana Ailenei. 2003. 'Social Innovation, Governance and Community Building – Singocom'. http://users.skynet.be/frank.moulaert/singocom/index2.html.

Mas-Colell, Andreu, Michael D. Whinston, and Jerry R. Green. 1995. *Microeconomic Theory*. Oxford: Oxford University Press.

Massarksky, Cynthia, and Samantha Beinhacker. 2002. 'Enterprising Nonprofits: Revenue Generation in the Non-profit Sector'. Yale, NJ: Yale School of Management and The Goldman Sachs Foundation Partnership on Non-Profit Ventures. http://community-wealth.org/content/enterprising-nonprofits-revenue-generation-non-profit-sector.

Matthews, Peter. 2012. 'From Area-based Initiatives to Strategic Partnerships: Have We Lost the Meaning of Regeneration?' *Environment and Planning C: Government and Policy* 30 (1): 147–61.

Maude, Francis. 2015. 'Letter to Sir Ronald Cohen from UK Government Cabinet Office', 27 March. https://assets.publishing.service.gov.uk/government/uploads/system/uploads/attachment_data/file/418433/Letter_to_Sir_Ronald_Cohen.pdf.

May, Jon, Paul Cloke, and Sarah Johnsen. 2005. 'Re-Phasing Neoliberalism: New Labour and Britain's Crisis of Street Homelessness'. *Antipode* 37 (4): 703–30.

Mayer, Margit. 2003. 'The Onward Sweep of Social Capital: Causes and Consequences for Understanding Cities, Communities and Urban Movements'. *International Journal of Urban and Regional Research* 27 (1): 110–32. http://dx.doi.org/10.1111/1468-2427.00435.

Mayo, Ed, and Glenys Thornton. 2001. 'Coalition for Social Enterprise: Development Plan and Proposal'. London: New Economics Foundation.

McGregor, Alan, Simon Clark, Z. Ferguson, J. Scullion, and University of Glasgow. 1997. 'Valuing the Social Economy'. Glasgow: Training and Research Unit, University of Glasgow.

McGregor, Alan, Andrea Glass, Simon Clark, and University of Glasgow. 2003. 'Valuing the Social Economy'. Glasgow: Training and Research Unit, University of Glasgow.

McKay, Stephen, Domenico Moro, Simon Teasdale, and David Clifford. 2011. 'The Marketisation of Charities in England and Wales'. *VOLUNTAS: International Journal of Voluntary and Nonprofit Organizations*, Published online 7 January 2014: 1–19.

McLaughlin, Kate. 2004. 'Towards a "modernized" Voluntary and Community Sector?' *Public Management Review* 6 (4): 555–62. www-tandfonline-com.gcu.idm.oclc.org/doi/pdf/10.1080/1471903042000303337.

Meadway, James. 2013. 'Why We Need a New Macroeconomic Strategy'. *New Economics Foundation.* https://neweconomics.org/uploads/files/66609d0b-b3c446660a_z6m6b6zxt.pdf.

Means, Robin, and Randall Smith. 1994. *Community Care: Policy and Practice.* Basingstoke: Palgrave Macmillan.

Mellor, Mary. 2010. *The Future of Money: From Financial Crisis to Public Resource.* Pluto Press. www.oapen.org/search?identifier=642725.

Mendell, Marguerite, Benoît Lévesque, and Ralph Rouzier. 2000. 'New Forms of Financing Social Economy Enterprises and Organisations in Quebec (from EU Local Economic Development Programme and US German Marshall Fund)'. Envision Canada, September. www.envision.ca/pdf/SocialEconomy/Financing-SocialEconomyQuebec.pdf.

Meyer, Samantha B., and Belinda Lunnay. 2013. 'The Application of Abductive and Retroductive Inference for the Design and Analysis of Theory-Driven Sociological Research'. *Sociological Research Online* 18 (1): 86–96. https://doi.org/10.5153/sro.2819.

Millennium Commission. 2000. 'Millennium Commission Announces Short Listed Applications To Manage The £100 Million Millennium Awards Endowment Fund'. Press release, 3 August.

Mintrom, Michael. 1997. 'Policy Entrepreneurs and the Diffusion of Innovation'. *American Journal of Political Science* 41 (3): 738–70. https://doi.org/10.2307/2111674.

Monzón, José Luis, and Rafael Chaves. 2008. 'The European Social Economy: Concept and Dimensions of the Third Sector'. *Annals of Public and Cooperative Economics* 79 (3–4): 549–77.

Morgan, David, and Richard Krueger. 1993. 'When to Use Focus Groups and Why. Chapter One'. In *Successful Focus Groups*, edited by D. Morgan, 1–20. London: Sage.

Morgan, Gareth. 1990. 'Paradigm Diversity in Organisational Research'. In *The Theory and Philosophy of Organisations: Critical Issues and New Perspectives* (Social Analysis series). Abingdon: Routledge London.

Morley, John. 2017. 'Local Economic Initiatives', 18 December.

Mort, Gillian S., Jay Weerawardena, and Kashonia Carnegie. 2003. 'Social Entrepreneurship: Towards Conceptualisation'. *International Journal of Nonprofit and Voluntary Sector Marketing* 8 (1): 76–88. http://dx.doi.org/10.1002/nvsm.202.

Moulaert, Frank, and Oana Ailenei. 2005. 'Social Economy, Third Sector and Solidarity Relations: A Conceptual Synthesis from History to Present'. *Urban Studies* 42 (11): 2037–53. https://doi.org/10.1080/00420980500279794.

Moulaert, Frank, Abid Mehmood, Diana MacCallum, and Bernhard Leubolt. 2017. 'Social Innovation as a Trigger for Transformations – The Role of Research'. Brussels: European Commission. https://ec.europa.eu/research/social-sciences/pdf/policy_reviews/social_innovation_trigger_for_transformations.pdf.

Mulgan, Geoff, and Charles Landry. 1995. 'The Other Invisible Hand: Remaking Charity for the 21st Century'. London: Demos. www.demos.co.uk/files/theOtherinvisiblehand.pdf.

Murgatroyd, Nick, and Smith, Peter. 1985. 'The Third Sector Economy'. *The New Cooperator. Journal of the Industrial Common Ownership Movement* 28 (2): 9.

Murphy, Joan. 1990. *Local Development Agencies Development Fund: The Second Evaluation of Funded LDAs*. London: LDA Development Fund.

Murray, Robin, Julie Caulier-Grice, and Geoff Mulgan. 2010. *The Open Book of Social Innovation*. London: Young Foundation. http://kwasnicki.prawo.uni.wroc.pl/pliki/Social_Innovator_020310.pdf.

Murray, Ursula. 2013. 'To What Extent Is the Voluntary Sector Colonised by Neo-Liberal Thinking?' In 8th International Critical Management Conference. 10–12 July, University of Manchester. www.independentaction.net/wp-content/uploads/2013/09/Voluntary-Sector-Neo-Liberal-thinking-Ursula-Murray.pdf.

Nathan, Lord. 1989. 'Working Party into Effectiveness of Voluntary Sector'. London: NCVO.

National Audit Office. 2009. 'Building the Capacity of the Third Sector'. London: National Audit Office. www.nao.org.uk/wp-content/uploads/2009/02/0809132.pdf.

———. 2011. 'Department of Health: Establishing Social Enterprises under the Right to Request Programme'. London: National Audit Office. www.nao.org.uk/wp-content/uploads/2011/06/10121088.pdf.

Newman, Janet. 2000. 'Beyond New Public Management? Modernising Public Services'. In *New Managerialism. New Welfare?*, edited by D. Clarke, S. Gewirtz, and E. McLaughlin, 45–61. London: Sage.

Nicholls, Alex. 2006. *Social Entrepreneurship: New Models of Sustainable Social Change*. Oxford: Oxford University Press.

———. 2010. 'The Legitimacy of Social Entrepreneurship: Reflexive Isomorphism in a Pre-Paradigmatic Field'. *Entrepreneurship Theory and Practice* 34 (4): 611–33.

Nyssens, Marthe, ed. 2006. *Social Enterprise: At the Crossroads of Market, Public Policies and Civil Society*. Abingdon: Routledge.

———. 2008. 'The Third Sector and the Social Inclusion Agenda: The Role of Social Enterprises in the Field of Work Integration'. In *The Third Sector in Europe*, 87–101. London: Routledge. www.academia.edu/30098374/The_Third_Sector_and_the_social_inclusion_agenda_The_role_of_social_enterprises_in_the_field_of_work_integration?email_work_card=view-paper.

Obinger, Herbert, Stephan Leibfried, and Francis G. Castles. 2005. 'Bypasses to a Social Europe? Lessons from Federal Experience'. *Journal of European Public Policy* 12 (3): 545–71. https://doi.org/10.1080/13501760500091885.

O'Donohoe, Nick, and Dormant Assets Commission. 2017. 'Tackling Dormant Assets. Recommendations to Benefit Investors and Society'. Gov UK, 3 March.

OECD. 1996. *Reconciling Economy and Society: Towards a Plural Economy*. Paris: OECD.

OECD. 2014. 'Connecting People with Jobs: Activation Policies in the United Kingdom'. Paris: OECD.

O'Mahoney, Joe, and Steve Vincent. 2014. 'Critical Realism as an Empirical Project A Beginner's Guide'. In *Studying Organisations Using Critical Realism: A Practical Guide*. Oxford University Press. www-oxfordscholarship-com.gcu.idm.oclc.org/view/10.1093/acprof:oso/9780199665525.001.0001/acprof-9780199665525-chapter-1.

Ortmann, Andreas, and Mark Schlesinger. 1997. 'Trust, Repute and the Role of Non-Profit Enterprise'. *VOLUNTAS: International Journal of Voluntary and Nonprofit Organizations* 8 (2): 97–119.

Osborne, Stephen P. 2000. 'Reformulating Wolfenden? The Roles and Impact of Local Development Agencies in Supporting Voluntary and Community Action in the UK'. *Local Government Studies* 26 (4): 23–48. www.tandfonline.com/doi/pdf/10.1080/03003930008434006.

Osborne, Stephen P., and Kate McLaughlin. 2004. 'The Cross-Cutting Review of the Voluntary Sector: Where Next for Local Government–Voluntary Sector Relationships?' *Regional Studies* 38 (5): 571–80.

O'Toole, Mo. 1996. *Regulation Theory and the British State: The Case of Urban Development Corporations*. Aldershot: Avebury.

Ott, Auguste. 1851. *Traité d'économie Sociale ou l'économie politique coordonnée au point de vue du progress*. http://gallica.bnf.fr.

Outhwaite, W. 1998. 'Realism and Social Science'. In *Critical Realism: Essential Readings*, 282–96. London: Routledge.

Owen, David. 1980. 'Cooperative Ownership'. Co-operative Party. https://catalogue.nla.gov.au/Record/1420219

Panel on the Independence of the Voluntary Sector. 2013. 'Independence Under Threat: The Voluntary Sector In 2013. The Panel's Second Annual Assessment'. London: Baring Foundation. http://baringfoundation.org.uk/wp-content/uploads/2013/09/IndependenceUnderThreat.pdf.

Parkinson, Caroline R. 2005. 'Meanings behind the Language of Social Entrepreneurship'. Institute for Entrepreneurship and Enterprise Development Working Paper No. 14, Lancaster University.

Parkinson, Caroline, and Carole Howorth. 2008. 'The Language of Social Entrepreneurs'. *Entrepreneurship and Regional Development* 20 (3): 285–309.

Parkinson, Michael. 1989. 'The Thatcher Government's Urban Policy: A Review'. *Town Planning Review* 60 (4): 421–45.

Parnell, Edgar. 2020. 'Notes for Leslie Huckfield', 7 March.

Patel, Raj, Andrew Carter, and Caroline Parkinson. 1999a. 'Dynamic Community Commerce: The Social Economy Framework for London (SEFfL)'. London: Greater London Enterprise.
———. 1999b. 'New Directions – Sustaining London's Communities'. London: Greater London Enterprise.
Pearce, John. 1979. 'Sources of Finance for Small Cooperatives'. ICOM Pamphlet ICOM Pamphlet No. 7. London: ICOM. Industrial Common Ownership Movement.
———. 1987. 'Strathclyde Community Business Ltd Annual Report'. Glasgow: Strathclyde Community Business.
———. 1993. *At the Heart of the Community Economy: Community Enterprise in a Changing World*. London: Calouste Gulbenkian Foundation.
———. 2003. *Social Enterprise in Anytown*, edited by Calouste Gulbenkian Foundation. London: Calouste Gulbenkian Foundation.
Pearce, John and European Network for Economic Self-Help and Local Development. 1999. 'EPOSE: Regional Report – UK'. Brussels: European Network for Economic Self-Help and Local Development.
Peattie, Ken, and Adrian Morley. 2008. 'Eight Paradoxes of the Social Enterprise Research Agenda'. *Social Enterprise Journal* 4 (2): 91–107. https://doi.org/10.1108/17508610810901995.
Peck, Jamie, and Adam Tickell. 2002. 'Neoliberalizing Space'. *Antipode* 34 (3): 380–404.
Peredo, Ana Maria, Helen M. Haugh, and Murdith McLean. 2018. 'Common Property: Uncommon Forms of Prosocial Organizing'. *Journal of Business Venturing: Enterprise Before and Beyond Benefit, Part 2: Prosocial Organizing* 33 (5): 591–602. https://doi.org/10.1016/j.jbusvent.2017.11.003.
Peredo, Ana Maria, and Murdith McLean. 2006. 'Social Entrepreneurship: A Critical Review of the Concept'. *Journal of World Business* 41 (1): 56–65.
Permanent Secretary to Department of Environment. Internal Departmental Letter. 1993. 'Letter from Department of the Environment Permanent Secretary to Department Officials and Other Departments', 4 November.
Pestoff, Victor. 2009. 'A Democratic Architecture for the Welfare State'. Dawsonera. www.dawsonera.com/readonline/9780203888735.
Pestoff, Victor, Stephen P. Osborne, and Taco Brandsen. 2006. 'Patterns of Co-Production in Public Services'. *Public Management Review* 8 (4): 591–95. https://doi.org/10.1080/14719030601022999.
Petrella, Francesca, and Nadine Richez-Battesti. 2014. 'Social Entrepreneur, Social Entrepreneurship and Social Enterprise: Semantics and Controversies'. *Journal of Innovation Economics & Management* 2014/2 (14): 143–56.
Pierson, Paul. 1996. 'The New Politics of the Welfare State'. *World Politics* 48 (2): 143–79. www.jstor.org.gcu.idm.oclc.org/stable/pdfplus/25053959.pdf?acceptTC=true&jpdConfirm=true.
Piore, Michael, and Charles Sabel. 1984. *The Second Industrial Divide: Possibilities for Prosperity*. New York: Basic Books.
Pirvu, Daniela, and Emilia Clipici. 2015. 'Social Enterprises and the EU's Public Procurement Market'. *VOLUNTAS: International Journal of Voluntary and Nonprofit Organizations* November: 1–27. http://link.springer.com/article/10.1007/s11266-015-9665-5-04/page-1.
Polanyi, Karl. 1944. *The Great Transformation: A Political and Economic Analysis of Our Time*. Boston, MA: Beacon Hill.
Policy Action Team 3. 1999. 'National Strategy for Neighbourhood Renewal: Draft Report of Policy Action Team 3 (Business)'. Neighbourhood Renewal Unit PAT Reports. London: Policy Action Team 3.

Policy Action Team 3, and Timms, Stephen. 1999. 'Enterprise and Social Exclusion: National Strategy for Neighbourhood Renewal: Policy Action Team 3'. London: HM Treasury.

Policy Action Team 9, and Active Community Unit. 1999. 'Report of the Policy Action Team on Community Self Help (PAT9)'. National Strategy for Neighbourhood Renewal. Policy Action Team Reports. London and New York: Home Office Active Community Unit.

Policy Action Team 16. 2000. 'National Strategy for Neighbourhood Renewal: Report of Policy Action Team 16: Learning Lessons'. National Strategy for Neighbourhood Renewal. London: Social Exclusion Unit.

Potter, Gary, and José Lopez. 2001. 'After Postmodernism: The Millennium'. In *After PostModernism: An Introduction to Critical Realism*, 1–19. London: Athlone Press.

Price Waterhouse Cooper. 2015. 'The Sustainability of Community Development Finance Institutions'. Price Waterhouse Cooper. London. www.british-business-bank.co.uk/research/the-sustainability-of-community-development-finance-institutions-december-2015/.

Prior, Cliff, and William H. Clark. 2014. 'Profit with Purpose Businesses: Subject Paper of the Mission Alignment Working Group'. London: Social Impact Investment Taskforce. www.socialimpactinvestment.org/reports/Mission%20Alignment%20WG%20paper%20FINAL.pdf.

Purdue, Derek, Konica Razzaque, Robin Hambleton, Murray Stewart, Chris Huxham, and Siv Vangen. 2000. *Community Leadership in Area Regeneration* (Area Regeneration series). Bristol: Policy Press and Joseph Rowntree Foundation.

Reed, Michael. 2005. 'Reflections on the "Realist Turn" in Organization and Management Studies'. *Journal of Management Studies* 42 (8): 1621–44. http://dx.doi.org/10.1111/j.1467-6486.2005.00559.x.

Rees, James, and Nigel Rose. 2015. 'New 'new Localism' or the Emperor's New Clothes: Diverging Local Social Policies and State–Voluntary Sector Relations in an Era of Localism'. *Voluntary Sector Review* 6 (1): 81–91. www.ingentaconnect.com/content/tpp/vsr/2015/00000006/00000001/art00005.

Regulator of Community Interest Companies. 2021. '2020/2021 Annual Report'. Office of the Regulator of Community Interest Companies (CICs). https://assets.publishing.service.gov.uk/government/uploads/system/uploads/attachment_data/file/1005991/cic-21-3-community-interest-companies-annual-report-2020-2021.pdf.

Rhodes, R. A. W. 2000. 'New Labour's Civil Service: Summing Up Joining-Up'. *Political Quarterly* 71 (2): 151–66. https://doi.org/10.1111/1467-923X.00290.

Rhodes, Robert. 1994. 'The Hollowing out of the State: The Changing Nature of the Public Service in Britain'. *Political Quarterly* 65 (2): 138–51. http://onlinelibrary.wiley.com/doi/10.1111/j.1467-923X.1994.tb00441.x/full.

Richardson, Pat. 1986. 'The Urban Programme: What Has It Achieved?' *Local Economy* 1 (1): 79–82.

Ridley-Duff, Rory. 2007. 'Communitarian Perspectives on Social Enterprise'. *Corporate Governance: An International Review* 15 (2): 382–292. http://onlinelibrary.wiley.com/doi/10.1111/j.1467-8683.2007.00568.x/pdf.

———. 2009. 'Co-Operative Social Enterprises: Company Rules, Access to Finance and Management Practice'. *Social Enterprise Journal* 5 (1): 50–68. www.emeraldinsight.com/doi/abs/10.1108/17508610910956408.

———. 2011. 'The Social Enterprise Mark: A Critical Review of Its Conceptual Dimensions'. *Social Enterprise Journal* 8 (3): 178–200.

Ridley-Duff, Rory, and Michael Bull. 2011. *Understanding Social Enterprise: Theory and Practice*. London: Sage.

———. 2014. 'Solidarity Co-Operatives: An Embedded Historical Communitarian Pluralist Approach to Social Enterprise Development? Keynote to RMIT Research Colloquium'. In *Sheffield Hallam University Research Archive*, edited by Rory Ridley-Duff and Mike Bull, 1–28. Sheffield Hallam University.

Ridley-Duff, Rory, and Cliff Southcombe. 2012. 'The Social Enterprise Mark: A Critical Review of Its Conceptual Dimensions'. *Social Enterprise Journal* 8 (3): 178–200.

Roberts, John Michael, and Fiona Devine. 2003. 'The Hollowing Out of the Welfare State and Social Capital'. *Social Policy and Society* 2 (4): 309–18. https://doi.org/10.1017/S1474746403001386.

Robinson, Joan, and Frank Wilkinson. 1977. 'What Has Become of Employment Policy?' *Cambridge Journal of Economics* 1: 5–14.

Robson, Brian T., Michael Bradford, Iain Deas, Ed Hall, Eric Harrison, and Great Britain Department of the Environment. 1994. 'Inner Cities Research Programme: Assessing the Impact of Urban Policy'. Centre for Urban Policy Studies, University of Manchester, and European Institute for Urban Affairs, Liverpool John Moores University. Inner Cities Research Programme. London: Department of the Environment.

Rochester, Colin. 2013. *Rediscovering Voluntary Action: The Beat of a Different Drum*. Basingstoke: Palgrave Macmillan.

Rose, Nikolas. 1996. 'Governing "Advanced" Liberal Democracies'. In *Foucault and Political Reason, Liberalism, Neo Liberalism and Regionalities of Government*. Chicago: University of Chicago Press. Governing "Advanced" Liberal Democracies.

———. 1999. *Powers of Freedom: Reframing Political Thought*. Cambridge: Cambridge University Press.

Rose-Ackerman, Susan. 1996. 'Altruism, Nonprofits, and Economic Theory'. *Journal of Economic Literature* 34 (2): 701–28. www.jstor.org/stable/2729219.

Ross, Kathleen, and Stephen P. Osborne. 1999. 'Making a Reality of Community Governance. Structuring Government–Voluntary Sector Relationships at the Local Level'. *Public Policy and Administration* 14 (2): 49–61. http://ppa.sagepub.com/content/14/2/49.abstract.

Rowthorn, Robert Eric, and Ramana Ramaswamy. 1997. 'Deindustrialization: Causes and Implications'. Washington DC: IMF working paper.

Rustin, Michael. 1996. 'The Clintonisation of New Labour'. *Guardian*, 18 November.

Salamon, Lester M. 1987. 'Of Market Failure, Voluntary Failure, and Third-Party Government: Toward a Theory of Government-Nonprofit Relations in the Modern Welfare State'. *Nonprofit and Voluntary Sector Quarterly* 16 (1–2): 29–49.

———. 1993. 'The Marketization of Welfare: Changing Non-profit and For-Profit Roles in the American Welfare State'. *Social Service Review* 67 (1): 16–39. http://ccss.jhu.edu/wp-content/uploads/downloads/2011/09/CNP_WP22_1996.pdf.

———. 1998. 'Letter to Non-profit and Voluntary Sector Quarterly'. *Non-profit and Voluntary Sector Quarterly* 27 (1): 88–89. http://nvs.sagepub.com/cgi/content/short/27/1/88

———. 1999. 'The Non-Profit Sector at a Crossroads: The Case of America'. *International Journal of Voluntary and Non-profit Organisations* 10 (1): 5–23. http://download.springer.com/static/pdf/892/art%253A10.1023%252FA%253A1021435602742.pdf?auth66=1393663960_9a0ab964165ca4c24795fa0e9038c153&ext=.pdf.

Salamon, Lester M., and Alan J. Abramson. 1992. 'The Federal Budget and the Non Profit Sector FY 1993'. Occasional Paper No. 13. Baltimore, MD.

Salamon, Lester M., and Helmut K. Anheier. 1997a. *Defining the Nonprofit Sector: A Cross-National Analysis* (Johns Hopkins Nonprofit Sector series). Manchester: Manchester University Press.

———. 1997b. *Defining the Nonprofit Sector: A Cross-National Analysis (Johns Hopkins, The State of Global Civil Society and Volunteering: Latest Findings from the Implementation of the UN Nonprofit Handbook).* Baltimore: Johns Hopkins University.

Salisch, Heinke. 1984. 'Report Drawn up on Behalf of the Committee on Social Affairs and Employment on the Communication from the Commission of the European Communities to the Council (COM (83) 662 Final) on Community Action to Combat Unemployment – the Contribution of Local Employment Initiatives'. Opinion of European Parliament, Working Document 1–35/84. Brussels: European Parliament.

Saunders, Mark N. K., Philip Lewis, and Adrian Thornhill. 2012. *Research Methods for Business Students*. London: Pearson.

Savio, M., and A. Righetti. 1993. 'Cooperatives as a Social Enterprise in Italy: A Place for Social Integration'. *Acta Psychiatrica Scandinavica* 88: 238–42.

Sawtell, Roger. 2009a. 'UK Worker Cooperatives: A Short History of Worker Coops: Part 1'. http://workerco-operatives.blogspot.co.uk/2009/07/short-history-of-worker-co-ops-part-1.html.

———. 2009b. 'UK Worker Cooperatives: Part 2: The Surge of the 1970s and Its Aftermath'. http://workerco-operatives.blogspot.co.uk/2009/07/part-2-surge-of-70s-and-its-aftermath.html.

Scottish Government. 2011. 'Public Social Partnerships'. Edinburgh: Scottish Government. www.scotland.gov.uk/News/Releases/2011/07/08133636.

Senior Management, London Cooperative Development Agency. 2015. Transcript of interview with Senior Cooperative Development Agency officer.

Social Investment Task Force (SITF). 2000. 'Enterprising Communities: Wealth Beyond Welfare: Report to the Chancellor of the Exchequer from the Social Investment Task Force'. London: SITF. https://static1.squarespace.com/static/5a6f0b584c0dbf-370367c95a/t/5b27ccd803ce643d6e7ccb10/1529335005229/SITF_Oct_2000.pdf.

———. 2003. 'Enterprising Communities: Wealth Beyond Welfare'. London: Social Investment Task Force. https://static1.squarespace.com/static/5a6f0b584c0dbf-370367c95a/t/5b27cd1ef950b7fedf445e0f/1529335086558/SITF_July_2003.pdf.

———. 2005. 'Enterprising Communities: Wealth Beyond Welfare 2005 Update'. London: Social Investment Task Force. https://static1.squarespace.com/static/5a6f0b584c0dbf370367c95a/t/5b27ce070e2e7236482eb363/152933530 5895/SITF_July_2005.pdf.

———. 2010. 'Social Investment Ten Years On: Final Report of the Social Investment Task Force'. London: Social Investment Task Force. http://forcatarefafinancassoci-ais.org.br/wp-content/uploads/2015/08/Social-Investment-10-Years-On.pdf.

Shaw, Eleanor, and Sara Carter. 2007. 'Social Entrepreneurship: Theoretical Antecedents and Empirical Analysis of Entrepreneurial Processes and Outcomes'. *Journal of Small Business and Enterprise Development* 14 (3): 418–34.

Skeffington, Arthur. 1969. 'People and Planning: Report of the Committee in Public Participation in Planning'. London: Ministry of Housing and Local Government.

Small Business Service. 2004. 'Lending to the Social Enterprise Sector'. London: Department of Trade and Industry. www.proseworks.co.uk/Downloads/dti.social%20finance%20report.pdf.

Smallbone, David, Mel Evans, Ignatius Ekanem, and Steven Butters. 2001. 'Researching Social Enterprise: Report to Small Business Service'. Middlesex University: Middlesex University Business School. www.mbsportal.bl.uk/secure/subjareas/smlbusentrep/bis/120401file38361.pdf.

Smith, Adrian. 2014. 'Technology Networks for Socially Useful Production'. *Journal of Peer Production* November: 1–9. http://sro.sussex.ac.uk/53574/2/Smith_2014_Technology_Networks_JPP_final.pdf.

Smith, Justin Davis. 2001. '*Volunteers: Making a Difference?*' In *Voluntary Organisations and Social Policy in Britain: Perspectives on Change and Choice*, edited by Margaret Harris and Colin Rochester, 185–98. London: Macmillan Education UK.

Social Economy Alliance. 2017. 'Social Economy Alliance: Manifesto for an Inclusive Economy'. Social Enterprise UK: Social Economy Alliance. https://socialeconomy-alliance.files.wordpress.com/2017/05/sea-manifesto-for-an-inclusive-economy-2017.pdf.

Social Enterprise Advisor. 2017. Interview with Social Enterprise Advisor Digital Recording.

Social Enterprise Coalition. 2002. 'Social Enterprise Strategy: "It's a Good Start!"' Inaugural AGM Details. London: Social Enterprise Coalition.

Social Enterprise London. 1998a. 'Social Enterprise London Steering Group Meeting Tuesday 09 June 1998'.

———. 1998b. 'Minutes of Steering Group Meeting of Thursday 09 June 1998'.

———. 1998c. 'Introductory Background Note on Social Enterprise London with Invitations to Become Members before AGM'.

———. 1998d. 'Minutes of the Inaugural General Meeting of Social Enterprise London. Thursday 15 October 1998'.

———. 1999a. 'Social Enterprise and Social Inclusion: A Major One Day Conference on Wednesday 27 January 1999 (Social Enterprise London Launch Event)'.

———. 1999b. 'Social Enterprise London: Strategic Objectives and Operating Principles: March 1999'.

Social Enterprise London Ltd. 1998. 'Certificate of Incorporation of a Private Limited Company: Company No 3502587'. Laws/Statutes, Companies House: 1–39.

Social Enterprise London Meeting. 1998. 'Presentation on Wednesday 08 April 1998. Social Enterprise London "A Vision for Social Enterprise London 2001"'.

Social Enterprise London Steering Group. 1997. 'Minutes of First Steering Group for Social Enterprise London from Friday 10 October 1997'.

Social Enterprise London Steering Group. 1998. 'Agenda for Social Enterprise London Steering Group Meeting on Tuesday 15 September'.

Social Enterprise UK. 2019. 'What Is It All About?' www.socialenterprise.org.uk/what-is-it-all-about/.

Social Exclusion Unit. 1998. 'Bringing Britain Together. A National Strategy for Neighbourhood Renewal'. London: Social Exclusion Unit.

———. 2000. 'National Strategy for Neighbourhood Renewal: A Framework for Consultation'. London: Cabinet Office.

———. 2001a. 'National Strategy for Neighbourhood Renewal: Policy Action Team Audit'. London: Cabinet Office. http://dera.ioe.ac.uk/9947/1/National strategy for_neighbourhood_renewal_-_Policy_Action_Team_audit.pdf.

———. 2001b. 'A New Commitment to Neighbourhood Renewal: National Strategy Action Plan'. Neighbourhood Renewal Unit., London: Cabinet Office.

Southcombe, Cliff. 2014. 'Email from Cliff Southcombe (MD, Social Enterprise Europe Ltd) to John Parman (PhD Candidate)'.

Spear, Roger. 1999. 'The Rise and Fall of Employee-Owned UK Bus Companies'. *Economic and Industrial Democracy* 20 (2): 253–68. http://eid.sagepub.com/content/20/2/253.abstract.

———. 2000. 'Support Organisations'. In *The Enterprises And Organizations Of The Third System: A Strategic Challenge For Employment*, Pilot Action 'Third System and Employment' of the European Commission, 57–86. Brussels: CIRIEC for European Commission.

———. 2006. 'Social Entrepreneurship: A Different Model?' *International Journal of Social Economics* 33 (5/6): 399–410. www.emeraldinsight.com.proxy.idp.gcu.ac.uk/journals.htm?issn=0306–8293&volume=33&issue=5&articleid=1550436&show=html.

Spear, Roger, and Eric Bidet. 2003. 'The Role of Social Enterprise in European Labour Markets'. *EMES European Research Network* WP No. 03/10: 1–46. www.oscrousse.org/programs/socialno/statii/ELEXIES_WP_03–10_Transversal_ENG-analysis%20in%20Europe.pdf.

Spear, Roger, Chris Cornforth, and Mike Aiken. 2007. 'For Love and Money: Governance and Social Enterprise'. Full Report for NCVO, Social Enterprise Coalition and Governance Hub. Milton Keynes: Open University. http://oro.open.ac.uk/10328/4/For_Love_and_Money_Full_Report_-_Final.pdf.

———. 2014. 'Major Perspectives on Governance of Social Enterprise'. In *Social Enterprise and the Third Sector*, edited by Roger Spear, Chris Cornforth, and Mike Aiken. Routledge.

Spear, Roger, Simon Teasdale, Fergus Lyon, Richard Hazenberg, Mike Aiken, and Anna Kopec. 2017. 'Social Enterprise in the United Kingdom: Models and Trajectories'. International Comparative Social Enterprise Models (ICSEM), ResearchGate, 31 May. www.researchgate.net/publication/317265021_Social_Enterprise_in_the_United_Kingdom_Models_and_Trajectories.

Spreckley, Freer. 1981. 'Social Audit – A Management Tool for Co-Operative Working'. Leeds: Beechwood College. www.locallivelihoods.com/cmsms/uploads/PDFs/Social%20Audit%20-%20A%20Management%20Tool.pdf.

———. 2015. 'Social Enterprise Brief'. Hereford: Local Livelihoods. www.locallivelihoods.com/cmsms/uploads/PDFs/Social%20Enterprise%20Brief.pdf.

———. 2017. Interview with Social Enterprise Advisor Digital Recording.

Stares, Rodney. 1982. *Local Employment Initiatives in Theory and Practice*. Edinburgh: Rodney Stares.

Stewart, John. 1978. 'The Inner Area Study Final Report: A Concluding Comment'. *Town Planning Review* 49 (2): 206–8.

Stewart, Murray. 1987. 'Ten Years of Inner Cities Policy'. *Town Planning Review* 58 (2): 129–46.

Stiller, Sabina, and Minna van Gerven. 2012. 'The European Employment Strategy and National Core Executives: Impacts on Activation Reforms in the Netherlands and Germany'. *Journal of European Social Policy* 22 (2): 118–32. https://doi.org/10.1177/0958928711433652.

Stoker, Gerry. 2004. *Transforming Local Governance. From Thatcherism to New Labour*. Basingstoke: Palgrave Macmillan.

Suchman, Mark C. 1995. 'Managing Legitimacy: Strategic and Institutional Approaches'. *Academy of Management Review* 20 (3): 571–610.

Teasdale, Simon. 2012. 'What's in a Name? Making Sense of Social Enterprise Discourses'. *Public Policy and Administration* 27 (2): 99–119.

Teasdale, Simon, and Alex Nicholls. 2015. 'Re-Evaluating Policy Paradigms: Social Enterprise Ideas and Policies in England under the New Labour and Coalition Governments'. In *EMES Working Paper*, edited by Simon Teasdale and Alex Nicholls, 1–22. EMES.

Thake, Stephen. 1995. 'Staying the Course: The Role and Structures of Community Regeneration Organisations'. York: Joseph Rowntree Foundation.

———. 2006. 'Community Assets: The Benefits and Costs of Community Management and Ownership'. London: Department of Communities and Local Government.

Thake, Stephen, and Simon Zadek. 1997. 'Practical People, Nobel Causes: How to Support Community Based Social Entrepreneurs'. New Economics Foundation. http://agallerymv.com/kindle/download/id=554725&type=stream.

The New Cooperator. Journal of the Industrial Common Ownership Movement. 1985. 'New Model Rules to Be Launched at Gala'. *The New Cooperator. Journal of the Industrial Common Ownership Movement* 28 (2): 3.

Thiemayer, Theo. 1982. 'The Challenge of the Market'. *Annals of Public and Cooperative Economics* 53 (3/4): 345–60.

Thomas, David N. 1996. *Oil on Troubled Waters: The Gulbenkian Foundation and Social Welfare*. London: Directory of Social Change.

Vaillancourt, Yves, Philippe LeClerc, and Marie J. Bouchard. 2013. 'The Co-Construction of Public Policy: The Contribution of the Social Economy'. In *Innovation and the Social Economy: The Québec Experience*, 127–57. Toronto: University of Toronto Press.

Vaillancourt, Yves, and LeClerc, Philippe. 2013. 'The CoConstruction of Public Policy: The Contribution of the Social Economy'. In *Innovation and the Social Economy: The Québec Experience*, 127–57. Toronto: University of Toronto Press.

Valentinov, Vladislav. 2007. 'Some Reflections on the Transaction Cost Theory of Nonprofit Organisation'. *Journal for Public and Nonprofit Services* 30 (1): 52–67. www.jstor.org/action/showPublication?journalCode=zeitoffegemeunte.

Van Gerven, Minna, Bart Vanhercke, and Susanna Gürocak. 2014. 'Policy Learning, Aid Conditionality or Domestic Politics? The Europeanization of Dutch and Spanish Activation Policies through the European Social Fund'. *Journal of European Public Policy* 21 (4): 509–27.

Van Kersbergen, Kees. 2003. *Social Capitalism: A Study of Christian Democracy and the Welfare State*. London: Routledge.

Van Opstal, Wim, Eva Deraedt, and Caroline Gijselinckx. 2009. 'Monitoring Profile Shifts and Differences among WISEs in Flanders'. *Social Enterprise Journal* 5 (3): 229–58. https://doi.org/10.1108/17508610911004322.

Venkataraman, S. 1997. 'The Distinctive Domain of Entrepreneurial Research'. *Advances in Entrepreneurship, Firm Emergence and Growth* 31 (4): 119.

Verschraegen, Gert, Bart Vanhercke, and Rika Verpoorten. 2011. 'The European Social Fund and Domestic Activation Policies: Europeanization Mechanisms'. *Journal of European Social Policy* 21 (1): 55–72. http://esp.sagepub.com/content/21/1/55.abstract.

Victor Hausner and Associates. 1989. 'Project Review (5): Successor Organisations'. Victor Hausner Associates for Inner Cities Unit. Action for Cities. London: Department for Trade and Industry.

Vidal, Isabel. 2005. 'Social Enterprise and Social Inclusion: Social Enterprises in the Sphere of Work Integration'. *International Journal of Public Administration* 28 (9–10): 807–25. www.tandfonline.com/doi/pdf/10.1081/PAD-200067347.

Vienney, Claude. 1980. 'Socio-Économie des Organisations Coopératives'. In *Socio-Économie Des Organisations Coopératives*. Paris: CIEM.

———. 2000. 'Qu'est ce que l'économie social ?' *RECMA – Revue internationale de l'économie sociale* 79 (275–6): 38–41.

Villeneuve-Smith, Frank, and Nick Temple. 2015. 'Leading the World in Social Enterprise: State of Social Enterprise Survey 2015'. London: Social Enterprise UK.

Viso, Mó. 2010. 'The Social Dimension of European Cohesion Policy in a 27-State Europe: An Analysis of the European Social Fund'. *European Journal of Social Work* 13 (3): 359–73. www.tandfonline.com/doi/pdf/10.1080/1369145 0903403909.

Vivet, David, and Bernard Thiry. 2000. 'Field of Study, Quantitative Importance and National Acceptations'. In *The Enterprises And Organizations Of The Third System: A Strategic Challenge For Employment*, Pilot Action 'Third System and Employment' of the European Commission, 10–35, Pilot Action 'Third System and Employment' of the European Commission. Brussels: Brussels: CIRIEC for European Commission. www.ciriec.ulg.ac.be/wp-content/uploads/2015/12/dgv_ciriec_fulltext_english.pdf.

Walloon Social Economy Council. 1990. 'Report of the Walloon Social Economy Council (CWES) 1990'. www.ces.ulg.ac.be/fr_FR/services/cles/notes-de-synthese/les-contours-de-l-economie-sociale-clarification-conceptuelle/la-definition-du-cwes.

Watkins, David. 1976. 'Industrial Common Ownership Act'. www.legislation.gov.uk/ukpga/1976/78.

Weakley, Kirsty. 2021. 'Government Commits to Release of £800m of Dormant Assets to Help Charities'. Civil Society, 9 January. www.civilsociety.co.uk/news/government-commits-to-release-of-800m-of-dormant-assets-to-help-charities.html.

Webb, Adrian, Lesley Day, and Douglas Weller. 1976. *Voluntary Social Service Manpower Resources*. London: Personal Social Services Council. http://discovery.nationalarchives.gov.uk/SearchUI/Details?uri=C6161509.

Weber, Heloise. 2004. 'The "New Economy" and Social Risk: Banking on the Poor?' *Review of International Political Economy* 11 (2): 356–86. www.tandfonline.com/doi/abs/10.1080/09692290420001672859.

Weisbrod, Burton A. 1988. 'The Role of the Non Profit Sector'. In *The Non Profit Economy*. Cambridge, MA: Harvard University Press.

Wells, Peter, Tracey Chadwick-Coule, Chris Dayson, and Gareth Morgan. 2010. 'Futurebuilders Evaluation: Final Report'. Sheffield: Sheffield Hallam University. www.shu.ac.uk/research/cresr/sites/shu.ac.uk/files/futurebuilders-evaluation-final.pdf.

Westall, Andrea. 2001a. 'Value-Led; Market-Driven. Social Enterprise Solutions to Public Policy Goals'. IPPR pamphlet. London: Institute for Public Policy Research.

———. 2001b. 'Initial Social Enterprise Mapping Group Invitation Letter from Andrea Westall Following Initial Meeting Convened by Barbara Phillips on October 09 2001'.

———. 2009. 'Business or Third Sector? What Are the Dimensions and Implications of Researching and Conceptualising the Overlap between Business and Third Sector?' University of Birmingham: Third Sector Research Centre. http://epapers.bham.ac.uk/797/1/WP26_Business_or_third_sector_-_Westall_Dec_09.pdf.

White, Linda A. 2012. 'Must We All Be Paradigmatic? Social Investment Policies and Liberal Welfare States'. *Canadian Journal of Political Science* 45 (3): 657–83.

White, S. G. 1998. 'Interpreting the Third Way: Not One Road but Many'. *Renewal* 6 (2): 17–30.

Whitehead, Jean. 2001. 'Towards a Charter for Social Enterprise and the Formation of Social Enterprise UK'. London: Social Enterprise Coalition.

Whitehead, Philip. 2015. 'Moral Economy, Markets and Privatisation: From 2010 to 2015'. In *Reconceptualising the Moral Economy of Criminal Justice: A New Perspective*, edited by Philip Whitehead, 61–82. Basingstoke: Palgrave Macmillan. http://link.springer.com/chapter/10.1057/9781137468468_4#.

Wilensky, Harold. 1981. 'Leftism, Catholicism, and Democratic Corporatism'. In *The Development of Welfare States in Europe and America*, edited by Peter Flora and Arnold Joseph Heidenheimer, 345–82. New Brunswick, NJ: Transaction.

Wistow, Gerald, Martin R. J. Knapp, Brian Hardy, and Caroline Allen. 1994. *Social Care in a Mixed Economy*. Buckingham: Open University Press.

Wolfenden, John. 1978. 'The Future of Voluntary Organisations: Report of the Wolfenden Committee'. London: Croom Helm.

Wood, Bruce, Jacki Reason, and Kathleen Egan. 1999. 'Social Enterprise in London: Case Studies in Economic Participation'. London: Social Enterprise London.

Woodin, Tom, David Crook, and Vincent Carpentier. 2010. 'Community and Mutual Ownership'. York: Joseph Rowntree Foundation.

Yeo, Stephen. 2001. 'Letter to David Blunkett for His Book *Politics and Progress: Renewing Democracy and Civil Society*', 12 April.

———. 2002. 'Cooperative and Mutual Enterprises in Britain: Ideas from a Usable Past for a Modern Future'. London: LSE. http://eprints.lse.ac.uk/29393/1/CCS_Report_4.pdf.

Young, Dennis R. 2003. 'New Trends in the US Non-Profit Sector: Towards Market Integration'. In *The Non-Profit Sector in a Changing Economy*, 61–7. Paris: OECD.

Young, Dennis R., and Cassady Brewer. 2016. 'Introduction to Social Enterprise Zoo'. In *The Social Enterprise Zoo*, 3–14. Cheltenham: Edward Elgar Publishing. www.dawsonera.com/readonline/9781784716066/startPage/19/1.

Young, Hugo. 2013. *One of Us*. Pan Macmillan.

Young, Ken, Deborah Ashby, Annette Boaz, and Lesley Grayson. 2002. 'Social Science and the Evidence-Based Policy Movement'. *Social Policy and Society* 1 (3): 215–24.

Younger-Ross, Sue. 1998. 'Better Government for Older People'. *Journal of Integrated Care*: Better Government for Older People 6 (6): 236–9. https://doi.org/10.1108/14769018199800048.

Yunus, Muhammad. 2007. *Banker to the Poor: Micro-Lending and the Battle Against World Poverty*. Penguin Books India.

Zadek, Simon, and Stephen Thake. 1997. 'Send in the Social Entrepreneurs'. *New Statesman*, 20 June. https://search-proquest-com.gcu.idm.oclc.org/docview/224371888/abstract/A247C28135114CACPQ/1.

Zimmerman, Brenda, and Raymond Dart. 1998. 'Charities Doing Commercial Ventures: Societal and Organizational Implications'. Toronto: Trillium Foundation. http://rcrpp.ca/documents/12736_en.pdf.

Index

www.ingramcontent.com/pod-product-compliance
Ingram Content Group UK Ltd.
Pitfield, Milton Keynes, MK11 3LW, UK
UKHW021909130225
454979UK00004B/32